CPR

Cold Starry Night

Other books by Claire Fejes:

People of the Noatak
Hardbound edition published by Alfred A. Knopf
Softbound edition published by Volcano Press

Villagers
Published by Random House

Enuk, My Son
Published by Pantheon

Cold Starry Night
An Alaska Memoir

Claire Fejes
illustrated by the author

Chena River

Epicenter Press
Fairbanks/Seattle

Epicenter Press
Fairbanks/Seattle

Epicenter Press Inc. is a regional press founded in Alaska whose interests include but are not limited to the arts, history, environment, and diverse cultures and lifestyles of the North Pacific and high latitudes. We seek both the traditional and innovative in publishing quality nonfiction tradebooks, contemporary art and photography giftbooks, and destination travel guides emphasizing Alaska, Washington, Oregon, and California.

Editor: Sue Mattson
Cover and Inside Design: Newman Design/Illustration
Proofreader: Lois Kelly
Printer: Best Book Manufacturers

Library of Congress Cataloging-in-Publication Data

Fejes, Claire.
    Cold starry night: an Alaska memoir / Claire Fejes.
        p.   cm.
    ISBN 0-945397-55-0 (softbound)
        1. Fairbanks (Alaska)—Biography. 2. Frontier and pioneer life—Alaska—Fairbanks. 3. Fejes, Claire. 4. Women artists—Alaska—Fairbanks— Biography. 5. Artists—Alaska—Fairbanks—Biography. I. Title.
    F914.F16F35   1996
    979.8'6—dc20
    [B]   96-43182
                                                              CIP

To order COLD STARRY NIGHT, mail $19.95 plus $4.00 for shipping (Washington residents add $1.64 sales tax) to: Epicenter Press, Box 82368, Kenmore, WA 98028.

Booksellers: Retail discounts are available from our trade distributor, Graphic Arts Center Publishing™, Box 10306, Portland, OR 97210. Phone 800-452-3032.

First Printing, October 1996
10 9 8 7 6 5 4 3 2 1
Printed in Canada

*

To my dearest husband, Joe,
the bravest man I ever knew, and
to the memory of Elmer and Hildur Keturi,
our best friends. Never an angry word or
misunderstanding came between us.

Table of Contents

Acknowledgments

I thank the Keturi family and the dear friends mentioned in this book, whose friendships have enriched our lives throughout fifty years in Alaska. This is a personal memoir of friends who have influenced my life — others too numerous to mention will know who they are and forgive my omission.

I thank our son, Mark, for his strength of purpose and his creativity. I thank our daughter, Yolande, for her artistic vision and calm strength. And I thank them both for their love and devotion to us.

I thank Angus Cameron, who believed in this book from the beginning.

I thank Wanda Stiles, who faced the major work of putting this book with its changes on a computer with patience and good humor.

I thank Esther Blanc, who opened her heart and home to me so I could work, and Bonnie Brody, for their positive enthusiasm and belief in this work when I floundered.

My deepest gratitude to Neville Jacobs, my wilderness painting partner, for her valuable suggestions; and to Jean Anderson, Peggy Shoemaker, E'Louise Ondash, Natalie Komisar, Nina Mollett, and Dorothy Drum, for their support of my work.

Claire Fejes

Foreword

Although I am not a sourdough who would know how truly Claire Fejes has reported what it was like to have lived last on our country's last frontier, as a vice president of Alfred A. Knopf and editor of her first book, *People of the Noatak*, perhaps I can judge how far she has exceeded the wonderful revelations of that earlier book. And to some extent I qualify to write the foreword by having spent five months on the Arctic coast myself during 1949 and 1952.

Claire and her husband Joe left their home in New York to make their fortunes in Alaska seeking gold. Basically, this was Joe's ambition, for Claire's was to become a sculptress and painter. Joe was a musician at heart, but he was also a jack-of-all-trades, and such men can make it on the frontier even if no gold is discovered. Claire's sacrifice, for it was surely that, was to leave the art world behind. It was a hard sacrifice, for Claire was an artist, period; she had no experience making a home on a wilderness frontier.

Happily for all the rest of us, Claire discovered that her artistic talents went further than painting and sculpture. She discovered, as all her readers have, that she was also a writer. Her first book told of her remarkable experience living with Eskimos. This book tells the story of the early years in an artist's life on America's last frontier. It teems with the detail of life, for she kept in her journal, for over half a century, a sensitive record of their lives.

The reader of this book comes as close as anyone is apt to come to knowing what life was like on that last frontier. And that reader will meet here a vast cast of remarkable people: sourdoughs, cheechakos, Eskimos, Indians, trappers, miners, fishermen.

Claire Fejes, the painter, is famous; Claire Fejes, the writer, soon will be, for this book is a frontier classic and will become a valuable record of the last phase of westering Americans.

Angus Cameron

CHAPTER

I

————

Leaving
Home

My father told me
the day I was born
a rainbow arched over
the concrete of New York City.

Forever after
I longed for colors
and hungered for
wild green forests.

From my journal

Never in my dreams had I wanted to go to Alaska. The farthest my sisters and I had ever traveled was to St. Petersburg, Florida. My wilderness was the Bronx Park in New York City.

My burning desire was to be an artist. I had longed to share a studio loft in downtown Manhattan. Alaska was as remote to me as Zanzibar.

I was not one of those women who can shoot a moose or a bear or even a rabbit. I could not and would not shoot anything. I have never trapped a mouse or caught a fish. I was afraid of bears and relieved that there are no snakes in Alaska. Flexibility and adaptability are what I have most admired in myself. Lighting a fire using one match was my outstanding survival skill.

Yet, how beautiful was my first sight of Alaska with its

rolling snow-covered mountains bathed in rosy light, arched over by a sky of purest azure blue! When we first came, I felt that with each footstep in the woods we trod on virgin earth. We drank river water everywhere and watched moose feeding.

Joe was drafted into the Air Force in 1942. We had been married only one year. After basic training, he was shipped to Fairbanks, Alaska, to work in the flight control tower at Ladd Field with the Air Transport Command. Since he could speak Russian, he was made an interpreter and gave landing and takeoff instructions to Russian pilots flying Lend-Lease planes from Fairbanks to Siberia.

When the war ended in 1945, he realized that he did not want to live in New York, to punch a time clock, or to fight the subways, the crowds, and the job scarcity.

He had caught "gold fever"! We were in love, and Joe, at twenty-nine, was adamant about seeking his fortune mining gold. He had a fierce determination to work hard and the patience to stick with a project no matter how difficult. We had been separated for four years during the war, and I was not going to be left behind again.

I decided I would have to adapt, to do my art work as well as I could in whatever circumstances I found myself. Although I had my doubts about Joe's get-rich-quick scheme, I packed my belongings — my art supplies and stone-carving tools — and I slipped in a chunk of alabaster, in case I could not find suitable stone to carve.

In the forties, even if a woman did think her career was as important as her husband's, it was a "Whither thou goest, I will go" world. No matter where I went, I was an artist. Perhaps I could carve stone while he mined.

When Joe had asked me to marry him, I had told him what my art meant to me. It was not a minor hobby but a deeply rooted part of my life. I had told Joe I would not marry him unless he understood that I would not be an ordinary housewife. "I'll always be an artist. It's my work, it's important in my life."

I left my heavy stone carvings with my family for safe-keeping; surely I would create others in Alaska. I said good-bye to Jose de Creeft, my teacher, and fellow artists at the Art Students League. My first stone carving, *Four Sisters*, was on exhibition at the A.C.A. Gallery in New York City, a good beginning. The carving depicted me and my three sisters with our arms around one another.

Our friends thought we were crazy to leave New York for Alaska. My mother and father were dubious but did not offer any objections. After all, they had been Jewish immigrants in their teens when they crossed the ocean by themselves from Europe to America. My mother fled from Poland by steerage, the money she had earned from sewing strapped around her waist.

My parents looked sad, and my three younger sisters cried as Joe and I left. They probably thought I was desert-ing them. But I left home without a tear.

My father said, "I waved casually to my family like any eighteen-year-old as I boarded the ship to America. Little did I realize then that I would never see any of them again."

"We'll strike it rich," Joe said. "We'll be back every winter, living off the gold we struck in the summer!" Such is the confidence of youth. As it turned out, it would be many years before I went home again, carrying their first grandchild in my arms.

I had come from a family of four sisters and had never been alone. As the oldest, I was the leader. I dragged my three sisters to the free W.P.A. art classes, where we were given free paint, paper, clay, and brushes. The teachers were professional artists, and models posed for us. It was an excellent beginning art education. Would I be able to carve and paint in Alaska? What would I make of the loneliness and separation?

Joe had a job waiting for him in Alaska as an oiler for the Moore Creek Mining Company, owned by Elmer Keturi. He would be paid a dollar and sixty-five cents an hour.

"I can learn all about gold mining from an expert," Joe said optimistically.

We arrived in Seattle in March 1946 after driving through the Rockies. We sold the 1936 Chrysler and boarded the *S.S. Columbia*, one of the Alaska Steamship Line's utilitarian ships, painted gray like a U.S. Army transport ship. I wondered if it was any more seaworthy than the line's *S.S. Yukon*, which had run aground a few weeks before.

As we headed north through the icy waters, seagulls followed our ship and dolphins leaped. It was my first sea voyage, and I was seasick most of the time. Joe, a splendid sailor, photographed the porpoises and kittiwakes and gloried in the high waves as the horizon tilted and lifted and sank. Sick and green, I staggered off to our small cabin, steadied by Joe's tall, slender frame.

The third day out, the ship ran into a storm and the waves hit the top deck. Everything in the room fell and crashed, and I was tossed out of my bunk. My mother must have suffered worse turbulence coming from Europe. Joe said I didn't realize how well off we were compared with passengers in steerage. The storm finally abated, and huge gulps of cold, fresh air, so different from the city fumes to which I was accustomed, helped to dispel my seasickness. A forceful wind was blowing. My feet were numb, my face burned red.

The ship docked at Ketchikan, which was nestled in a big harbor. Cedar, hemlock, and spruce trees surrounded the buildings, and a colorful array of fishing boats lined the harbor. The town was built on pilings, and nothing seemed level. Green moss grew on rooftops due to the constant rain. Men in heavy boots lounged against warehouses that lined the wharves. The fishermen and loggers were dressed in checkered jackets and windbreakers, with knitted caps pulled down over their ears. They were unlike any of the city men I knew in business suits and ties, men who rarely held a hammer or chopped wood. The women we saw used no makeup. They wore pants and bulky jackets and walked with easy strides in comfortable boots.

The totem poles were inspiring. I had visions of the large murals or sculptures I would create, and I filled a small notebook with sketches. When I was a child, we lived across the street from Bronx Park, and every day we explored the park and its animals. There, in the zoo, I saw my first totem pole, never dreaming that I would someday see the real thing in Alaska.

To steady our sea legs, we walked to a cafe and had our first taste of Alaska coffee, served in big white mugs. The waitress punched two holes in the top of a can of evaporated milk and slapped it down in front of us.

After a brief stop at Juneau, we continued to Seward, where we boarded the Alaska Railroad for Fairbanks. Among the passengers were Eskimos, Indians, trappers, and miners dressed like characters from a Jack London novel. The train crawled along the tracks that curved through snow-capped mountains bathed in rosy light. Spruce, heavy with snow, cast long blue-purple shadows. The only sign of man was an occasional log cabin or railroad shack with its wood pile and smoke streamers. We caught a glimpse of a moose on a snow-covered plateau. Mountain sheep — tiny white spots — dotted the high stony ridges.

At 4 A.M. we arrived at Curry, the halfway stop. During dinner at the Curry roadhouse, a grizzled miner regaled us with stories of roadhouses of the past. "We went by dog sled or horses, bundled up in furs." He stopped to chew a huge helping of ham and potatoes. "We stopped at the roadhouse before dark, and it was full of travelers. After supper, everyone went to bed in a room where the bunks were stacked four high. No train then."

The next day, after a hearty breakfast of sourdough pancakes, we boarded the train for Fairbanks. The train rumbled over high bridges and frozen rivers. Looking back along the tracks, we could see the rear of the train snaking around the hairpin curves, maneuvering carefully on the icy tracks. A moose loped away from the train. We watched him until he was just a moving speck. "Good steaks," mumbled the old-timer. "Those damn moose stand on the tracks till the trains hit 'em!"

A few hours after leaving Curry, the train stopped, and the old-timer climbed off with his packsack, strapped on his snowshoes, waved goodbye to us and went on to his cabin and trapline.

As we traveled farther north, we were surrounded by silent, endless snow and relentless cold. The winds blew, making patterns in the snow reminiscent of desert sand dunes.

Although my usual style was to plunge headlong, trusting to luck, I was anxious about our new life. Still, Joe was confident, and living with little money in crowded New York apartments had made me adaptable. I was accustomed to being a fighter with all against me; I had always been a yeasayer.

I had known at an early age that I was an artist. I made drawings all over my school papers. At fifteen, without consulting my parents, I switched from a neighborhood high school to an art high school downtown. I had to get up an hour earlier to ride the subway, hanging on to the strap, swaying as I dozed, supported by the rest of the morning commuters. My father did not object when he realized how eager I was to study painting and sculpture.

When I graduated from high school during the depression, the only work available was menial factory jobs. I finally found a job painting flowers on umbrellas. Ten girls in a stuffy room painted flowers all around the opened umbrellas.

Sometimes I managed to finish one hundred of them a day. For each umbrella we were paid five cents. We used large, flat brushes loaded with three colors; I could have painted roses with my eyes closed. We used lacquer thinner for the paints, and, in the confined quarters, the smell made me cough continually.

Every Tuesday evening, I attended a sculpture class. I had seen Saul Baizerman's hammered copper sculptures at an exhibition, and I was determined to study with him. I found his studio in Greenwich Village, above a delicatessen on Sixth Avenue. I offered to be his class model in return for lessons. When I admitted that I had never posed nude, he turned to his wife Eugenie, who was a painter, and then said to me, "We were once poor students, too. We already have a model, so you don't have to pose. You can have free lessons if you clean up after each class." I was greatly relieved that I would not have to pose naked, but I would have, in order to study with the great sculptor.

I loved drawing and sculpting in clay from the nude models, and I turned out to be their hardest-working and most enthusiastic student.

What would Fairbanks be like? The books I had read of Alaska depicted the terror of the cold: A Jack-London-frozen-land with wolves ready to devour people and bears abounding in the forests, ready to rip you apart. The pioneer women in books shot bears, had babies alone in the wilderness, and made decorations out of popcorn when they weren't rendering bear fat for pie crust. I had read of a life of survival, lonely trappers, gold miners, starving hunters, and snarling dogs. Danger, disaster, blood everywhere, and death to the weak was the message!

I wondered whether or not I could deal with the demands

of such a country, where temperatures dipped to sixty below zero. What did I know of wilderness life? When I was ten I spent one week at Ella Fohs Camp. It was the first time I ever sat on a horse or swam in a lake. It was the first time I had ever seen a lake. I was born in the Bronx tenement section of New York, where going to Manhattan by subway was an adventure.

Would those tough pioneer women accept me? And what of my dreams to be an artist? Sculpting what? Ice? I wondered how Alaska would influence my work. I leaned my head against Joe's strong shoulders and tried to sleep.

When I awoke and opened my eyes, I saw the vast dome of sky and the shadowy passing forests. The night sky opened up and a new world appeared filled with myriad constellations. It was unlike any sky I had ever seen in New York. It was unsettling to my city eyes, as though my old world had disappeared and a new, cleaner and purer world had taken its place. Ice had frosted all the windows. It was three in the morning, thirty-two degrees below zero, and pitch black on that March 12, 1946, when the train pulled into Fairbanks, the innermost heart of Alaska.

Second Avenue

★

2

Frontier Living

The reason I came to Alaska was because I had nothing to lose, but danged if I didn't lose that . . .

Anonymous

Elmer and Hildur Keturi were waiting when we stepped from the train. I was nervous, not knowing what to expect. I could hardly breathe; icicle-like cold frosted the inside of my nostrils. An icy sensation crept into the space between my glove and coat sleeve and I shivered.

The middle of the night was eerie and dark, with halos around the street lights and automobile headlights. Everything was shrouded in the exhaust pluming from idling cars at the train station. A hearty voice boomed out in the dark. It was Elmer Keturi, who had spotted Joe. "Welcome to Alaska," he shouted, slapping him on the back and enveloping my hands with his big paws. A huge man, his face hidden by the wolf ruff of his bulky parka, he piled our bags effortlessly into an old Chevy. He scraped the ice that covered the windshield, and in a booming voice cheerfully introduced me to Hildur.

I had corresponded with Hildur for three years. Her letters were warm, funny, and full of information. Photos of her showed a smiling, blonde woman with a nose that curved up at the end, "like Bob Hope's nose," she had written.

"Wait till you hear her giggle!" said Joe. They had befriended Joe when he was a sergeant on the base, inviting him to dinner often. Elmer had offered him a job working at his gold mine beginning in April, freighting equipment and supplies over the frozen ground to the mine.

The Keturis were so cordial that I felt I was indeed coming home to people I had always known. They made us comfortable, serving tea and sandwiches near the wood range in their kitchen.

Without her heavy coat, Hildur was a slender, sandy-haired woman with a brisk, cheerful way. Her eyes looked as if she were laughing all the time. In spite of our weak protests, they insisted that we take their bed, and we sank into its warmth, covered by flannel sheets and a down sleeping bag. We slept blissfully, no horns, no fire engines, no city noises. We awoke to the smell of bacon and coffee and a peaceful, white new world of small log cabins, wood smoke, and cheerful laughter.

"How would you like sourdough pancakes, Claire?" called Hildur through the door.

"Come and get it!" said Elmer loudly behind her. I had never met anyone like him before. Joe had told me about his prowess with all kinds of machinery and his reputation as a gold miner. At twenty-one in 1929, he had walked in a blizzard from Nenana to Flat, 400 miles in seventeen days, over Lake Minchumina and the old trails. He was the first man to break a winter ice trail from Fairbanks to Koyukuk; now it is the road used to reach the northern oil fields. Elmer had forged the trail through snow blizzards by compass, through Stevens Village up the Dall River, making a landing strip on the river with two rows of spruce boughs for the pilot to land on skis.

Hildur, a schoolteacher, was taking a leave to be home with their baby, Hilda, who lay gurgling in her crib with a toothless grin. Their ten-year-old son, Ray, was at school.

It was snowing heavily, and huge snowdrifts were piled window high. The radio reported thirty-seven degrees below zero.

We needed a place to live, and rentals were scarce after the war, but the Keturis had located a small, furnished cabin for rent two blocks away. After lingering over coffee, we dressed warmly and went to investigate the cabin. It was a great effort for me to walk two blocks. My hands and face were so cold that I pulled my scarf over my face, leaving only eye slits.

The one-room cabin had a Lang woodstove in the middle of the room for cooking and heat; an outhouse, but no running water or plumbing. The rent was thirty dollars a month. "This place is not much," said Hildur, "but it's all that's available."

We moved into our cabin, six blocks from Second Avenue, the main street. It had a fine sink, and though it sported a faucet, no running water came out; a bucket caught the contents when it drained. "Where do I dump this?" I asked. Joe lifted the bucket and tossed the water out the back door, letting in an icy blast. Water was precious. Snow from the five-foot bank outside our window tasted oily, unsuitable for drinking, but the view of snow-laden trees made me happy.

Only eight city blocks in town had running water; the water was hard and orange-colored. We put a big card in our window when we wanted water. The four-sided card had a number along each edge: 5, 10, 15, and 20. I would set it in the window with the number of gallons we wanted displayed on top.

Chuck Wehner, owner of Pioneer Wells, drove up in his water truck equipped with a woodstove emitting smoke. The stove kept the water from freezing, and the coffeepot on it kept the driver warm. A 50-cent five-gallon jug lasted two days if we were careful. "Boughten" water was used over and over in ingenious ways: leftover potato and egg water for mopping floors, the shampoo water for cleanup jobs, and if our water supply was very low, we washed our faces, then our hair, and finally our dirty socks in the same soapy water.

The Keturis, whose house was on the water line, were kind enough to invite us for showers, or for two dollars we went to a bathhouse downtown. First we sat on the wooden benches of the sauna, splashing water on the hot rocks. The floors leading to the showers were wooden slats. We soaped each other and luxuriated under the abundant, hot running water. It was our special weekly treat.

We returned to our little cabin energized and clean. We scrubbed the shelves and floors, unpacked our books and records, pots and dishes, and our few clothes. When we played Mozart on our record player, the music filled the little cabin and vibrated, overflowing in that silence.

We slept on an old couch that separated at night, one side higher than the other, an acrobatic challenge. There were two rickety chairs and a table. Since rooms were scarce, I was glad to have a shelter of our own.

When a passerby walked in the stillness, the snow crunched. Sometimes a dog team and rider whizzed by; I watched until they were a speck on the horizon. The snowy trees and sky I could see from our window made me aware of the vast space beyond, and I gave a sigh of profound joy. Smoke plumed from every small cabin, and the Chena River, which flowed through Fairbanks, was frozen to a seven-foot depth, enabling us to walk and drive across it. Everywhere we looked it was beautiful. It filled my heart and satisfied my artistic yearnings.

Our outhouse behind the cabin was right in the middle of town. When I complained about the icy seat, Elmer suggested, "You can always get a caribou-skin seat, like the old-timers." However, when it was thirty-five degrees below zero I balked at going out, and improvised with a Hills Brothers coffee can "chamber pot" which I would later dump in the outhouse. Joe, however, used the outhouse, and I felt a bit ashamed at my lack of hardiness.

The Keturis' home was a haven to us that first winter, for it had plumbing. Hildur and I spent many hours together. She taught me how to bake rye bread and graham bread from a recipe of her mother's. I liked to knead the dough, and when I punched it down, it felt alive.

Our house smelled fragrant on baking days, and I learned to make all kinds of baking powder and yeast breads using dried fruits and seeds. I cooked simple things on the large black stove, which was slow to boil water. Under Joe's tutelage, I was able to build a proper wood fire.

I marveled at the skillful way Joe split the spruce wood. It looked so easy. The ax was a foreign tool to me even though I had used gouge tools for carving wood and a chisel for carving stone sculpture. Joe feared for my life and loss of toes when I swung the ax, but slowly I made progress.

Joe made bookcases from planks and cement blocks, and I put our books and small clay sculptures on it. I hung paintings on the wall and hung new yellow print curtains. We struggled with our lumpy sofa bed, and lack of water and plumbing. We bathed in galvanized tubs with water heated on the woodstove. We worked hard to make our one room a cozy nest.

My father wrote us that if I was not happy in Alaska, I could come home again, that it was no terrible thing to admit we had made a mistake. It was no mistake. We were living a pioneer life in a frontier community, and comfort was secondary to our young natures. We were in love and content.

My artistic nature was ecstatic over the beauty of the landscape. Birches, cottonwoods, and spruce covered with snow surrounded every cabin. Aspen, tamarack, and willows also grew in the harsh climate, and they stretched out from our door for hundreds of miles in every direction. We felt part of a small community inside a large wilderness.

In 1946, Second Avenue, the main street of Fairbanks, was two blocks long and had paved sidewalks. Eighth Avenue, where we lived, was a dirt road under snow and ice. Twelfth Avenue was the end of town. On the trails and on the streets everyone smiled and said, "Hello," whether we knew them or not.

The largest store in town, the Northern Commercial Company, or the N.C. Company, owned the power plant that supplied electricity, water, and telephone service. The store sold everything from mining machinery to groceries and clothing, everything for gold mining and creek living.

I knew what it was to be poor in New York when a chicken was a luxury, so it was not such a hardship for me to do without salads or fruits, our "luxury items." I made do with dried prunes and apples instead of the more expensive fresh fruits. We seldom had salads until I learned to use dandelion leaves, fireweed shoots, and other wild greens.

Eggs were shipped in by boat from Seattle and were at least a month old when they arrived. They came in three prices — ranch, boat, and airborne. When fresh eggs were flown in, the old-timers, used to stale eggs, would not eat them.

Waechter's Meat Market cut frozen beef carcasses by electric saw while the customers waited. Butter came in cans, and milk was delivered from Creamer's Dairy by a truck that had a wood-burning stove in it to keep the milk from freezing. Charlie Creamer had bought the dairy in 1928, from a man named Hinkley, who brought the cows up on the boat from Seattle to Nome. When Nome's gold strike slowed, Fairbanks became the center of population and Creamer moved the Holsteins down by barge.

Hildur suggested it was cheaper to buy by the case at the Alaska Market, where canned goods were stocked high.

There were a few onions, potatoes, carrots, some wilted lettuce, and apples and oranges. I bought staples and bread-makings, oatmeal, beans, a dozen boat eggs, flour, salt, sugar, yeast.

"I'll take a case of peas and a case of corn," I said grandly. "And make that a case of Borden's milk and a can of Hills Brothers coffee." No one drank any other brand but that red can with the old man in a white nightgown carrying a candle. We bought Log Cabin Syrup, its can shaped like a log cabin, to use on sourdough hotcakes. Mort Cass, the owner of the Alaska Market, gave me silver dollars in change, and waved aside my pennies and nickels. Stores didn't bother to deal with petty change then, nor with paper money.

After stocking up on groceries and paying the rent, we had fifty dollars left over. However, we were given moose, caribou, and fish by new friends. Our needs were small; we did not feel poor at all. In New York City we would have felt desperate. In Alaska we felt the country was bountiful.

We had each other and our love of music. We lived on beans, homemade bread, caribou, and moose. I developed the coffee habit from the Keturis, but I never could drink it without canned milk.

It snowed almost every day, covering each tree branch with a white blanket, blurring snow into sky. The sun shone on the snow, glinting like strawberry ice cream, shadowing a house front here, a tree there. I felt lazy, with time to dream, more time than I ever had in my life. My whole being slowed to a steady, contented beat.

In the woods, the birch branches bent, arching with the burden of snow. Green spruce had white capelets extending to each tip. We saw split-hoof moose tracks near grouse tracks. The snow was free of human footprints until our big ones came — huge webbed, snowshoe tracks, and an indentation where I fell, tripped by my clumsiness. Eventually, I managed not to step on the webbing, and to keep the snowshoes far apart and parallel, but it was not easy to learn that straddle-legged gait.

In a snowy clearing, a red bushy-tailed fox was hunting mice, pacing around and around, sniffing the frozen earth — a white landscape except for the living flame of the fox.

Bird songs echoed from hill to hill, and a hawk circled above us. I gulped the air like water. We ate our lunch sitting on a fallen log in a patch of faint sunlight, listening to the cold snap of branches and the whine of a saw miles away.

C H A P T E R

3

Sourdoughs

They called us cheechakos, or newcomers. The
old-timers were called sourdoughs. (Sourdough,
a fermented flour and water dough, was used
by prospectors to make hotcakes and bread.)

From my journal

As she served us hot cinnamon rolls and coffee, Hildur told me what it was like in Fairbanks in the early 1900s. "Fairbanks was just a clearing in the wilderness, more dogs than people. Felix Pedro, an Italian prospector, discovered gold and the stampede was on." Hildur passed me the canned milk in her china pitcher. "Captain Barnette built a trading post on the banks of the Chena River and soon there were five hundred cabins, a row of saloons, cigar stores, a newspaper, bathhouses and barber shops, as well as a grocery and meat store."

Elmer joined in on his favorite topic. "They took out six million dollars in gold from the creeks in 1905. The men cut wood all winter to feed the boilers that powered the mining equipment." Elmer took a bite of his bun. "Crews worked with pick and shovel all day for about six dollars. The Finns thought it would be easy work, but after a month their hands couldn't open from the cold and shoveling." Elmer looked at his huge hands and flexed them.

"Was it really like the movies, those murders over gold claims?" I asked.

"You bet. Claims were staked, sold, and resold. Many a time they sprinkled gold dust to fool the buyer. When there was a murder, the miner's court used to hang men without a trial."

"Did you get your claims by staking them?"

"No, I mined with my Uncle Gus; he had already bought a mine. There's only about three thousand people in Fairbanks now. There were five thousand in the early 1900s, but gold profits are down. Gold is only thirty-five dollars an ounce. Everyone wants to get rich, but it's not that easy, as you'll find out at Moore Creek this summer."

"You know what a 'sourdough' is, don't ya, Claire?" he went on. "If you're really of this country, you have to pee in the Yukon, sleep with a squaw, and shoot a bear. That's supposed to define a sourdough."

"Don't pay attention," laughed Hildur. "Those miners made that up. If it weren't for the Indians around here none of them would have made it."

"Well, a sourdough is one step up from a cheechako," grinned Elmer. "You're a cheechako, Claire."

"Anybody can be a cheechako, a greenhorn, but only men are supposed to be sourdoughs," explained Hildur, turning up her nose.

"Men think they're the only ones who discovered this country, but it was the women who made this a civilized town, don't forget. They're the ones who scrubbed clothes in lye soap and river water, used egg boxes for drawers, and baked bread and pies with bear grease. They tended the gardens while the men worked, and they brought up books. Aunt Aina hemstitched sugar sacks for curtains. What was a rude camp became a home."

"The men provided the moose, bear, and caribou haunches that hung in caches," said Elmer, jumping up to add two logs to the wood fire. "Don't forget that."

"Elmer, what about Fannie Quigley?" said Hildur, passing more buns around. "She was as good a shot as any man. She and her Joe mined at Kantishna."

I had seen the clipping from the *Fairbanks Daily News-Miner* when Fannie had died in 1944. The photo showed her to be a square-faced woman, her hair pulled on top of her head, dressed in a wool shirt and men's pants. "She sure could out-shoot, out-cuss, and out-drink most men," granted Elmer.

Alaska seemed to be the last refuge for rugged individuals, a motley crew from every state in the union. It was a place for them to get far away from organized civilization. On the whole, Alaskans were tolerant of one another's foibles and many individual acts that would have seemed out of place elsewhere were tolerated here.

But as we put on our fur-lined boots and bundled up, ready to walk home in the frosty night, Elmer said, "Everyone here is friendly to newcomers, Claire. You'll find that people are generous in sharing their catches."

Nineteen forty-six was a time of change, the founding of a more stable population in Fairbanks. It offered new beginnings for young people like us coming after the war.

An influx of construction workers came to build the army barracks, roads, and the post hospital. New fortune hunters came to stay, bringing their wives. Still, women were scarce. Some of the single men eventually married the few school-teachers and nurses.

More pickup trucks than cars were seen on the dirt roads, and the N.C. Company sold draglines, tractors, and other mining and heavy equipment. The Alcan Highway linking Alaska with Canada was being upgraded from a military supply route to a civilian highway. During the day, float planes carrying government officials took off from under the Cushman Street bridge on the Chena River, heading for northern villages.

Looking at the globe, Fairbanks was not the remote end of the planet, but the growing center of Arctic trade, close to Japan and Russia, the crossroads of the world.

Fairbanks, the end of the Alaska Railroad, was halfway between New York and Tokyo. It was located in the Tanana Valley, known as the "Golden Heart of Alaska," the jumping-off place and supply center for Arctic villages. The nearest town, Anchorage, was 450 miles by railroad, and Seattle was 1,460 miles by airplane.

Bob Bartlett and Ernest Gruening represented us in Washington, D.C. We often felt locked away from the mainstream of political and economic life. As a territory, our delegates had no vote in the United States Congress — the feeling persisted that we were isolated and ignored by the federal government. Sometimes I felt very much like our territory, outside the pale, and isolated.

The highway built during the war connected us with Canada and the rest of the United States. It was a narrow, two-lane dirt road used mostly for military transport. People taking a trip to the States said they were going "outside." We were "inside"; the rest of the world was "outside." It was not uncommon to chip in to raise the fare if someone needed to go "outside" and did not have money. Sometimes a person who seemed unsavory would be "blue-ticketed" — given a one-way ticket out of town.

Nonconformists abounded and delighted in this last outpost; they could dress any way they wished and could live miles from other people in a cabin they built themselves with logs from the land. They could hunt, trap, and fish. They did not care whether they had plumbing or the latest fashion in furnishings. What they chose to do was their business as long as they did not infringe on others or break the law. Some people threw out slop water and used an outhouse, but no one ever trashed the streets with tin cans.

The men in Alaska seemed larger than life, and the pioneer women equal to any task. People talked to one another without ceremony. Friends became family, bonded by coping with the same challenges of weather and hardships. Few people were from New York, most were midwesterners, some came from the "old country" — Finland, Russia, Sweden, or Yugoslavia.

People came to Alaska because they wanted to get away from wherever they were — to get away from some trouble, or a "rat race" job. They wanted to "make it" in another place. They wanted to find a fortune in gold; they wanted free homestead land. Some were rejects from society, remittance people and misfits. Loners. Many loved fishing and hunting, and some thought they could live off the land. Most wanted to get rich quick. We were a boom or bust town.

They came for the higher wages, not realizing that it took more money to live here; everything was more expensive than in the States. Some did not come for gold or higher wages; they came lured by the wilderness call of the North. We were making friends from all walks of life and from every state. We met mail-order brides married to trappers and ex-prostitutes living with gold miners, but I didn't meet any artists who were serious about art. People needed jobs, lumber, money for wells, roofing — basics, not culture. However, I needed art, books and music. I felt alone in a cultural wilderness.

Our only connection with the outside world was our mail, the radio, and the *Fairbanks Daily News-Miner*, which featured Drew Pearson's column and Westbrook Pegler, who held opposing views. *Jessen's Weekly* kept us abreast of all the comings and goings of trappers, miners, and visitors to Fairbanks.

My favorite column in *Jessen's Weekly* was by Lydia Fohn-

Hansen, who worked for the University of Alaska's Extension Service. She told us how to extend butter with gelatin and canned milk, and how to make easy ice cream. (Mix a can of evaporated milk with a can of fruit, beat it and freeze outdoors.) We learned how to make plum pudding in Hills Brothers coffee cans and how to make slipcovers. She told us how to use Sta-way, condemned by the health authorities as a mosquito repellent, but "excellent for removing black rubber marks from linoleum."

Jessen's want ads were interesting, with gold scales, guns, gold claims, bear hides, and trap lines for sale. Cotton dresses were ten dollars each. Ernest Spink, the fur buyer from Seattle, bought sixty thousand dollars' worth of beaver pelts from the trappers. Building lots were offered for two hundred dollars each, and if we could afford to buy a log cabin, the price was two thousand dollars. That was a lot of money to us. I was focusing on a new way of life. My days now revolved around the huge woodstove, chopping wood and keeping the fire going, learning to cook on a temperamental stove. It took all day just to do chores. The stove never got hot enough and I never got warm enough. When would I ever find time to paint?

★

4

A Different
Drummer

*"If a man does not keep pace with his companions,
perhaps it is because he hears a different
drummer. Let him step to the music which he
hears, however measured or far away."*

Thoreau

I lingered alone over a breakfast of oatmeal, reading
Lydia's latest column, a new recipe invented during the war
by a pioneer woman, called the "Eggless, Milkless, Butterless
Cake." It was perfect. I had no eggs, no milk and instead of
butter, I had been mixing a white, waxy concoction called
oleomargarine with some yellow dye in a bowl. The recipe
sounded terrible but it tasted delicious, and the raisins and
spices filled the house with fragrance. It was surprisingly
moist and dark and kept for a long time.

The buildings on Second Avenue revealed their false
fronts. They had not been too obvious before, with the
heavy snow cover on the roofs and the picturesque icicle
trim. The downtown bars smelled of stale beer, and the men
coming out in the daylight looked unkempt. Joe and I
counted the bars and churches when we first arrived; there
were thirty-two bars and thirty-two churches for fewer than
three thousand people.

Crooked, awkward cabins with sunken storm porches and

leaning stovepipes squatted next to the wooden sidewalks.
When I walked, I was careful to avoid the howling huskies.
Hildur told me of a child mauled by a dog in our neighborhood, evidently not an unusual occurrence. I walked often
to the Thomas Memorial Library, housed in a picturesque
log building. The white clapboard Catholic church was the
most graceful wooden building in town, with stained glass
windows and a madonna in a cupola topped with a spire.

I painted small watercolors on the kitchen table, but soon
learned that what Alaskans held in high esteem were Sydney
Laurence's realistic paintings of Mount McKinley. People did
not seem to care for my simplified forms and brilliant colors,
my impressionistic style. It was no use telling them that the
world of painting had changed since the early 1900s. I
painted alone without any encouragement. My influences
were Picasso, Gauguin, Van Gogh, Hartley, and Rivera.

I liked Ted Lambert's paintings at the University of
Alaska. They were fresh and impressionistic. Ted, named
after Theodore Roosevelt, was twenty-one when he landed
in Cordova with $3.65 in his jeans pockets. "I had to make
that do for ten days during which I traveled on foot 220
miles to Nazina where I first found employment and my first
square meal in the country," he wrote in his journal.

His paintings of dog teams, wilderness, and Native people
came from his own experience. He wrote, "I have been on
the up side of the Arctic Circle a few times and punched
dogs in as low as sixty-seven degrees below zero, but the
nearest I ever came to freezing to death was in Chicago
waiting for a train."

Ted moved to the Kvichak River to trap when he and his
wife Lovetta "split the blanket" or divorced. He built a cabin
at Mentasta Lake, "where grizzlies were thick as rabbits." In

1960, his boat was found on the lake nearby, his easel spotted up in the mountains by Indians, but his body was never recovered. A strange parallel existed between his life and that of the artist Thom Thompson of Canada, who was also presumed drowned in a northern lake. Both men were artists who loved the wilderness, both were very handsome, and both died young.

People who remembered Lambert said that he had a vibrant personality. I wished I could have met him. He wrote about painting: "If there is any road to art, it is to live utterly what one wants to express and then be willing to sacrifice society of others and comforts of a gregarious existence to give all one's energy and emotional strength to its expression." He lived that philosophy. However, after giving up his wife, he became a misanthrope, bitter about people. He paid for living in isolation with his life.

Sydney Laurence, Alaska's best known artist, was born in New York. He had lived and painted in St. Ives, England. Lured by gold, he took off for Alaska, leaving his wife and two sons. In Anchorage he opened a photography store. "Like all the other suckers, I went broke mining gold," he said. "But I found enough painting material to keep me busy for the rest of my life."

He found his greatest subject matter in Mount McKinley. His snow-covered mountains are depicted with skillful brushwork and mastery of composition. Sometimes he painted a lone trapper or an Indian tending a fire, but the majority of his work consists of landscapes devoid of humans.

I hungered for art talk with my peers. Unfortunately the library at that time had few art books. Art was not important in a pioneering community.

I met Eustace Ziegler in Fairbanks when he had an

exhibit of his paintings at the radio station, the only place he could find to hang his paintings. He confessed to me that he often painted "pot boilers"! An itinerant preacher, Ziegler was recruited by the Episcopal bishop to do missionary work in Alaska at $750 a year. A small man weighing 135 pounds, he traveled along the railroad camps among the construction workers and miners. He was an excellent camp cook, a likable, modest man. He painted miners, mountains, and horses as well as portraits of Indians and Eskimos.

During the summers, he drifted down the Yukon with Lambert, painting along the way. Just as Remington and Russell captured the Old West, Ziegler's work captured the feeling of early life in Alaska.

Rusty Heurlin, a popular illustrative painter, lived fourteen miles out of town at Ester. He confessed to me that he did not like "perverted modern art, especially Van Gogh's work," and that "Picasso was the root of all evil." I did not want to get into a controversy with him over something that had been settled by the rest of the world years ago.

An itinerant "artist" painted on velvet and sold his work at the Tanana Valley Fair. The work of a fellow who burned cabin scenes and moose onto fringed moose hide was also in popular demand.

Sydney Laurence had to trade a lot of paintings to pay his bills; his canvases were stacked up like cordwood in an Anchorage drugstore and sold for fifty dollars each when he first came to Alaska, even though his work was well-known in England. Lambert did hard physical work on the river to make a living, and Ziegler sold most of his work out of his Seattle studio.

Years later, I discovered Emily Carr from Victoria. She had painted without recognition in Canada until Lawren Harris brought her into the "group of seven." Her feeling for nature and her forms of expression were not understood by the people of her town. I felt a kinship with her. She painted the Indian life of the Northwest coast and its forests and also wrote about her life in many books, taking in boarders to support herself.

Paintings and sculpture filled our home, but visitors rarely mentioned them. I had framed Van Gogh's print of *Starry Night* and no one mentioned that either! I worked on the kitchen table as well as I could.

The fact that I was a woman painter seemed strange; surely I painted only on weekends or in my spare time as a "hobby." Most of the women felt that their working day should be spent house-cleaning and cooking — the day belonged to their husbands and to their families. When viewing my work, they said, as a compliment, "It looks like a man painted it." I could not think of a smart retort that would not be rude, so I kept quiet.

At the Art Students League I had worked just as hard as the men, drawing from models, chopping and lifting fifty pounds of limestone, carting my own marble, creating what I wanted, my own vision strong. Comparing a "woman" artist with a "man" artist never entered my consciousness.

The indifference I found in Alaska was a contrast to my family's atmosphere of mutual encouragement. My three younger sisters and I were happiest sitting around our big dining room table painting in watercolor, each sister's work different. It was a special language, like writing, only we used brush and colors. It was a driving need in all our lives.

My father made scrapbooks for us, and on rainy days we children pasted in the photographs he cut out of magazines — mostly the *National Geographic* — photos of paintings, sculpture, architecture, castles and exotic gardens, people in strange costumes from other lands. This world we had never seen shaped our tastes and broadened our views.

At the Art Students League, I had enjoyed a camaraderie

working with other artists. The Master, Jose de Creeft, criticized our work on Fridays — the highlight of the week. The students and the nude model gathered around him, listening to what he said about our sculpture. A generation before, women and men were not allowed to draw from the model in the same classroom.

At home during meals, my family talked about painting. We visited the great museums and galleries, especially the Kurt Valentin Gallery, which showed Henry Moore's and Lembruch's sculptures, and Emile Nolde's watercolors.

The treasure house, the temple where I had worshipped, was the Metropolitan Museum of Art. In the forties, I worked across the street as a typist for the Audubon Society. At the stroke of twelve, my lunch hour, I entered the museum and headed for the Greek, Egyptian, or Rembrandt room. I caressed the marble head of a Greek boy when the guard was not looking. Years later, when I returned to New York, one of the first things I did was to visit the Greek sculpture room at the Metropolitan. I found the boy's head. My fingers touched his curving cheek as I kissed him on the lips.

What had been the single most important factor in my life now lay like a subterranean stream, submerged in my struggle to be a housewife. The general consensus was that women could not possibly be serious about art.

I decided to do something about that and advertised for children to attend art lessons. Four little girls signed up. Art in the school consisted of children tracing pumpkins at Halloween and Christmas trees at Christmas.

My students painted to "Peter and the Wolf" and Bach concertos. They painted events out of their lives, depicting their bouts with measles, their first fishing experiences, their snowy houses, log cabins, and dog teams; whatever came to them. They were their own ideas — their paintings, not mine. I hung the children's brightly colored paintings on the wall and put their soap carvings on the window sills.

The Fairbanks symbol of "kultur" was the German music teacher, William Gorbracht, who had heard Liszt and Strauss play in Europe. A bandmaster in the Army, he was supposed to have played the trumpet and French horn for Madame Schuman Heink at the Metropolitan Opera. After his lip muscles gave out, he left New York with his wife to seek his fortune in the North.

Gorbracht climbed the Chilkoot Pass, mined in the Klondike, then opened a roadhouse in Dawson, playing for the "Lousetown" prostitutes as well as for the formal grand balls. In 1904, he went by horse and cutter to Fairbanks to get rich on the gold strike. Instead of striking it rich, he wound up giving piano lessons to pioneer children. His wife, "Tante" Wilhelmina, acted as a midwife and knew how to give abortions. Gorbracht was a strict teacher and formed the first band in Fairbanks. He was in his eighties when we met him, a dignified, heavy man with a gray mustache.

The only music we heard was on the radio or on our record player. One day Joe came home early with a large package under his arm. I was baking bread and yelled, "Hi Honey," from the kitchen.

I heard music coming from the living room and thought it was the radio. I went to the living room to investigate. Joe had a violin under his chin and was playing Tchaikovsky. I had been married to him for four years and he had never played the violin before.

"But... you never told me you could play like that." I was stunned. "Why haven't you had a violin before?"

"Well, I had one, but I sold it. I was broke."

"Where did you find this one?"

"I just bought it from a woman for two hundred dollars."

Joe put down the violin. "When I was a kid," he said, "I used to take the wooden sticks out of the bottom of the window shades, place one under my chin and use the other as a bow. I was imitating the Gypsy violinists at Hungarian dances.

"When I was twelve, my folks bought me a violin. They paid a dollar a week for fifty-two weeks for the lessons and the violin. Later I studied in Cleveland with a famous gypsy, Horvath Vili. In 1932, I played with a gypsy ensemble."

Joe organized a 16-piece band, called it the Russ Kayne Orchestra and played the saxophone and the clarinet in nightclubs around Cleveland.

In 1944, while in the Air Force in Alaska, he played the sax and clarinet with an Air Force band called the Northernairs.

Joe's violin became his primary interest. He played Hungarian songs with a haunting quality that he could not express with words. Playing the violin without telling me he was so accomplished was typical of Joe's understated way of communicating.

Our evenings were now enriched with Joe on the violin playing both jazz and classical music. Gypsy songs were my favorite. Joe sang, "Csak egy kiss lany vana vilagon." (There's only one little girl in the world for me.)

Hearing Joe play gypsy songs reminded me of our engagement dinner. Joe, with his old world courtly manners, had invited my parents out to a Hungarian restaurant, buying gardenias for me and my mother, a carnation for my father, and a bouquet for the table. It was his old-fashioned way of letting my parents know that he wanted to marry me. The gypsy violinist came to our table and played. We shared a love of music, which remained as one of our strongest bonds.

When the Keturis came over, we coaxed Elmer to sing. Hamming it up, he waved his arms over his head and raised his eyes heavenward. Without any coaxing, he sang his favorite Finnish folk song, with Joe playing violin accompaniment:

> *"Run my horse, run*
> *For the clouds are so dark,*
> *And the trees,*
> *They are shading my way."*

Then he sang an old miner's song:

> *"In the land of the pale, blue snow,*
> *when it's ninety-nine below . . ."*

Hilda and washing clothes

★

CHAPTER

5

Our Mothers

And in the sweetness of friendship let there be laughter, and sharing of pleasures.

The Prophet
Kahlil Gibran

I saw Hildur almost every day, warming to her hospitable manner. She was eight years older than I, and experienced in frontier living. The Keturis had opened their home and hearts to us. We treasured the comradeship between us and the open flow of good communication, especially the heart-to-heart talks between Hildur and me. Our men usually talked about machinery, mining, and practical things, rarely discussing their feelings.

Hildur knew we had no running water or washing machine.

"Come on over and bring your laundry," came her invitation. "I'm heating water now." She'd meet me at the door with a wide grin, little Hilda on her hip.

Wash day was an adventure. While the water heated in big washtubs on Hildur's wood stove, we drank coffee and ate her homemade graham bread and blueberry jam. On her kitchen floor, we sorted the dirty clothes into piles according to colors, washing our clothes together. I brought Oxydol soap powder for her wringer washing machine, vintage 1940. We washed the white clothes, then the colored ones, then the men's dirty, greasy overalls last. After we wrung them out, we hung them on wooden racks and lines near the stove to dry. It was an all-day job, but we enjoyed the companionship, looking forward to our weekly wash get-together. I remembered my mother washing clothes on her knees, leaning over the bathtub. Picking up another batch of clothes to put in the soapy wash water, I said, "At least we don't have to use the metal washboards our mothers used, scrubbing up and down with harsh soaps." Hildur and I lifted the washtub and poured hot water into the machine.

Hildur looked up and brushed her hair out of her eyes as she added more Oxydol soap. "I remember my mother doing that until she got a washing machine. We lived in a two-story wooden farmhouse in Spencer, New York. My mother cooked on a big kitchen range. My father chopped all the wood. We had another wood heating stove in the middle of the living room. My mother did a lot of the farm work. She milked the cows, tended the potatoes and big vegetable garden. I never had to milk the cows, thank goodness, but I did help during the haying and the digging of the potatoes." She threw in a batch of clothes. "We do have it easy compared to our mothers."

"Being poor on the farm is not like being poor in the city like we were," I said, dragging Joe's wet flannel shirts through the wringer. "They didn't throw your family out on the street for not paying the rent, and you had enough to eat and plenty of milk to drink on the farm."

"You think you were poor in the city," Hildur grinned. "We lived one year on apples, milk, potatoes, and bread."

"The last year of high school, I wore one skirt, two blouses, and one hand-me-down olive-green sweater, which made me sick of that color forever. My black coat pockets were so worn I painted them with India ink." I pulled the clothes through the wringer, setting them aside in a pile.

"So what?" Hildur countered. "Everyone was poor in those days during the depression. I never had any clothes either. I had only one dress I wore the first year through school. Everyone wore hand-me-downs."

In New York City, we had always lived in the poor neighborhood, gazing at the things we could never possess, but in Alaska, the town millionaire walked around in bib overalls. "Cap" Lathrop owned the Lathrop Building, the radio station, the Healy coal mine, and other properties. People said no matter how much money Cap made, he still froze his ass in the cold weather same as the rest of us.

Hildur looked at me, not with the sympathy I expected, but with a gesture I still remember. "It doesn't matter now, here in Alaska. Who cares if you were rich or poor, an artist or a housewife?" Her arm waved, and with one stroke she freed me from my past. "It's what you are now that really counts. Money is not the criterion here that it is in the cities. People here count for themselves, not for their families or bank accounts. You are judged not for your clothes, but for your character."

After washing other loads we emptied the dirty water through a hose into the sink. Then we filled the machine with cold water and rinsed the clothes. We took another coffee break while the machine whirred away, so heavily loaded it did little dances on the floor. We sipped our coffee in companionable fashion while I thought of what Hildur had said.

Joe had not yet received a paycheck so we were careful with every dollar. Before I spent money, I asked myself if I really needed what I wanted to buy; invariably the answer was no.

Hildur, with her usual flip, had quipped, "We do more without in Alaska than we do with."

It reminded me of my whole life, scrimping and stretching every cent. "I wanted to go to college," I told Hildur, "but my family needed the money I earned. It broke my heart. Perhaps if I had been a son, my father would have encouraged me to go to college. He probably thought a girl's destiny was to get married! My mother had no illusions, she just wanted me to marry and have children. According to her, had I not married at twenty-one, I would have been an old maid." I snapped a shirt and hung it on the rack.

"At sixteen, after graduating from high school, I found a job in a factory for twelve dollars a week, spending two dollars for lunch and carfare and giving the rest to my dad." I laid Joe's overalls on the line, just missing little Hilda as she crawled underfoot.

Hildur picked up the baby with one arm and fed clothes through the wringer with the other. "I wanted to go to college, too," she said. "I wanted to be a schoolteacher. I managed college for one year, then taught in a rural one-room school. I was seventeen, and the oldest boy in the class was fifteen!" Hildur poked a bottle into the baby's mouth and whirling her around she danced a little jig, singing, "Enchy enchy meanchy . . ."

I marveled at Hildur's lightheartedness. She never seemed to get moody or introspective as I did — all angst and seriousness. In New York, I had been a serious young woman. Besides attending the Art Students League's night sculpture class with Jose de Creeft, I worked in a factory, marched on picket lines, and attended rallies to help families who could not afford to pay the rent and were thrown out on the streets. In Alaska, no one was thrown out of their homes. If they were, they could go into the woods and build a log cabin. Here it was not dog-eat-dog. The skills I needed were precisely those our mothers knew. I tried not to take everything so seriously, to lighten life with humor. My mentor was Hildur.

Hildur and I could talk about any subject, usually agreeing on political and social issues. We were both avid readers, exchanging and discussing books. We enjoyed each other's company, never tiring of each other. She was the leavening in my daily bread; we laughed over everything.

Life was funny to the Keturis. They didn't take themselves seriously. They plugged along, doing their best every-day, and they laughed about it.

Hildur had an easy, no-nonsense way of bringing up her children, doing away with nonessentials. Her children wore the usual cast-offs that the women shared. She recovered her old couch with new fabric using a staple gun. She put anything she wanted to freeze on a shelf outdoors. She knew how to dress for the cold; how to put mittens over wool gloves to hold in the warmth; how to stretch the dollar; how to cook with limited supplies; how to sew her own clothing; how to knit sweaters and crochet afghans.

She taught me how to knit a wool scarf for Joe. "The scarf," Joe explained to Elmer, "is a mile long. It started out wide, then ended up narrow — besides, maroon isn't my favorite color." That was the end of my knitting.

When Hildur's mother came to visit her from Spencer, New York, I liked her immensely. She was a farm woman who wore kerchiefs; a plain country woman with a Finnish accent. Her hands were worn from milking cows and she wore wide, worn black shoes with high laces, the kind my mother wore. Hildur had her kind eyes, gentle ways, and dignity.

Hildur's mother reminded me of my own mother, my Yiddish mother. She had the same humble simplicity. My mother could not read English, and my father worked nights and could not help us, but we were all good students. When it snowed, our mother brought our galoshes to school, waiting outside, her babushka on her head, her housedress under her old black coat. I felt embarrassed by the way she dressed, but of course all the other immigrant mothers must have worn kerchiefs.

Hildur was very much like her mother in her unpretentious ways. She was nonjudgmental, never saying a mean thing about anyone. Her advice was sound, but she never gave it unless I asked. If she said something, she meant it. Of different backgrounds, we felt a strong kinship, sharing a love of learning.

My mother never knitted, and she didn't sew much anymore. Her hands sat idly on her lap. In the evenings while my father worked as a waiter, my mother read the *Forward* laboriously, her glasses at the end of her nose, the glasses my father chose for her at Woolworth's.

I had loved to go to the market with her to see the fresh fish swim in the tank, to enter the butcher store where they plucked the chicken feathers while we waited. The fruit man hawked, "Fresh tomatoes today!", his fruits and vegetables arranged in colorful pyramids. In the bakery, my mother squeezed the onion rolls and bought a Pechters Rye bread. Walking home, we heard the roaring elevated subway overhead and smelled the pervasive malt of the beer factory. We carried the heavy paper sacks up four flights. Stewing cabbage wafted from the crowded tenements across the alley. From our window we could see a man in long underwear scratching his belly as he opened his refrigerator. A Russian neighbor exchanged meat-filled piroshkis for my mother's cheese blintzes on holidays.

Coming from a small Polish village on the Russian border where survival was an everyday struggle, she never adjusted to the big city. She never learned to ride the buses or subways alone. Our parents spoke in Polish when they did not want us to know what they said. They never talked to us about their lives before they came to America, not about the pogroms from which they had fled to this land of opportunity. They wanted us to have a good life like other young girls.

Mother never drew attention to herself. She accepted her poverty, the temper of my father, and the revolt of her children with meekness, showing us a steady devotion. She never raised her voice in anger. Our apartment was her world; she was truly a "house" wife — shopping, sewing, cooking, and keeping everything clean was her main occupation. Her life was spent within a radius of ten blocks. She never had the spirit to overthrow any of her burdens or to fight them. Her greatest joys were her four girls; her sorrow was that she could not give my father a son. Her lack of education was not her fault, and neither was her life bound by kitchen and children.

From early photographs, I could see that my mother had been a beautiful woman with delicate features and blue eyes. People who were strangers to me used to ask to see my hands because hers had been so beautiful. They said she loved to sing and dance, and they remembered her pretty clothes. Her smile was sweet and childlike, and she enjoyed having her girls make a fuss over her hair.

When I left home, she had begun to deteriorate slowly. She could not remember where she put her purse or how to set a table. She seemed depressed, had no friends and stayed home most of the time.

My mother needed help now, and I was thousands of miles away. The burden was on my sisters.

I loved my mother, but I didn't want to be like her. I rejected her way of life every day. I rejected her narrow ideas of the world. Contrary to her wishes, I had married outside of her religion.

Yet she was a part of me, as Hildur's mother was part of her. As our mothers had, we would transmit our inner fiber, our aspirations and dreams to our children. I remembered my mother's rare joyous moments, but tried to bury memories of her sadness and loss of memory. Unconsciously, I painted my mother in every painting.

Everyone who came North began afresh, with a new slate. I had brought a heritage rich in love and family traditions. In Alaska there was no landed gentry as in other states. The second generation of pioneer Alaskans were our age or younger, so Hildur and I decided we would create our own traditions.

★

6

―――

Spring
Thaw

You, whose day it is,
Make it beautiful.
Get out your rainbow colors
So it will be beautiful.

Nootka Indian

April marked the spring thaw. The birches were etched
against a pale, watery sky, their broken branches ravaged
black, flimsy shreds of bark waving in the wind. Spruce trees
were faded to the shade of a green plush chair left out all
winter. Bits of dried leaves lay uncovered in the ice and mud.
Roads were quagmires, deeply rutted, crisscrossed with
streams.

Garbage that had been buried all winter was now exposed
and lay frozen where stray dogs had dragged it. Windows
were dirty from the winter's grime. Within their houses,
people felt just as bedraggled, for they, too, had been beaten
by cold and storms all winter and eagerly awaited the sun.
Adults felt sluggish, and children were pale; dark rings
circled their eyes. When people congregated, they yawned
continually.

Joe and I had to find a larger place to live, preferably with
running water. People were sleeping in church basements,
spare rooms, hallways, even the jail.

My wet hair was wrapped in a torn towel and I was mopping the floor when there was a knock at the door. The washing hung across the rope in our one-room cabin, and the stacked, dirty dishes sat in the sink.

A tiny woman with a toothy grin stood there. "I'm Mrs. Karstens, the lady with the one-bedroom house for rent. You were recommended by Hildur Keturi." Her elbows seemed to fill the narrow doorway so I invited her in, trying to hide the mop and pail, ducking under the wet clothes on the line.

We needed a place with plumbing, I needed a place to paint, and rentals were hard to find. I served her tea, then showed her photos of my family. I knew that I had passed inspection when she said, "You can have the rental for $75 a month."

"I feel like I won the sweepstakes," I said, restraining a loud whoopee.

Slightly deaf, she answered, "No thanks, I had my dinner."

The new house had a woodstove in the kitchen, working plumbing in the sink, and a cabinet with a white enamel counter containing a flour bin. The living room and small bedroom were paneled in stained plywood. The bathroom had a claw-footed bathtub and running water! No matter if the water ran rusty with algae and minerals; no matter if the iron-red stains in the tub never came out. No matter if the water had to be boiled and allowed to settle in a kettle overnight before it could be used for coffee or cooking. It was running water and we appreciated every blessed drop.

A storm porch shielded the main room from the cold, and there was a garden space on one side of the house. Our refrigerator was a hole in the dirt basement dug into permafrost, the permanently frozen ground which lay under nearly all of Fairbanks. A rain barrel caught the runoff water from the roof, great for shampoos. Joe bought logs and hired a woodcutter to cut eighteen-inch cordwood with a circular saw, then threw the logs down the basement steps and stacked them.

The poorly insulated house never got warm. My feet were always cold, even when I wore several pairs of woolen socks. I solved the problem by doing my reading and writing in front of the stove with my feet in the oven. The kitchen was so small I could sit at the table by the wall and touch the woodstove.

Except for a few ice patches, snow melted in small rivulets and disappeared in front of our cabin. The sun was out longer each day, and it was getting warm. Shedding my heavy winter coat, I gave a deep sigh.

As I looked heavenward I witnessed a rare phenomenon, a para-helios, occurring when ice crystals in the high altitude reflect the sun. To the west, a second sun was surrounded by a rainbowing light, and in four places in the sky were the beginnings of rainbows.

My father told me I was born after a rainstorm when a rainbow arched over the sky. Here we could see four rainbows and the northern lights!

I stomped in Joe's overlarge rubber boots, helping him to shovel channels in the ice so that the water would flow away from the house. Icicles melted from our rooftop and big chunks broke off. Joe, the more practical one, saw icicle drips as proof of bad insulation. "Heat loss, needs fixing," he muttered. I was his impractical, unsalaried apprentice.

Joe chopped the remainder of the ice and snow from the wooden sidewalk in front of our house, and I carted three loads of ice in a wheelbarrow to dump on the road to melt.

To Joe, Elmer, and the other miners, the first trickle of melting snow meant that the creeks would be flowing. Miners would then be freighting supplies on the trails over the hills and creeks.

The Keturis' log cabin seemed to have been built by the previous owner without plan in order to get indoors before winter came. In the front storm porch they hung parkas, mukluks, storm boots, and other paraphernalia. The back porch held the woodpile, shovels, sleds, and shelves for tools, food, and other equipment. Like everyone else, the Keturis rarely locked their doors.

Joe had the habit of walking through their house to warm up. He entered their storm porch and went through the living room to the large kitchen that held a wood stove, washing machine, and big, round kitchen table. He checked the table for any pies, or Hildur's homemade graham bread, used their bathroom if he had to, then went out their back door to our house, a few blocks away. He usually left a humorous note if they were not home. One day, Hildur was visiting with three club members when Joe happened to come in. "Don't mind me," he waved. "I'm just passing through."

Mrs. Karstens, my landlady, came often to check up on me, especially when I least expected her. No sleeping late! She would appear at the back door, grinning like a Cheshire cat because her dental plate never fit quite right. She would look at the stove, making sure I didn't burn down her real estate holdings. Invariably, I would have unwashed dishes in the sink. I should have planted dust balls in the corners to make her happy.

Her husband, Harry, was an unfriendly, grumpy person, who rarely smiled. It was some months before I discovered he was the same Harry Karstens of the Park Service, who, with Archdeacon Hudson Stuck and Walter Harper, had climbed Mount McKinley with a primus stove and a ton-and-a-half of food and supplies relayed on their backs. They ground sheep and caribou meat to make frozen pemmican. Their trek was long before the days of scientific expeditions with modern equipment and air-dropped fresh food supplies. It was the first time anyone had reached the top of the mountain, a remarkable feat.

Even when I asked Mr. Karstens to see his photos of the climb, he did not change his glum expression. The same obdurate trait in his character that had enabled him to withstand the strenuous climb had soured him in his old age.

Mud was tracked constantly into our small house, and I wielded the mop with a vengeance. Kept busy with the basic things, I was living a "simple life," but found out that it took longer to do things, and that life was not as simple as it appeared.

I was comfortable without a refrigerator, gadgets, or appliances. I had used them at home in New York, but I didn't miss them. I could hear De Creeft talking in sculpture class, "Sure, you can go out and buy an electric sander to finish your stone and polish it, but if you do it by hand, it has a truer polish. The sander makes a slick finish, and takes all your hand tool marks away, your individual stamp. Besides, the hand is quicker than your brain, so you have to be careful."

I had romanticized the "glamorous north," raving to Hildur about the purity of life away from the big city. Her retort was, "Baloney, nothing pure about it. You're just going through a phase. You'll change."

In the winter, the frozen Chena River had been the main thoroughfare for walkers and cars. It had felt strange to be in a car going across the frozen river, but it was solid, seven feet thick. Now with spring coming, and ice melting, it was not safe anymore. The ice was covered with black soot, and children had to be carefully watched lest they fall into it.

On the back porch, I held my face up to catch the rays of the sun. "The sun feels so good," I said. "It soaks out the waterlogged places within me."

Hildur, ever the pragmatic humorist, retorted, "For God's sake, Claire, if you're so waterlogged, why don't you just go to the bathroom?"

My new neighbor, Minnie, was born in Huslia, north of the Yukon River. Married to a white-faced, silent man, a house painter who eventually left her with three children, she later married again and had three more children. She told me many stories of village life, especially of woman's work, cutting fish and game. "Life in town is much easier with washing machines and running water," she said as she hung her clothes on the line we shared.

As a child, she had suffered from tuberculosis, as had so many people in the Arctic, without immunity to white man's diseases. Thousands had died from smallpox, flu and T.B. Minnie's handsome head, wide cheekbones, and sparkling black eyes served as a model for a foot-high chunk of lime-stone. I sketched her, preparatory to carving on the back porch as soon as it was warm enough to work outdoors. Our house was too small to chip stone inside. I would eventually change my medium to oils in spite of ten years of studying sculpture with my teachers, Jose de Creeft, William Zorach, Saul Baiserman, and Aaron Goodleman in New York.

Minnie sang beautiful Indian songs. The melody seemed to be a residue from the Russians who had settled in Nulato and Huslia years ago.

Minnie and I visited each other's houses and chatted over the clothesline. A good seamstress and fur sewer, she made

Joe a trapper's hat from a beaver he had trapped and shot. It was Indian style, with flaps tied on top of his head. He wore that hat for ten winters until it was stolen in a theater on his first visit to New York.

The miracle of nature would not forsake us. Even here in the frozen North, the trees would bud and the wild grasses would turn green. Redpolls, tiny gray birds with a splash of red on their heads, gathered outside our windows. Melting snow formed a miniature pond in our backyard, full of slush and flotsam. The air was crisp, and fragrant cabin smoke quivered in the wind. Spring was in the air.

Fairbanks had a slow-moving, quiet pace; there was plenty of time to talk to people, especially at the post office where I lined up at the General Delivery window. Dog teams were common transportation. Cars could drive now on solid ground instead of ice, and they could be started without a firepot under them, or without being plugged into a headbolt heater.

"You must go downtown and meet Eva," said Hildur one day. She was sewing curtains, and Elmer was hammering nails into the trim to put up the rods.

"Who's Eva?"

Hildur took the pins out of her mouth. "You have got to let Eva know you are new in town. She knows everyone. You can't have a wedding or a baby without Eva McGown. We call her or Adler's Bookstore to let them know our club is having a dance or a tea, just so they check the calendar to make sure there's no conflict.

"If there's a funeral, Eva is there. At parades, she is driven around in a float waving to everyone. She attends more weddings and funerals than anyone in town."

I dressed in my black coat and wound my black turban around my braids, New York style, added earrings, and walked downtown to the Nordale Hotel.

Eva was sitting at her desk at the hotel, wearing a hat with a green veil. She smelled of Yardley's violet perfume. "Oh, my dear, top of the morning to you," she exclaimed in a thick Irish brogue. "Welcome to Fairbanks." Her gray hair had just been marcelled and she dressed like a southern belle of another generation — high heels, dark suit, pearls, and a flower pinned on a green chiffon scarf.

A young woman interrupted us. "Can you find us a place to live? I'm not going to put up with this dump. I came here to get married; my boyfriend is in the military. We have no place to go. I'm ruining my shoes, mud up to my ankles from the holes in the streets. I'm going home if I can't get a place. They told me to ask you."

"Sit down, dear, sit right down. Oh, my dear, we'll soon fix that." Eva lifted the phone. Before she hung up she had persuaded someone to open her home for two strangers. I could hear the woman on the other end of the phone say, "But Eva," and Eva saying, "Yes, I know that woman at Clara Rust's has been there for over a year, but there is no other place for her to go. You really will like them. He's in the military. She's on her way over. I knew you had that spare bedroom and wouldn't mind. Thank you, dearie. God bless you." She handed the address to the young woman, who thanked her and left.

"So you're that artist from New York," she said. "I heard about you giving art lessons, just what this town needs is an artist. You must show me your work soon.

"Would you like a cup of tea? I was just going up to my room, do come." I followed her as she waved, in bird-like fashion, to the old-timers sprawled around the lobby reading the *News-Miner.*

Letters were stacked high on her desk. Above it a sign read, "Do It Now!" Books were jammed on her shelves among porcelain figurines. Dominating the small hotel room was her bed piled with clothes and boxes. Nearby a rack hung with hats and scarves stood in the corner. A dried bridal bouquet hung on the wall among small paintings and photographs.

We drank Irish tea in flowered china cups. "You will love it here," Eva predicted. "'Tis a beautiful country. Have you got a place to live?"

"We live in Mrs. Karstens' place. My husband is going to work at Keturis' gold mine."

When she heard we were in such good hands, she beamed. "Oh, the dear woman, Hildur. Do let me know if I can do anything at all for you."

During her fast chat she mentioned Ireland, Paris, Kentucky. She had friends all over the world, and she made me feel as though we were not so isolated after all. It was said it took Eva one-half hour to walk the half block to the post office because so many people stopped to talk. Before I left she sold me two tickets to the Nenana Ice Pool. I had to guess the date and time of day the ice would break up on the Tanana River at Nenana.

At the Keturis' house, Hildur had finished the green chintz curtains from fabric I had purchased for her in New York before I came to Alaska.

"How do you like Eva?"

"I really liked her. She certainly knows everything that is going on around here."

"Eva ignores the climate as much as possible," said Hildur, shaking her head. "We stomp in heavy boots, she walks on heels; Eva wears fur pieces, veils and dainty boots. Most of the women wear head scarves or fur hoods, but Eva wears hats: real hats with big brims, veils, flowers, velvet and velour. And her ears don't freeze!

"Eva came from Belfast to marry Arthur McGown, who

used to own the Model Cafe. When we first came up here," Hildur recalled, "she kept chickens and one rooster in her back room. She named them Harry and Gloria, after her friends. She had planned to kill them before winter freeze-up, but she couldn't. Didn't have the heart, so they moved into her back room that winter.

"She nursed her husband the last five years, cutting wood, shoveling snow and keeping fires going, all without running water," said Hildur. "After he died she began visiting lonely women who had just come to Alaska, and going to the hospital to see the sick people."

Hildur looked up from her sewing. "She is really the heart of this town. The city and the governor finally appointed her Alaska's Official Hostess, and she was put on the city payroll to welcome people to Alaska, greeting dignitaries at the airport, presiding over teas.

"Ever since she was on 'This Is Your Life', she's been getting letters from mothers looking for their sons and all kinds of requests from people. It keeps her busy."

Everyone bought tickets on the Nenana Ice Pool to guess the date of breakup. The Chena River usually went out about a week earlier. We walked down to the Chena every day to see the condition of the ice. We all took the ice pool business seriously.

On May 15, the ice went out of the Chena with a terrifying crash. Hildur and I rushed down to watch as the ice and water rushed swiftly under the wooden bridge at Cushman Street. The river front was lined with debris, and broken ice chunks cascaded downriver so strongly that they knocked out sections of land. The breakup of ice washed away the winter's overburden — a loosening of bonds for everyone. The Indian villages of Galena and Minto on the Yukon reported flooding and homelessness again, a frequent occurrence at breakup.

Joe won the electrician's minute ice pool. The men went to the Northern Tap Room and drank up every cent of his winnings. One of the electricians, on his way home, hit a truck and wiped out his new Dodge. Another electrician smashed into a Cadillac. The superintendent on the job fell in his bathtub and cut his head!

Runoff water swelled the stream that fed the Chena and Tanana rivers, and the last icicles dripped from the low eaves of cabins. Mud turned to dust on the roads, and the willows took on a red-violet tinge. From the dark days of winter, we now turned toward the summer solstice. Distant, snowcapped ranges seemed faintly pink.

I awoke at night startled by an insistent throbbing sound — an atavistic drumbeat. Roused from sleep, I knew instinctively what it meant, even though I had never heard the sound in the city. The raucous cries came closer, and craning my head out the window, I saw wild geese flying in wide arcs above the birches.

The Canada geese and snow geese flew in graceful formations, skimming the silvery weeds as they landed, ravenous for grains, roots, and seeds. The wet fields were a commotion of feeding, honking, and splashing. Mallards, sandhill cranes, pintails, and ducks by the hundreds landed with a skid, the sun glinting on their wings. Someone reported seeing thirty-two white swans, but they were gone when we arrived. Plovers landed to rest and feed, as well as rare Peregrine falcons, loons, widgeons, and grebes.

An Athabascan Indian, Fred Stickman, wrote a letter to the editor published in the *News-Miner* telling the world how he felt about spring and geese at Nulato on the Yukon.

"I built a canoe and camped out seven miles from Nulato. I was hungry for my own food, dried fish and wild meat. You talk about a miserable spring camp, snowing wind every direction. I was living on smoke. I set a muskrat trap in a muskrat house the first night. I caught fifty muskrats and I ate thirty-six in thirty-six days, besides the ducks and geese.

"I've never seen geese and ducks so fat and in good shape. They fatten up at Creamer's Field, then come here and are tame. They flew so close that I was ashamed, and sorrowed for them. I quit!"

The geese flew against the gray hills, landing in ponds crackling with ice. The hills behind them misted and fogged over the rosy growth of new birch before its greening. Soon the flocks would head north in flashes of white and gray, with black ducks crisscrossing beneath them.

I saw my first loon among the white geese as they fed at the fields at Creamer's Dairy; the only loon I had seen before was stuffed or in a book. It was much later at a lake near Mount McKinley that I heard the loon call, a most haunting, unforgettable sound.

Many years later, on a painting trip to Point Hope, where I lived with a shaman, Killigvuk, and his wife, I learned of his identification with the loon. When I left, he gave me his rare loon headdress, which he wore when he drummed and sang at the Eskimo dances. The loon, his symbol, was sacred to him and had great power. I felt a strange affinity to loons that would last all my life, as if Killigvuk's gift had opened my vision to another dimension.

How nourishing were the manifestations of spring, the greening of the land, and the geese and ducks in the ponds. I sensed a powerful force in the woods, the dark earth breathing, its juices pouring into the soil and trees. I had hungered for trees and a life without cement, and here in the woods, I felt that mine was the first footstep to tread on the mossy trails. There was a sense of creating history, seeing things for the first time.

Homesteader's Cabin

★

7

Homesteaders

*Here was no man's garden, but the
unhanselled globe, not lawn, nor pasture,
nor mead, nor woodlands, not lea, nor
arable, nor waste-land. It was the fresh
and natural surface of the planet Earth,
as it was made forever and ever . . .*

Henry David Thoreau

Tight, sticky leaves on the branches unfurled after a rain
shower, and the sun burst out. New trails were cut into the
wilderness. Spruce and birch fell to the homesteaders' axes,
black earth still clinging to their roots. Cabins were going up
log by log. Stumps smelled full of sap, a pungent fragrance. I
brought earth into the house in flats to begin flower seedlings on the windowsill.

Our neighbors had an outhouse and chicken coops in
their back yard, and we awakened to the crowing of their
roosters. The town was a mixture of old and new. One could
see its beginning and its future within one block of each
other. The crooked cabins, sunk in permafrost, had more
charm for me than most of the new buildings, which were
built, out of necessity, of the shoebox design from the cheap,
quick school.

Old washing machines lay rusting in the yards of some of
the homesteaders a few miles out of town. They collected

old trucks, surplus World War II Quonset huts, worn-out generators, engine parts, old buses, fifty-gallon drums, stoves, and old machinery of all kinds. The junk sat on the land until it collapsed. Later, we had a law prohibiting billboards, but the junk on private property was a permissible eyesore.

Some people built their houses on swamps, and were plagued with mosquitoes. Others built on permafrost, and watched their houses sink and tilt lower each year. Others built on gravel tailings that the gold dredges had left, then hauled dirt and planted grass on top. Still others bulldozed their land clear of every tree and bush, taking away the topsoil, and built their houses in the middle of that manmade desert. They built without plan, using outcast lumber, to have minimal shelter. There were tent dwellings, discarded army barrack homes, converted garages, and sod houses. Skinned rabbits hung on the sides of small cabins near galvanized bathtubs.

Others made a thing of beauty of their homesites in the wilderness, cutting away only the necessary trees, leaving the mosses and wildflowers.

Our friends, the Tordoffs, hauled hundreds of rocks to their garden site, split each rock with a chisel, hauled peat from the woods, then transplanted wild delphinium, iris, ferns, daisies, and bluebells. They had no money for plumbing, but rocks and wildflowers were free.

One homeowner made the siding for his house out of gasoline cans hammered flat, with embossed metal ceiling panels for trim. The men chopped down spruce trees, peeled off the bark with an ax or draw knife, then trimmed the sides of the logs to fit tightly, chinking between them with peat moss to fill in the gaps. Some of the old cabins had logs more than two feet in diameter and fifty feet long.

The oldest cabins had weeds, wildflowers, and often small spruce trees growing from their sod roofs. Many stovepipes were crooked, and the floors, doors, and cupboards went

askew as the melting permafrost settled the house into
the ground.

The highway cut through the center of the wilderness. To
one side, power lines were strung on pole tripods, cut from
the surrounding trees. Ravens sat on spruce trees, watching
men cut the freshly peeled logs. Crude metal mail boxes and
wispy smoke rose from the scattered homesteaders' cabins.
The sound of the tractors rumbled as the homesteaders
plowed the potato fields.

Many of our new friends had filed on 160-acre home-
steads, with a promise to clear and cultivate twenty acres a
year. They did without plumbing, electricity, or running
water. Mosquitoes were a constant nuisance. They bulldozed
a clearing, heaping the trees and brush high in the fields, and
then building their cabins. They planted gardens, but the
rabbits and moose ate most of the produce. Potatoes were a
good crop, and the homesteaders could winter on the
money the crop brought. Usually, man and wife worked side
by side, putting each dollar into tools, insulation, and lumber. Their roads cut right through the wilderness. Rain and
snow had made their trails slick and full of ruts.

The first summer, homesteaders cut the trees and peeled
the logs; the second summer, they put up the walls and roof
of their cabin; the third year, they did the inside work and
cabinets; by the fourth year, they had to add on a new entry,
or a bedroom for a baby.

Some homesteaders, instead of building a barn for their
livestock, as they do in the states, built a shelter for their
pickup. Without a warm truck, they could not get to work in
town, and could not support themselves. Our friends the
Mackiowaks settled on their homestead by snowshoeing all
around the place in winter to find the best view when the
trees were bare, then they picked the highest spot, cleared
twenty acres, and dug a room in the hillside for themselves
and their truck. Their well was three-hundred feet deep, and
provided delicious water. They planted barley and a large

vegetable garden, and kept horses.

Joe and I talked about homesteading. We could get 160 acres easily. "Let's do it . . . all that land." But we put it off. We had no car and no money, and Joe had a job waiting for him at the Keturis' mine.

When some friends homesteaded, I said again, "Let's do it." But Joe objected. "I can't clear roads, build a house, live miles out on a dirt road and work in town. It's too hard; no roads, no running water, and an outside john." So that was that.

The homesteaders' efforts went into keeping warm. They felt lucky if they had water so that their kids could go to school with clean clothes. They had to chop wood, keep the roads open, go to work to earn money, and do all the extra chores, starting their trucks with firepots in the winter.

The homesteaders had little time for talk, music, or cultural pursuits. Their children would have an easier way of life — washing machines and more money to spend — but it was the third generation who would have the most benefit from the money and comforts that the land would eventually bring. Today they are the landed gentry.

As Fairbanks began to grow, in the early 1950s homesteaders settled on a high, rolling hill west of town known as Chena Ridge. Among the first were Joan Koponen and her Finnish husband, Niilo, who were proving up on their 160-acre homestead, clearing and cultivating twenty acres, building a rambling log house.

When I went to visit, a German Shepherd with yellow eyes leaped up to greet me without barking. I retreated as Joan shouted at the dog to back off. "That's Gemini," she said, as I quickly went indoors, leaving the dog to attack an old sneaker, which he threw into the air.

"I haven't been comfortable around big dogs since I was attacked by a German Shepherd when I was a child," I explained to Joan, as she took my coat.

The Koponen house had two sections: living quarters and a barn, separated by a Dutch door. The cabin walls were made of rough-hewn logs with a sleeping loft for the children. A goat nosed the hay, while horses poked their heads into the warm kitchen, where Joan fed them sugar from her pocket. Cats, chickens, tame mallards, and geese waddled around the barn under the horses' and cows' feet.

"You're wondering if dirt doesn't get tracked in, but hay on the barn floor keeps shoes clean and the good smell of the barn seems to stay. It beats having to bundle up and trudge through fifty-below weather to give the horses their grain. It helps keep that side of the house warm. I like to hear them snorting on the other side of the wall."

It looked cozy. I liked the arrangement. I looked out her window and saw her dog leap into the air. "That dog looks pretty strong."

"He's a she," said Joan, "and she's not a dog. She's a wolf! I've raised her since she was two weeks old. She looked like a little bear then, six inches tall with blue eyes. Ten months old now, and getting leaner and rangier. She plays pretty rough sometimes."

"Is she toilet trained?" I asked after my initial astonishment. Looking again, I could see her head was bigger and her legs longer than most dogs.

"I tried, but failed. I taught her like a dog, giving commands, like 'sit,' 'bring it here,' or 'lie down.' She's lived in and out of the house. I taught her to leave food on the table, but if I go out of the room, she steals the food."

Joan sliced large chunks of blueberry bread and boiled water for tea. "I always wanted to have a wolf to see if I could train it," she said. "We always had dogs and cats in the house."

Her cat put her paws on my chest and peered into my

eyes. Her husky, curled by the stove fire, had an old man's
way about him. Arthritis of the hip, most likely.

Joan loved all animals, especially horses, which she rode
in all weather, her long hair flowing. "I read somewhere that
animals can't learn from other animals. They learn from
man."

"I doubt if that's true," I said. "Animals don't start wars,
thank God."

"An Eskimo from Anaktuvuk sold me this wolf," said
Joan, pouring rosehip tea and stirring honey in it from a
wooden spoon. "I wanted an intelligent animal to study. I
wondered if a tundra wolf's wild ancestry becomes evident if
he was brought up by man."

"Does she have the killer instinct?"

"No stronger that that of our dog puppies. It seemed to
me proof of how much a wolf learns from its parents in
order to survive. It wasn't until she was six months old that I
saw Gemini go after a rabbit. When she didn't catch it, she
gave up quickly. She couldn't survive if we let her go.

"She did bite our hens, and bit me when I tried to smack
her and take one away. 'No,' I said, and smacked her, 'Bad
dog!' I never could say 'Bad wolf!' Ingrained, I guess. Later,
she didn't hold a grudge, but rolled over in the cabbage bed
and looked so apologetic and happy when I petted her. But
It didn't stop her from continuing to catch hens and pull out
their feathers. Went after ducks, too, and bit our daughter
once."

Joan poured more tea. "Gemini's really wonderful with
our children now, and loves strangers, but she never had a
dog's willingness to please. She always jumped on strangers
unless I intervened. Once she leaped into the air and
tongued a friend of ours who visited us in twenty-five-
below-zero weather. She slurped her wet tongue across his
glasses and they instantly collected thick frost. He was
almost blind without the use of his glasses. Good thing he
didn't fall over our woodpile."

Gemini never barked, just wagged her tail, but she howled a sad howl, like singing to herself, or a response to a dog's barking. It was singsong and beautiful, but Joan thought the moon had nothing to do with it — she howled around midday.

About a month later, I visited Joan again. I brought my watercolors, and this time painted the view from their window, a spectacular panorama of the Tanana River snaking in glistening curves.

One of the problems on Chena Ridge was that water was so deep in the ground. "How do you get water if you have no well?" I asked.

"I used to carry jerry cans of water from the university. Niilo finally got two airplane wings to use as tanks. Now we pump the water out. We also get water from the rain gutter, and use that for washing clothes and to water the garden." I was not so sure I would be happy giving up my running water to have her view.

"Niilo works as an electrician, and also drives a bull-dozer," said Joan. "I was alone so much of the time. The first winter, Niilo and I hopped the train to Curry, stayed two nights. We took baths all day in those big bathtubs. It was such a thrill.

"I grew up with horses, and thought it would be easy to have horses here, but it was difficult. We sent for two broncs, which came from Montana by train. They were so wild, it took me a week to catch them after Niilo let them out in the pasture. I finally trained and rode them.

"There was no extra hay; the dairy farmers didn't have extra hay. So we just cut grass from the roadsides. It got to be such a problem between Niilo and me, what with Niilo feeling he was spending all his spare time building a fence and getting hay for them, that I decided to get rid of one horse. Couldn't find a buyer, so I took the horse into the woods and shot it. I thought Niilo would appreciate my sacrifice for his sake, but he was very upset, and not pleased at all — felt he'd done all that work for nothing!

"All that work," said Joan. "I lost my sense of self. Some days I didn't know if it was worth it. I asked my mother for an electric chain saw for my birthday. Having all those animals was colossal work. I felt I had to do all the chores. We sold eggs, milk, and garden stuff."

"I heard you never farmed before. Did you have a comfortable lifestyle in the states?" I asked.

"I grew up in the East in a big house with all the fixings of an easy life," answered Joan. "When you have everything, it's hard to know who you are. I hadn't tested myself. I used to envy those who had less. Everything was made easy for me. When Niilo asked me to marry him, and wanted to homestead in Alaska, it really appealed to me. I knew horses, but I just didn't know how to take care of them in the Arctic."

Their sauna, a part of Niilo's Finnish heritage, became an institution on Sundays up on the Ridge, as few homesteaders had running water. On Sundays, the barrel stove in the sauna bloomed cherry red.

Their sauna was a small, windowless room with wooden plank seats against one wall, the top for the strongest of heart, the floor for youngsters. The neighbors and friends came — then they brought their friends.

Steam permeated the air, sweat ran, and tight muscles relaxed. Shadows explored the resin-beaded logs. Dippers of water sloshed over glowing skin. No more spit baths in small basins, but a real sweat bath.

Unable to stand the suffocating heat, people ran out into the snow, jumping into the tub outdoors, breaking the ice layer. Some brave souls stood under a spruce bough, shaking the tree to rinse with snow. Snow stuck to their bare feet as they ran back. Afterward, they lolled around in towels and drank tea sweetened with honey.

Everyone in town talked about the Koponens' Sunday saunas. Joan chuckled. "We have a reputation for having

orgies up here, but it's nothing of the kind. The women go
in first, and come out with towels wrapped around them,
then the men go in. Some people go out in the back porch
to cool off and look at the stars. I never do, it's too cold.
People bring their own towels and cookies. I just make tea."

Joan invited me back to paint from her window again.
She was interested in my work, as she had studied art at
college, and she felt my paintings were "incredibly imaginative."

Homesteaders Liza and Heinz Borchard had escaped the
Holocaust, and come to Alaska, sponsored by the Griffin
family. They filed on a homestead on Chena Ridge near the
Koponens, living in a tent while Heinz found a job repairing
watches.

Liza began to build their house with her own hands, and
she did not know a thing about carpentry, except that they
needed shelter before winter came. A tiny, slim blonde, she
had tremendous raw energy. With her ax, she cut willows,
cottonwoods, and small spruces, then forced earth between
the logs to build the house. Nothing daunted her; she made
their first stove out of an old oil barrel.

When I first visited the Borchard homestead in the early
1950s, they were butchering a bear Heinz had shot. Liza,
with her usual energy, was cutting the bear meat into steaks.
Over a wood fire, bones, liver, and scraps for their dogs
boiled in an old washtub. A black cat with white paws
chewed on a bear rib nearby.

Heinz had shot a caribou the previous year, and was
cutting the frozen steaks with a chainsaw. That year they had
raised and butchered fifty chickens and three pigs. Liza froze
and canned her vegetables until her larder could hold no
more. In addition to baking loaves of pumpernickel bread,
which she sold, they kept a cow, goats, and rabbits. Her

produce won prizes at the fair. The only things they had to buy were sugar, flour, salt, and other staples.

When Liza became pregnant, she told Heinz, "Don't worry, Heinzy, I will tell you what to do, and you can help me. We don't have the money for doctors, and besides, I know what to do. It's easy."

When the time came for Liza to have her baby, Heinz had the fire, the boiling water, and the knife to cut the cord ready. The delivery went easily. A few months later, Liza took in other babies to care for so she could earn money.

For Heinz's birthday, Liza built him a study over the kitchen with stairs leading up to it. She bought him a secondhand desk and built crude shelves; the room was crooked, but the view from the window was superb.

Liza decided to face the logs with rocks, so she hauled rocks in the pickup. Then she mixed cement in a wheelbarrow, and put up the rocks. An expedient builder without experience, she never figured that the weight of the rocks would separate them from the walls. She had to prop up the rocks with logs to brace them.

They invited us to eat bear stew with them, delicious with her pumpernickel bread and spruce-tip jelly. Her blueberry pie had a delicious flaky crust made with bear grease, which was considered a delicacy. Liza also used it for frying doughnuts. Heinz talked about the nine-foot-deep indoor swimming pool he planned to build, a first in Fairbanks. He was a champion swimmer, daring to swim across the Yukon River at Eagle, where the water is freezing cold and full of silt.

We talked about the ice breakup. Liza talked about the war in Europe. "The noise of the ice hitting the banks frightened me. It sounded like gunshots."

When we left, Liza gave me her recipe for the spruce jelly. "Claire, you pull those little green spruce bud ends in the spring, and you boil them in water. Boil for an hour, then strain the needles out. Add sugar until it's jelly-like."

The Indians had used spruce syrup for everything —

headaches, coughs, stomachaches, and burn poultices — so I welcomed Liza's recipe.

Eager to learn all he could about gold mining, Joe left with Elmer to freight supplies to Moore Creek Mining Camp. They would be freighting over the mountains and frozen rivers for about forty miles. It was unlikely that there would be any letters. Joe and Elmer flew to the Kuskokwim River. The crew loaded about one thousand barrels of fuel oil, five hundred barrels of gasoline, grease, lumber, and grub on three sleds hooked in tandem, pulled by tractors. They would cross hills and streams through bear country.

Looking forward to joining Joe at the mine, I had already packed my paints and stone-carving tools. Elmer said, "Moore Creek is surrounded by wilderness, whole mountainsides for the taking, if you need rocks."

I found crocus among the gravestones in the old cemetery, and felt as if I had come across a rare treasure.

The frogs croaked in the ponds, and soon I was scratching with the first stirrings of mosquitoes. "The time of the birds is come and the voice of the turtle is heard in our land," I quoted to Hildur with a deep contentment.

"Voice of the turtle? Voice of the mosquito's more like it," she retorted, slapping one on her arm.

Our Moose Creek Cabin

★

8

Moore Creek
Mining Company

*More money is put in the ground than
is taken out.*

Old miner's saying

The ice had gone out, the sun was hot, and riverboats
roared down the Chena River. Sap ran like blood in the
trees. Eyes seemed brighter, people ran instead of walked;
movements became freer as the days grew longer and
warmer. Rivers were full of beaver sign. My seedlings sat in
the sunny windows, ready for planting out-of-doors. Nights
were still cold, and the danger of freezing had not passed.

The days were growing longer, and by June 21, we would
have daylight all day. The summer solstice would be celebrated with a midnight sun baseball game.

I prepared to fly to the Moore Creek Mine to join Joe.
Bush pilot Tony Schultz, in his Gull Wing Stinson, surveyed
the landscape and swooped down to buzz a black bear.
"Elmer Keturi saved my life many times," said Tony. "Whenever I was lost in the fog, I'd fly low and look for his Cat trail
over the hills, then follow that."

Hours after leaving Fairbanks, we landed at Moore Creek,
a cluster of five small buildings surrounded by cabins and
low hills and many small mounds resembling anthills, which
turned out to be "tailing piles," residues of mining operations.

Even though it was June, ponds were still covered with ice and patches of glacial snow. Faint beginnings of green touched the willows, and sticky little leaves were opening on the birches.

A man wearing striped overalls and a heavy growth of beard came running out of one of the small cabins perched up on a hill. As he ran, he slipped on the muddy hill and slid to where I was standing. Only then did I recognize Joe, his back and shoulder muscles hard, his face deeply tanned. He needed a haircut. He had not known when to expect me, as there was no communication to such an isolated place.

After a muddy embrace, Joe carried my bags uphill to our spruce log cabin, called Charley's Cabin after the miner who built it. The cabin had a wood plank floor, a bed with a tropical mosquito net around it, a handmade willow table, and two chairs. A gun and a broom stood in the corner, and Joe's wet socks and overalls hung on a nail to dry near the Yukon stove. The outhouse a few feet away had a view of the surrounding mountains through the half-moon cut out of the door.

Joe's job as an oiler required him to keep machinery oiled and ready to go. He tried to explain his work to me. "I refuel all the equipment, grease the roller, climb the boom, oil the shiv, and lay pipe from the ditch to the cut." Black smudges dirtied his hands and face, and he smelled of grease. Joe also operated a Cat and "bulldozed pay dirt into the sluice boxes." He dreamed constantly of mining on his own land, and was learning all he could.

Eager to see the Keturis, Joe and I walked hand in hand down to the messhouse. In the large room, the aromas of spruce wood and fresh bread mingled. The huge, black Lang stove, which had been hauled in by dog team, presided over an enormous pot of coffee, kettles, four loaves of bread, and two kinds of pies.

The miners in their work clothes sat on wooden benches around the red-checkered, oilcloth-covered table. They worked day and night shifts, seven days a week. Ten men eyed me as I was introduced as Joe's wife.

The youngest miner was Art, the oldest Olaf, grizzled and gray, with a back bent from years of prospecting. Everyone wore overalls and rubber boots, and they ate until the huge mounds of food on white crockery plates disappeared. It was a Sunday dinner of canned oyster stew, followed by ham, mashed potatoes, three canned vegetables, homemade rolls, pickles, olives, strawberry jam, and three kinds of canned fruit swimming in juice. For dessert we ate apple and blueberry pies, with lots of hot coffee.

Some of the miners ate thick slices of homemade bread and strawberry jam with their soup, meat, and vegetables. Hildur explained, "They are starved for sweet stuff. They lived out in the bush all winter eating beans and moose."

Elmer noticed me examining big gashes in the ceiling above the table. "Before we got here this spring, bears broke in through the window. There was bear dung all over. They knocked down this wall. Went right through the partition. That's claw marks over the stove."

"They broke up all our canned goods," added Hildur, passing the jam. "Made an awful mess to clean up. They must have smelled the grease; they stood on the stove and licked and clawed the grease on the ceiling. They ruined the cans of molasses."

There were three women in camp — Hildur, Elmer's sister Lempi, and me. A blonde, comely woman, Lempi had cooked for a family in New York until Elmer sent for her. All the miners, single men, paid homage to Lempi, but she favored Art, the dragline operator — the shyest man in camp, a good-looking Swede.

The men followed solitary occupations, working in the gold mine in the summers and trapping, prospecting, or logging in the winters.

Olaf, at seventy-two, was one of the hardest workers, bent over in a perpetual stoop from panning gold. "For fifty

years I've followed the creeks looking for pay dirt. I almost
hit it last year. I was right on the edge of a paystreak, but I
ran out of grub and had to quit. Next year I'll hit it for
sure." Olaf's blue eyes glowed in the prospector's eternal
belief that next year he would strike it rich.

When I asked if he was married, he answered, winking at me,
"Wouldn't have any woman who couldn't keep up with me."

A couple of years earlier, Olaf had prospected on
Henderson Creek. "By March we put in a mess of holes. We
didn't hit pay dirt and our food was running out. 'Just one
more hole,' I urged my partner, 'we'll hit it.' He threw
down his shovel and said, 'God Almighty, you want to dig
up the whole country in one winter. I'm quitting!'"

"What would you do with the money if you did hit
gold?" I asked Olaf.

His watery, aged eyes sparkled, and his work-bent back
straightened. "I'd get me the purtiest gal in camp and have
her sit on my lap."

Elmer sat at the head of the table and talked shop, ". . .
the track came off the sprockets."

When there was a lull in the conversation, I asked Elmer,
"How did you get all the machinery here in the middle of
nowhere with no road?"

"We freighted machinery cross-country in the winter
when the ground was frozen," he answered. "The tractors
pulled the sleds, carried all our supplies over the mountains."

Elmer paused to eat his pie. "Every nail has to be
brought in. If we forget something, I have to make it. I can't
run to the corner store." It seemed like a monumental task,
but he made it sound simple.

Hildur talked of her fear of bears, but the men talked
continually of cleanups, tailings, bedrock, and sluicing. A
favorite topic was the mosquitoes. "Millions of mosquitoes.
They're black clouds," said Elmer, scratching. "Can't open
your mouth because you'd swallow them."

"Last year I couldn't hear a thing," said Olaf, shaking his

old head. "Those damn bastards were stuck in my ears."

In addition to being in mortal danger from mosquitoes, the men realized that if they were mauled by a bear or hurt by machinery, it was a long way to a doctor.

"Fannie Quigley was tough," Hildur said. "Her husband got mauled by a bear out at their mine in Kantishna. She found him at the cut with his face torn off. She raced back to the cabin, got a needle and thread and sewed him up. That's the kind of woman she was."

"I don't know if I could have done that," I said.

"You'd have to," came her retort.

"The old-timers called her 'Fannie the Hike'," said Elmer. "She used to carry a pack on her back with her Yukon stove, bacon, beans, and flour. Then she set up a tent and sold meals at the gold strikes. That's how she got her handle, 'Fannie the Hike.' I reckon she set her tent and hung her 'Meals for Sale' sign at most every strike in the North."

"Did you hear about Mrs. Barrack who went to Kantishna with Dr. Sutherland and ran into Fannie's team on the trail?" asked Hildur. "The dogs went berserk when they saw Mrs. Barrack. Fannie put her hands up and shouted, 'My God, they never saw another woman before!'"

Elmer had hauled heavy equipment over hundreds of miles by landmark and compass in the winter — over frozen rivers and over the mountains — in sub-zero temperatures. He had an absorbing interest in machinery, and could fix anything mechanical. His fingers were long, and his hands were twice the size of mine.

"Pure gold is thirty-five dollars an ounce; gold mixed with silver or quartz, twenty-nine," said Elmer. "I take it to the bank at Flat. They have a little smelter, and they smelt the gold, removing the impurities, and cast it into bricks, which they sell to the mint."

The Keturis had done well at Moore Creek. "We bought another mine at Gold Bench on the Koyukuk, and sunk the money into heavy equipment," said Elmer.

"Elmer was the first man to freight with heavy equipment," said Olaf. "He made that trail straight up to Bettles on the Koyukuk River. It will probably be a road someday."

The men mined twenty-four hours a day in the summer when the ground was thawed. They worked in ten-hour shifts, digging up the gravel and sluicing it through the sluice boxes. The night shift would come into the messhouse for supper and a last cup of coffee before they fell into bed, exhausted; the day crew would eat their breakfast, then replace the men on the machinery while the engines were still warm.

The earth was torn up by the bulldozers and piled into round pyramids, despoiling the wilderness surrounding it. It upset me to see such destruction, but Hildur assured it would soon covered with birch trees.

On the hottest summer day, snow lay in the great pocks of crater-like earth at Moore Creek, yet a few hundred miles away, hot mineral pools erupted in a steaming boil all winter long.

Oscar Winchell, the bush pilot, flew over and dropped meat and mail. Once he dropped a frozen side of beef, and it slid under the moss and was never found. Winchell had a standing order not to bring any alcoholic beverages to the mine. One of the miners had ordered four fifths of 151 proof Demarara Rum from Bert's Drug Store in Anchorage. We were having lunch, but the miner ran out to check the items dropped. When he finally got his package, it was wet, all four bottles broken. He got down on his hands and knees, sniffing the moss. "That is it, all right," he yelled, "That's it! Damn that Oscar!"

Joe ran out and caught a roll of toilet paper as it fell and unwound all over the tundra. There was a message for Elmer in the tube.

The virgin wild of thick spruce, birch, wild rose, and willow, and the pungent scent of Hudson Bay tea, or Indian tea, rose from the mossy earth. Caribou lichen and cranberries lay in every shovelful, and were thrown aside and trampled. The men would have shoveled aside rubies in their blind search for gold.

When a designated area was mined out, there was a cleanup, usually every other week. Bulldozers pushed the gold-bearing gravel to the sluice boxes, and the men washed it through with high-pressure water nozzles. Gold, being heaviest, remained in the boxes, while the gravel fell through.

After mealtime in the messhouse, Hildur and I put the old records on the wind-up Victrola or played pinochle.

One evening I heard Art say, "He had the nerve to come up to my cabin this morning. I didn't mind that, but when he stuck his head in the door, that was too much. So I shot him." That explained the fresh bearskin, flayed and nailed across the side of his cabin, the head gory with blood, the claws huge. Joe Stuver had already nailed a seven-foot black bear onto his cabin.

Joe built a roaring fire on the Yukon stove each evening, to heat up wash water. We slept in our cozy little cabin under the mosquito net, the only sound the crackling fire.

Dawn was pink and cool; the hills were peaceful in the suspended stillness. I listened to the bird song and recalled the rush hour of New York. When I thought of all the space, the vast horizons of changing sky, and the starry nights, I wondered how I had ever found any peace in the tumultuous, crowded city.

I thought about Fannie, living out in the wilderness by herself after her husband died. I liked Fannie's spirit; she was a fighter, a fearless hunter for meat and subsistence. Maybe I did not have to go out and shoot meat to survive. I was hungry for something else — my quest was for my artistic survival.

In the Sauna

✷

9

Sauna
and Bears

Wilderness Woman

Alone in a wilderness cabin
Surrounded by mountains
That swell and dance around me,
I am pregnant with life;

Grasses vibrate the colors of the earth,
Clouds embrace me,
Wide spaces of sky give me joy,
The sun warms the child within me;

Flowers lean over the creeks,
Birds walk beneath them,
Streams of water rushing over stones
Liven the fragrant air;

May our unborn child know of the peace,
May his life be blessed,
May he gather strength
To live in our world.

From my journal,
1946

Numerous bears pestered the camp. We found tracks around the meat house, an open structure with screened sides where hams and bacon hung on hooks, swaying in the wind. Cuts of beef and pork were kept in a kerosene-operated refrigerator. Lempi lived near the meat house, terrified at the thought of bears.

When one of the miners was sent up to check the ditch, and did not return through lunch or dinner, Joe Stuver (nicknamed "The Cowboy") went up to see what was wrong. The man had thrown his pick at a bear and missed. He was up a tree in the pouring rain, his teeth chattering. He was relieved to see The Cowboy, who promptly shot the bear.

Hildur and I, left to our own pursuits, helped Lempi do the dinner dishes, then took a walk. Hildur wore an African safari sort of hat with a black net dangling below her chin. On her feet were high boots with green wool socks pulled over her pants.

"Where did you get that hat?" I asked, giggling.

"Is that how you're going?" she asked, eyeing my bare head and short-sleeved sweater. "You'll be sorry."

"I thought we were taking a short walk, not going on a hunt!"

"You'll be glad I'm taking this mosquito dope along."

We walked up a narrow trail, past the men at work. As we walked farther away, I noticed Hildur taking long side glances into the thickness of the forest.

"What's the matter?"

"I'm just making sure we don't run into a bear. That's all."

The remark spoiled the walk for me. I kept seeing a bear in every dark clump of bushes. I was afraid of bears, but relieved there were no snakes — too cold!

I discovered why Hildur wore a headnet. The mosquitoes were so thick we had to brush them out of the way in order to see. They buzzed around our heads, biting and clinging to our life's blood. I slapped and scratched until my walk resembled a fox-trot. My hands and face and every part of my exposed legs were bitten to an angry welt. The mosquitoes had the audacity to bite right through my sweater and jeans.

I spent the rest of the afternoon looking at nature through the cabin window, using binoculars to search the hillsides for bears, and at the same time, applying cold vinegar packs to my bites.

Olaf refused to wear a headnet, even when the crew had to walk miles to repair a break in the water ditches. With each cut of the moss, clouds of gnats and mosquitoes rose up. Joe and the others wearing headnets and dope withstood the onslaught, but Olaf swallowed them with every breath. He became ill with the poisons, and was bedridden for several days.

On a sunny day in July, Joe and I took a stroll a mile away from camp, and this time I was adequately dressed. When the mosquitoes swarmed towards me searching for a crack in my armor, they could not get up or down my pant leg because I wore two pairs of heavy woolen socks and a heavy, leather jacket. "I hope they break their teeth," I muttered. Joe had sprayed me with the newest type of repellent, citronella and tar oil. The smell was terrible.

We crossed the river on a narrow, rotting wood plank suspended twenty feet over the water. The Cowboy's team of mangy huskies was tied to stakes in the ground, straining in our direction, howling. Joe walked through the double line of dogs and signaled for me to follow. The dogs growled, as if they knew I was a coward, and the last dog snapped at me, ripping the seat of my jeans. I tried to defend my bare fortress and ran to our cabin.

The Cowboy, a slim, taciturn Montanan, had a rollicking walk and slim hips. Hands in his pockets, he apologized the next day. "Sorry about my dog," he said through his thin lips without moving his face. "She just isn't used to women. Don't know what happened. Hope she didn't get you?" I showed him the rip I had sewn up with red thread, the only color I could find. He apologized again for the way his dog, Lady, had behaved. "She usually behaves like a lady," he smirked, brushing back his hair, revealing a receding hairline.

I gave his dogs a wide berth after that, but the men were right; bears and vicious dogs were nothing compared to the mosquito plague. Every time I slammed the cabin door, hundreds of the bastards sneaked in with me. I made a dash for the bed, drew the bed net around me, collapsed and stayed there for three days. I knew when I was beaten. Joe brought my meals up to me, and we burned Buhach, a punky, smelly repellent powder, all day and night. The Buhach bolstered my morale, but I doubt if it killed any bugs — it just rendered them helpless for awhile. I cringed inside my net throne, and took fiendish pleasure in killing every bug that dared to invade my privacy, staying up half the night trying to kill them.

Elmer came to cheer me up on the fourth day. He told me he had heard of bears being bitten in the eyes and nose by mosquitoes until they became blind, wandering helplessly until they starved to death. Then he told me an equally encouraging story of how some miners had to go to the doctor to have their ears and noses cleaned of dead mosquitoes.

I hated the mosquitoes. I was frightened of the huskies and the bears. I did not feel like going outdoors. I wanted my mother. I wanted to pull the covers over my head, stay there a week reading ten-year-old *Reader's Digests*, and take my meals in bed under the mosquito net.

On the fifth day, bolstered by pep talks from Joe and cheerful Hildur, I finally convinced myself that I was the bigger and stronger opponent. Venturing down to the messhouse for breakfast, I found that I had become the butt of camp jokes.

The men politely inquired, "Seen any mosquitoes lately?" I became known in camp as the woman who spent four days under a bed net.

Actually, it was not just the bears and the mosquitoes that had kept me in bed. The truth was, I was nauseated and I did not feel well. I consulted with Hildur about the morning nausea. We both decided that it could mean only one thing. I must be pregnant, because I was too healthy to be nauseated for any other reason. In New York, no one had a baby without verifying it with a doctor, and here I was at a mining camp for three months without a doctor, or even a nurse. No orange juice! No vitamins! My teeth would rot! I was having a baby, and I was acting like one.

Joe was excited about the news, and urged me to take care of myself. We wanted a baby; we felt we were married for life, and wanted to begin a family.

When Hildur and I took our walks, I was careful not to trip over rocks, and when we passed the creek and had to wade through icy water, I was careful, and when we climbed the hills to find the rare, white fireweed, I climbed slowly. Joe ordered a case of canned orange juice to be sent in by plane from Flat, the nearest village, and I wrote to Dr. Schaible to mail me vitamins.

Hildur and I sat in her cabin after breakfast while we went through the nausea routine. "Now, Claire, it's all in the head," she said, handing me saltine crackers. "Just eat these." It worked, for I never did vomit.

Joe and the other men worked twelve-hour shifts. Except for washing dishes and clothes, and helping Lempi with the messhouse chores, my life was easy. I had time to paint in watercolor and write poetry.

One day, exploring the rocks in the tailing piles, a chunk of coarse lava rock with a hole in it caught my imagination. The twelve-inch chunk, weighing about sixty pounds, was an unusual sandy color, and not as hard as I thought it would be. With Joe's help, I found a chisel and one of Elmer's big hammers. I worked near a running brook, using a large tree stump for a working table. I cut stone every day until I finished the carving of a pregnant woman, a free-form woman's shape, a la Henry Moore. It was good to be carving again; it made me happy.

To my regret, we had too much weight in the plane

going home, and I had to leave the carving at the mine. The next year, Elmer offered to bring it home. I had left the carving at the airstrip where I had set it while waiting for the plane, and one of the tractor operators working nearby had accidentally driven over it, destroying it. Perhaps the worker thought it was just a big rock with a hole in it, and didn't realize it was a work of art

Every time I think of it, I still feel angry. All that work!. I lost something important to me forever. I often wonder what some future anthropologist might make of those carved fragments in the wilderness near the tailing piles of an abandoned gold mine. Would they believe it was the art of some lost Indian tribe?

The nausea was gone and the mosquitoes died down, only to be replaced by tiny gnats. These delightful tidbits were called "no-see-ums," for they bit and fled from the scene before you could see them. We never had the satisfaction of squashing them, but by then, I was a hardened veteran, plenty battle-scarred.

It was light twenty-four hours a day, and I enjoyed waking up at three in the morning, seeing daylight flood our cabin. It was eerie to hear bulldozers on the night shift, stripping the earth to bedrock. Gold had to be found before the earth froze.

I loved the Moore Creek housekeeping system. Every Wednesday, I warmed water on our Yukon stove, added soap, then threw it all over the wooden plank floor, swooshing it around with a broom. Joe had drilled holes in the floor for the water to drain. I made the bed and walked out, leaving a clean-smelling cabin full of sunlight.

The Keturis, staunch Finns, naturally would not dream of living without a sauna. Tuesday was ladies' turn at the sauna. The bathhouse had two rooms: one held a huge barrel stove covered with stones; the other was the dressing room, containing a washing machine and various tubs.

On the afternoon of bath day, we started a fire in the

stove, and by afternoon, when a good steam arose, the sauna was ready. Hildur, Lempi, and I soaped and scrubbed with a hard brush until our skins tingled. We poured buckets of water over each other until we were scoured clean and boiled to a tomato color, then lay on wooden boards to be baked like fish, oozing and wilting in the hot vapor, the steamy air so thick we could scarcely see. If cleanliness was next to godliness, we were certainly godly on Tuesdays. We dried our hair outdoors in the flower-scented evening air. My skin glowed; I felt like a newborn baby.

We washed clothes in an elderly washing machine powered by a gasoline engine, dumping in our men's greasy work clothes last. When the clotheslines were full, we hung underwear and overalls from tree limbs to dry. When the water drained out, we invariably found tiny gold nuggets, nails, and occasionally Elmer's gold watch, which he had left in his pants pocket.

Hildur had washed his watch for the third time, and it still ran. Feeling a bit guilty, she sidled over to where he was sweating under the tractor, changing the oil.

"Elmer," she yelled, as he poked his head out. "What time is it?"

"Sorry, I left my watch in my other pants."

"Oh," said Hildur as she walked away. Several times that afternoon she asked Elmer the time, and he answered, "I left my watch in my pants pocket."

When the men were seated at the dinner table, Hildur plunged into her act. "Elmer," she said as she passed the mashed potatoes, "Elmer, I washed your watch again."

He looked up from his dinner, opened his mouth, then closed it. Ever the consummate actor, he took the line she fed him. "So that's why you kept asking me what time it was." The men at the table laughed so hard, Olaf nearly choked on a piece of ham.

Ray, the Keturis' son, played with toy draglines, often composing mining scenes with hoses and water boxes, just like his daddy. One day The Cowboy put some brass filings in his dirt and hung around to see what Ray would do. Ray said disgustedly, "Aw, shucks, it's just brass."

The year before, Ray had fallen out of a tree and broken his arm above the wrist. The plane to Fairbanks was delayed because of weather. When the doctor finally saw Ray's arm, he said Hildur had done a good job of splinting, and the arm had healed well.

One of Joe's duties at the mine was to check the water ditch three miles away. On a trip with Olaf to the ditch, they saw a black bear. Olaf rattled stones in a Hills Brothers can. The bear ran. "It always works," said Olaf, beaming, but Hildur and I had no trust in rocks in a can. Hildur never said what we would do. Scream and run, I guessed.

We picked blueberries, eating in silence until our tongues were purple. Sitting on the tundra plopping berries into our cans with two hands, we watched for bears. At the messhouse that evening, Lempi made three pies with our blueberries.

The next morning, I walked to the Keturis' cabin. The air smelled of freshly dug earth and spruce smoke. "Smells like bear to me," said Hildur. That evening Joe and I watched in silence as a dignified moose with his ludicrous nose drank from the creek. We brought back large bouquets of yellow daisies, yarrow, poppies, forget-me-nots, iris, bluebells, monkshood, and magenta and white fireweed.

Not long afterwards, during the night, we were awakened by wild screams. Joe rushed to the window, and I hid behind him. A black bear about fifty feet away was chasing Lempi, barefooted in her white nightgown, up the hill. Elmer came running downhill, wearing longjohns, barefooted, but with his hat on. He was leaping and whooping, firing his rifle into the air.

Grabbing his rifle, Joe yelled, "Where's my shells, where's my shells?" He finally ran outside without the shells, without shoes, but with gun and pants. There were more shots coming from every direction, but the bear had disappeared. When I finally found the shells, I handed them to Joe, who loaded the gun and set it by the door.

Lempi told us she had been awakened by a noise at the window. "There was a black bear; his head was enormous. I screamed and ran."

Lempi spent the rest of the night in bed with me, and Joe slept on the floor in his sleeping bag. The wind howled all night, and at every scratching noise, Lempi and I sat up, looked at each other, then at Joe, who snored through it all.

I hated to leave the mine at Moore Creek, for I had never known such perfect peace. Joe had learned more about operating a gold mine. Lempi and Art were getting married. After the initial nausea, I had spent the first months of my pregnancy feeling wonderful. Joe and I were ecstatic about the coming birth.

The summer had been a great gift to me — I had painted and sculpted and written poetry, and had my meals cooked for me. The Keturis and the Fejeses were bonded in a friend-ship that was to last all our lives.

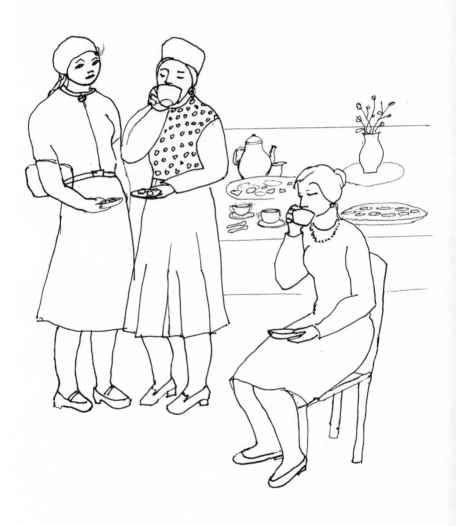

✳

10

——

Gatherings

*I found myself saying . . . I can't go where I
want to — I can't do what I want to. I can't
even say what I want to. I decided I was a very
stupid fool not to at least paint what I wanted
to . . . that seemed to be the only thing I could
do that didn't concern anybody but myself.*

Georgia O' Keeffe,
1923

Back in Fairbanks, the hillsides seemed to have turned
from green to gold overnight, and the fields that had been
thick with flaming fireweed now blew cottony seeds all
through the wilderness. The seeds burst into silvery wisps
that clung to our hair.

We settled down in the Karstens' house, getting ready for
the baby. My body was changing, and on the cold mornings
I struggled out of bed with my eyes half shut to make Joe's
breakfast on the woodstove. Joe had a job as an electrician
on the Ladd Field buildings. After breakfast, I groped my
way back to bed.

Dr. Arthur Schaible and Dr. Paul Haggland were the only
two doctors in Fairbanks. Haggland, called the "bone man,"
had a good reputation for surgery; Schaible, the internist,
seemed gentler, so I chose him to deliver the baby.

After examining me, he confirmed that I was four-and-
one-half months pregnant, and in perfect health, but needed

to check with a dentist. "Try not to exceed twenty-five pounds," he said. He did not say anything about diet or exercise.

Hildur and I pored over the Sears catalog, carefully ordering baby blankets and diapers. I bought flannel and began making receiving blankets and little nightgowns, blanket-stitching them around the edges.

We were invited everywhere, making new friends. New people were coming up, and soon we were helping them get adjusted. We were not called "cheechakos" anymore.

Some of the women in Hildur's circle belonged to Beta Sigma Phi, a social club, not an academic society. Each club was given a planned program with various topics to discuss at their meetings. Hildur brought me to one meeting, and I was asked to join. It filled a need for isolated women, lonely for social life. When it was my turn to speak, my topic was art. I gave an impassioned talk, showing prints of Van Gogh and Gauguin and other Impressionist artists. Afterwards, the hostess apologized for the paint-by-number painting on her wall.

Mary Woolford was president of Beta Sigma Phi. What endeared her to us was her giggle. Although very proper and reserved, she shared a nutty kind of humor with us, and the three of us became good friends. The women I met were natural; they did not use makeup, except a bit of lipstick. These women had a sense of honor — they did not gossip.

When it was my turn to host the Beta Sigma Phi meeting, I scrubbed and waxed the floors on my knees and polished every surface in the house.

It was wonderful to get out of slacks and sweaters and get dressed up for a meeting. Our men made fun of us, calling it the "Beta Sigma Phoo." They hated to get dressed up, and could not understand our need to look pretty and act lei-surely, away from children and chores.

The meeting went well. We discussed the business of having a silver tea to raise money for the children's room at the hospital. The talk went around and around about where to have the tea, for teas were serious business. I could not stand the indecision anymore, and in jest I offered, "Why not have it in the post office?" There was a shocked silence. I stifled a laugh. Hildur was absent from that meeting. It was finally decided to have the silver tea in the Nordale Hotel lobby.

When the judge's wife gave her yearly tea, Hildur took in a seam in her best dress, and I ran to Gordon's Store to buy a pair of new stockings, the kind with the seam in the back, held up by a garter belt.

Instead of the colorful skirts and long earrings I used to wear, my clothes had taken on a utilitarian look — boots, pants, sweaters. Style had not seemed important here; warmth was uppermost, nail polish and mascara all but forgotten. But for the tea I wore one of my New York dresses.

My neighbor, last seen in the back yard with frowzy hair and a safety pin in her blouse, was at the tea all starched up, wearing a hat and gloves. She smiled graciously as she accepted a cup of tea, served in a bone china cup, poured from a silver service set, complete with silver tongs for sugar lumps. Dainty plates held small, trimmed white-bread sandwiches and fancy homemade cookies.

About seventy women, most of them in hats, crowded into the judge's parlor. Eva was there, wearing white gloves, a hat with a veil, and a corsage pinned to her suit lapel, smelling of violets. Talking to a group of women, she opened her purse and took out extra gloves, English lavender smelling salts, a package of mints, and a hanky. "Oh, here it is, the letter from London I was telling you about . . ." She smiled at her best friend, Maisie Stoddard, also from Ireland, all dressed up in the latest fashion.

The principal of the public school, Marietta Pilgrim, a striking woman with black hair pulled back into a bun, stood talking to the judge's wife as she held her tea cup. Her husband owned an antimony mine. There was an unspoken pecking order of judges, doctors, lawyers, bankers, and businessmen, followed by schoolteachers and government officials. Most of the women were married to construction workers, struggling miners, or pilots. Few men owned a car; if they could afford a vehicle, they bought a pickup truck, useful for hauling garbage, firewood, and building material. The women I met came from every part of the states — they, too, had followed their husbands north.

In New York I had lived among bohemian artists, free souls. I did not know anyone my age who was a housewife. These northern women were ladylike and restrained, nothing like the uninhibited artists I had known. They spoke softly, sat with their backs straight and their knees clamped together, and made small talk. The *Ladies Home Journal* had articles against crossing your legs, as it was not supposed to be ladylike. Real social prestige consisted of displaying a complete silver service with a silver tray. Was it a reminder of their stateside homes? It did not remind me of my home. I had never gone to a tea in my life. Neither had Hildur or most of the other women.

Some of these women could nail a roof, hunt and fish, haul buckets of water and cut kindling, yet they were more socially conscious and straitlaced than any women I had ever met. We all shared the inconvenience of everyday living far from our families.

These were stoic, practical women, and I learned much from them. I was a dreamer, a writer of poetry, an artist, full of imagination, but impractical. It was always Joe or Hildur who yanked me to my feet with plain horse sense.

At one tea, I spilled the contents of my cup as I tried to balance the plate, cookies, and my purse on my lap. I was horrified. A homesteader's wife told me about the university tea she attended. "I got myself all gussied up. Living out on the homestead, I had forgotten how to talk to people. What with the cows, horses, chickens, building the house, and raising the kids, I was so out of touch I dropped my tea cup."

Soon after that, I bought an imported English china cup at the N.C. Company, with big red roses on a black background. Even women who lived in shabby houses without water or plumbing, whose kitchens had a curtain hiding the slop pail under the sink, displayed a row of china cups, a symbol that they, too, had once possessed fine things. Some women lived in a basement with electrical wires and pink fiberglass insulation exposed. The china cup was their link with their mothers, their past civility, and their present primitive Alaskan way of life.

A month later, fed up with that symbol of gentility, I poured a cup of coffee in my china cup and managed to drop it. Leaning against the sink, I contemplated ten dollars, smashed to bits. That was the end of my trying to be what I was not. An artist, clumsy, different, perhaps too direct, I resolved to be myself, to throw away whatever was not true to my nature. I went out and bought some mugs.

My family had not lived for one hundred years in one area with the same neighbors. We did not have to prove anything, or live up to the Joneses. Learning and being creative were what my father thought important, not material objects.

I said what I thought, wore no mask or social smile. I was friendly and open, and must have irked others not used to such forwardness. Once at the Beta meeting, I said I was sure we could win first prize making a float. One of the women whispered, "Don't pat yourself too hard, or you'll fall off the fence." We did win first prize, because I knew I could design a good float, but to her, it was unseemly bragging.

I did not want to go through life being excessively timid, or smiling when I did not feel like it. I wanted to be natural, expressing my true feelings.

Some of the women in Fairbanks acted like leftovers from the Victorian Age. Their children were "seen but not heard." Their husbands would "never let them work outside of the home!" Their husbands were the chief topic of their conversations. These women seemed to be adjuncts to their men, without identities of their own.

In the late forties, in our small town, this was the role of women, except for the single nurses and schoolteachers. A few of the women worked in stores. Sandy Fenton worked with Mac in their drugstore, but the majority of women stayed home and took care of the children. Hildur had accepted a job as part-time teacher substitute at the Fairbanks Public School, which was feeling the crunch of all the young families with children arriving after the war.

Since there were no places of recreation other than churches or bars, we had to find our own way of socializing. We did not call them parties — they were "gatherings." They did not resemble any party I had ever gone to in New York before I was married, where wine was usually served, and bohemian artists talked about the latest cultural event, art exhibit, or books.

These Fairbanks gatherings were sedate, quiet affairs. Married couples politely inquired about the latest happenings. The men invariably gravitated to one side of the room, away from the women. I thought it strange at first, but it happened every time, as if women could not possibly converse on such serious, manly, intellectual topics as mining, septic tanks, plumbing, hunting, planes, and motors. People rarely discussed ideas; the discussions were usually practical. The men would stand lumped together, in their best shiny Filson whipcords with their Pendleton shirts, or heavy sweaters, wearing string bolo ties, usually embellished with a moose carved in ivory, and a gold nugget fastened in the middle. Neckties were out and bolos were in; ties were rarely seen even at funerals and weddings. Some successful miners wore gold nuggets and jade-embellished wristwatches from Avakoff's Jewelry.

Their wives wore gold nugget earrings, rings, necklaces, bracelets, and pins formed in their initials. The miners from the creeks gave their wives nuggets emblazoned with diamonds as Christmas presents. Huge nuggets displayed on their breasts were the height of style. Not for Hildur and me. "Too ostentatious," she stated, her pert nose in the air.

From the men's corner, Elmer's baritone boomed, "The damn jack hammer wouldn't work." The men were right. We women were not interested in their mining conversation and their laconic discussions of valves, joints, gaskets, grease, and paydirt.

The men depended on one another for advice, tools, and support; the women also depended on each other for the same things. Women clustered on the couch and chairs, or made coffee and prepared snacks in the kitchen. Often we shared a potluck. We wore our one good dress, or a blouse and skirt. The hair-do was a bouffant back-comb job, but I wore mine up in a braid, easy to do. No one wore very high heels. Most of us wore fur-lined boots to the gathering, then changed shoes in the entryway.

The women talked about their children, chicken pox, and the two doctors in town. We exchanged recipes. We complained about the condition of our houses and the lack of water or plumbing.

To change the subject, I offered, "Did anyone see the new ball gowns in Lucille's windows this week?"

"You mean that black dress — low-cut in front and in back?" said cute little Marcel Colp, who lived across the street from me. She was a wonderful cook and housekeeper, and her house was always neat — just the opposite of mine.

Edna Lawson, the telephone operator who was born in Fairbanks, interrupted, "You think that dress is something, you should have seen my mother's dress for the Moose Hall dance. It had rose-colored bead spangles. She looked so elegant with combs in her hair. They had balcony boxes where the socialites sat. My father wore a swallow-tailed coat and white kid gloves. There were about a thousand people in Fairbanks then, but they had a fancy dress shop and a hairdresser."

"When the railroad was built in 1923," Edna continued, "they had a huge celebration — a masked ball and a torchlight parade. Mrs. Gillespie, the doctor's wife, shocked the town by coming in black tights with a garland of fake roses around her waist, wearing a black mask. They had 'tombolas', or skits written for them. Dr. Gillespie, who usually came to work in hat, gloves, and cane, dressed up in a wig and silk stockings, taking the women's parts."

Toward the end of a gathering, coffee and cake were served, and the men would join the women. Sometimes men told bear stories, bragging for our benefit. Sometimes loganberry wine was served, or slides were shown. The Argus camera was the new rage.

People seemed to be thrifty and hardworking; a do-it-yourself and help-your-neighbor philosophy existed. Dishonesty was quickly discovered in the small town. As Joe said, "There are only three ways out of town: you fly, take the train, or drive south on the only road to the states. The police will be waiting at the other end."

I noticed that Elmer, Doug Colp, and Joe were talking about mining every chance they had. Joe had not forgotten his dream of finding gold in Alaska. He had gold fever, as did most of the young men who came to Alaska. He planned to start out in a small way, and Elmer encouraged him.

We were making new friends, and were delighted to be invited for dinner at the home of Elkan and Anne Morris.

Elkan was an electrical contractor with an adventuresome spirit. He and his diminutive wife, Anne, came to Alaska on their honeymoon by canoe, portaging over the St. Lawrence River, through Canada and finally to Alaska, camping on the Porcupine River near Fort Yukon.

There they lived in a log cabin, making a bed and chairs using diamond willow and caribou hides. They made a table from a hand-hewn spruce plank and diamond willow legs. Anne stuffed their mattress with grasses as the Indians did. They trapped and shot game, living off the land. Anne learned to cut and dry salmon as well as any Indian woman.

As a young man, Elkan had worked for the Natural History Museum of New York. He had an absorbing interest. Snakes! He must have brought the first snakes into Alaska.

Armed with bottles, a net, a pickup truck, and a trailer, the Morrises traveled to South America to hunt snakes. They lived for six months in the heart of the South American jungle. "Snakes?" They asked the people in Spanish. "Do you know where there are snakes?"

Anne helped in every way, holding the receptacle while Elkan maneuvered the reptile. Underneath their trailer bed were snakes of all sizes and descriptions in boxes and jars. The Morrises slept peacefully over them, but I certainly would not have closed an eye all night.

They had traveled to Hong Kong, India, China, and Australia to find reptiles. Elkan gave the snakes to San Francisco's Steinhardt Collection. He had been offered the Smithsonian's highest job as a herpetologist, but he said, "Why would I want to sit in a stuffy office all year when I can go freely and hunt snakes?"

Elkan housed his snakes off the living room, behind a sliding door. When we visited them, a python slithered over their daughter's shoulders as she sat doing her homework. My pathological fear of snakes was so strong I would not go to the snake house in the Bronx Zoo. The Morrises had to put all their snakes away, locking the large pythons in their closet before I would come in.

Anne entertained us in her living room and brought out refreshments, while I sat uneasily. Elkan expounded on various scientific subjects — the stars, economics, the Earth, a rare blind dolphin he saw in India, and the colocynth off Australia. We discovered that he had a photographic mind; he looked at a written page and memorized the contents. It was impressive.

After three cups of tea, I asked Anne, "Where is your bathroom?"

"Follow me," she replied.

As I followed behind her, she opened the door. They kept another python in the bathroom. He was draped gracefully over the shower rod above the cool bathtub. I backed off hurriedly and said, "It's okay, I really don't need to go."

She called to Elkan, who lifted the snake and put him behind the sliding doors. "He is funny, isn't he?" Anne chuckled. "I swear he's saying 'peek-a-boo' to me. When I sit on the toilet seat, he leans over the sink as if on one elbow, while the other end coils over the shower rod. He looks at me as if he could talk.

"One day I left the toilet seat open and found him buried half way down the hole. I quickly called Elkan to come home from work. I was afraid he would disappear and plug up the plumbing. Elkan came and lifted him out."

The Morrises affectionately fed their snakes live chickens and mice, and went hunting for frogs in the pond. Their freezer held frozen mice in the summer. They often carried snakes in their pockets, which I found repulsive. We became friends, although I never overcame my fear of snakes.

I rebelled against the drudgery of housework, hating the everyday repetition. There were always errands, shopping, cooking, and cleaning. By the time I chopped the kindling, got the fire started in the stove, and made breakfast, it was time to clean up and do chores. Whenever I had to fill in a form, I never, but never, wrote housewife — I always wrote artist. I hated to give up sculpture, but it was impossible to chop stone in the living room. I painted watercolors, then turned to oils, painting on the kitchen table.

"My neighbors never notice my paintings when they come over," I complained to Hildur as I sat in the lamplight, sewing a flannel baby's nightgown with blanket stitch embroidery around the edge. "They pretend not to see them, and turn away."

"I never met anyone so interested in art. You see life through art," said Hildur seriously as she crocheted. "At Moore Creek, when we pick berries, you notice the color of the blueberries against the yellow tundra. I looked at it as food, like a farmer would. To you, it was a painting. You opened up a new world for me."

"Well, my eyes were trained for color and shapes. That's my work." Pleased by her warm empathy, I bit off the blue embroidery thread and looked at my stitching. It was not art, just a practical blanket stitch. Patting my stomach, I was conscious of the real creation growing within me.

"About them not saying anything," commented Hildur, "they probably don't know what to say. Forget it."

★

II

—

Reaching
Out

*Songs are thoughts which are sung out with
the breath when people let themselves be
moved by a great force, and ordinary speech
no longer suffices.*

Netsilik Eskimo

Villagers from the surrounding area and from the Arctic
found their way into the main streets of Fairbanks. Eskimos
in sealskin parkas, huge wolverine ruffs framing their
bronzed faces, roamed the main street and the banks of the
Chena River. Their women sewed geometric border designs
around their mukluks, or fur boots. Accustomed to village
trails, Eskimo women usually walked behind their men in
long, flowered calico parkas lined with fur. Babies snuggled
on their mothers' backs, stuck their heads up out of the fur
ruffs in order to breathe. I longed to paint them.

Many Indians in marten and beaver hats came to
Fairbanks from the nearby villages of Minto and Nenana,
and from the Yukon River villages. Since moose meat was
their staple food, the women tanned the skins and made
their men fringed moose-hide jackets, beaded with elaborate
designs. Long moose-hide gloves with fur and bead trim
were tied around the neck with bright red yarn. Indian

women usually wore hip-length parkas with wool pants. Indian footgear had moose skin rather than sealskin soles, with distinctive beadwork.

Indians walked around town proudly, with their hands in their pockets, as if their feet were an extension of the land. They did not walk carefully as we did, afraid to fall on the ice; their moose-hide slippers gripped the contour of the land.

Eskimo women rocked from side to side when they walked; I was told that the tundra in their villages was uneven. I did not fully understand this until I lived in an Eskimo village years later, and noticed that I was walking in the same fashion.

Eskimos and Indians congregated around the Co-Op Drugstore on Second Avenue, or gathered near the Chena River so that other villagers could find them. When I shopped for aspirin at the Co-Op, I saw them drinking coffee or having a hamburger with fries at the lunch counter. They brought their baskets and ivory carvings to sell at Charlie Main's store or Kaye's Curio. The women seemed calm; nothing flustered them, and they did not scold their children. There was a mystery about their lives, and I longed to see for myself how they lived in the Arctic.

Along the banks of the Chena were small wooden shacks, "wanigans," and ramshackle log cabins. Old trappers and Indians lived there without running water or plumbing, as they lived along the Yukon. We called the area "Rabbit Island."

I went to paint the picturesque, sunken cabins, some with old tin bathtubs hanging under the rafters. I painted an Indian woman as she sunned herself near her cabin door. Was this the way it looked in an Indian village on the Yukon? Was this the harbinger of the subject I enjoyed painting — the merging of a figure in the landscape, painting the people of the land?

Joe and I watched the Indian dancers of Minto perform at the University of Alaska. An elder, wearing a fringed moose-hide jacket, carrying a feathered stick, led the dancers. Around his forehead was a beaded moose-skin headband. The women, in long fringed dresses embellished with beads and feathers, danced to the drumbeat in small steps, their motions dignified, holding scarves as they looked down modestly. The men stomped in the center with strong head and arm movements. The drummer, a short wiry man with missing front teeth, led the singing. They sang of the hunt, of husbands lost. They sang songs of the squirrel: "he jump from tree to tree." The children danced randomly, imitating their elders. It was my first introduction to Indian dances and I shook my shoulders, enthralled with the beat.

After the dance, I sought out the dancers to tell them how much I enjoyed it. When I met Louise Titus, one of the dancers, at the doctor's office, I invited her and her husband to visit me.

"I'm expecting my baby in February," I confided. Mrs. Titus promised to visit us after they returned from a potlatch in Nenana.

Walter Titus, a thin man in thick bifocals, smiled warmly when he and Louise arrived at our home a few weeks later. I offered them coffee and cake in our living room. Louise had a soft, giving expression. "I brought this to show you, Clara." Her arms hugged a birchbark baby basket, the edges bound with spruce root.

"A long time ago we used animal claws along the back as rattles. Our babies rest their backs against part of a tree," she explained as she stroked the birchbark. "My grandmother used moss or squirrel's nest for diapers." She sipped her coffee and added more milk, then sampled my butterless, eggless, milkless cake. "She used birch baskets for cooking.

She heat stones in fire, then put stones in baskets with water. Then put in meat.

"Some women wear a soft, tanned strap of caribou skin under the stomach when they're pregnant," Louise advised me. "Some women have their babies alone. They kick off their snowshoes, lay down on a caribou skin. Give birth right on the snow. After the baby come, tie the cord, wrap the baby in rabbit fur and walk into camp.

"The winters," Louise whispered, "drop to sixty below. Snow is deep and winds terrible."

"I hope it's not 60 below this winter," I said. I knew I could never have a baby alone in the snow unless I had to, but the conviction was growing within me that I could have it without drugs. Naturally. Like an Indian woman.

"Clara, you'll have to come and visit us in Minto after your baby is born." Minto was a short hop by plane or a long dog team ride away.

In addition to child-raising and cooking, Indian women had to tan and sew all of the family's clothing, haul water, and gather dry willows for fire. They wove the netting on snowshoes, sewed birchbark on canoes, gathered spruce pitch to seal the seams of the canoes. They took fish from nets, cleaned them, and made snares for rabbits and other animals. The women also skinned beaver, mink, and other animals. When I thought of all the hard physical work Indian women did, I realized how easy our lives were in comparison.

I asked Louise, "What do you teach girls now?"

"How to bake bread, make slippers, tan moose hide, take care of babies, skin rabbits, and cut fish." She added sadly, "But the girls don't want to learn anymore." Indian girls wanted the same easy life as town girls.

"What is the most important thing to tell your children?"

"How to make a fire," Walter said emphatically. "Use dried black birchbark dust to start the sparks, with thin shreds of birch paper. Clara, always remember matches, an ax, and a hatchet. Without those you can't live in the woods."

"What is the second thing you tell your children?"

"To be kind to everyone, not to hurt people; be good to everyone. 'Love thy neighbor.'"

The third thing he said was, "Teach children not to be careless. Save thyself, thy life. When they are young, they think they can swim across a river or shoot with a gun. They are careless sometimes, they don't think."

Walter looked out the window. "We didn't need money when I was a boy," he said proudly. "My father trapped for a living. I was brought up like that. There was no way to work for wages till the war. Then I got work on the railroad. Most Indians still hunt and trap. A long time ago, Indians shared everything, but times are changing. When white people need something they go to the bank to get money, and when we need something we go to our land and that's our bank!"

I liked that — it appealed to my nature. The Tituses had shared another reality of life that I had been unaware of. I witnessed their warm relationship to each other, and understood how closely they had to work together. I was appreciative of their coming to visit me, and delighted that Louise would part with the birchbark baby basket. Louise needed the money. "I can make another one," she reassured me. The spruce root binding around the edges of the basket was dyed with blueberry juice and red ochre. The baby basket was a useful work of art, and I loved it. Their invitation to visit them in Minto planted a seed within me, but it would be many years before I was free and ready to go.

The first time I got up enough nerve to ask an Eskimo girl, carrying a baby in her parka, to pose for me, she turned out to be Charlie Brower's granddaughter from Point Barrow. Brower was the trader at Point Barrow and a whaling captain; a white man married to an Eskimo woman.

Mary Brower had come to Fairbanks to visit her relatives, wearing a muskrat fur parka. Her ruff, made of wolverine, was chosen because it would never gather frost. Underneath her ruff, her beautiful face glowed with naturally reddened cheeks, brown eyes, and glossy black braids.

Accustomed to seal and reindeer meat, fish and pilot bread, she enjoyed our lunch of Ritz crackers and cheese, hamburgers, bananas, and cake, all rare then in Eskimo villages.

Mary Brower sat for me in her parka, while I asked her about her life in Barrow. "We go caribou hunting. Sometimes I climb the cliffs for murre eggs and I shoot ravens for dog food."

"I've never shot anything. It must be great to be able to hunt for what you need to eat." I mixed my oil paint and looked at her and her baby, sleeping contentedly while I painted them both.

To northern villagers coming to Fairbanks for the first time, climbing a flight of stairs was a new experience. Electricity, running water, and washing machines were objects of great value, not to mention flush toilets, bathtubs, and electric stoves. The painting of Mary was my first Eskimo portrait, and her first meeting with an artist.

Linda Badten was one of the first Eskimo teachers in Fairbanks. Her living room was conventional; her kitchen had all modern conveniences. A widow, she supported her two children.

Linda went from Saint Lawrence Island to Sheldon Jackson College in Sitka, then completed her teacher's training in Kansas. She was the first one from her village to get a college degree. "I was a stubborn, curious youngster. I wanted to see the world. A good reader, I taught the other children and helped the teachers. They were good teachers. There were two classrooms for all the children." Linda was short, her movements decisive as she walked around her living room.

"I had two brothers and three sisters. I was next to the baby. They all died of T.B. except me and I wonder why to this day. Why me?

"My nose was always in books, in that dim light. I would repeat what I had learned in school to my parents. I tried to tell them about atoms and molecules, but I realized that our language was inadequate to describe this to them.

"I loved adventure, but I was never brought up as a completely traditional Eskimo woman. I longed to get out of the village, to try another lifestyle. Other Eskimo girls who went 'outside' felt differently — they felt they were sent into exile away from home.

"My parents did not want me to leave home. I was the only child left, but I persisted. They finally consented to let me go away to school.

"Later, I taught school at Fort Yukon, an Indian village on the Yukon, then at Kotzebue, an Eskimo village. It was there that I met my husband, Ed, who was a Wien Airlines bush pilot. We fell in love and married. Our daughter, Jayne, was seven months old, and I was pregnant when Ed crashed, sucked in a downdraft. He was flying some miners out for an exploration dig. It was a terrible time for me."

After her son, Ed, was born in Fairbanks, Linda carried on alone, teaching school. I imagined her house in the Arctic, an old Siberian type with walrus-skin covering and seal-oil lighting. I looked at her with admiration. She had learned a new language, left her family and her village to become a teacher, and raised her two children alone with perseverance and courage.

"Sometimes," Linda said, looking around her living room, then at her blue wall-to-wall rug, "I feel like I am a thousand years old. I have come from such a primitive beginning and I could see so far back."

It was through Linda that I met Otto Geist, whom she had known when he lived at Saint Lawrence Island. Otto, originally from Germany, was a short, stocky man of dignified demeanor, distinguished by a wide forehead, a strong nose and chin. No stranger to archeology, he had collected Roman artifacts as a boy. In Fairbanks, he found a job as caretaker and handyman around the university. Inspired to go into the Arctic to live with Eskimos, he collected many anthropological and archaeological artifacts.

Linda said he was greatly beloved by Eskimos and spoke their language "with a thick German accent!" The great passion of his life was collecting mastodon specimens, and his great feat was whale hunting with Eskimos and living with them as an Eskimo. He had been initiated by them and called "Aghvook" (whale), because he hunted whale like an Eskimo. He lived with an Eskimo family and became close to their daughter, Florence, who taught him much of the old culture. Florence was a gifted self-taught artist, who made beautiful drawings of her life and culture.

I listened to every word Linda and Otto said about the Arctic. Otto spoke seriously without any pretensions of his work and life with Eskimos. White men, like Otto, were rare in the Arctic. Rockwell Kent, with whom I corresponded and finally met in the seventies, lived with an Eskimo woman, Salamina, in Greenland. If white men could live in the Arctic with Eskimos, why couldn't I? If Rockwell could paint in Greenland, why couldn't I paint in the Alaska Arctic?

Otto's house was interesting for two reasons — he possessed a caribou-fur-lined toilet seat in his outhouse, and his driveway was distinguished by a rare fence made of discarded Pleistocene mastodon bones unearthed by gold miners in the Fairbanks area.

Otto, with his cigar tucked into his mouth, reminded me of my father. After dinner he and Joe discussed Truman and

politics. Joe took his pipe out to emphasize a point, and
both sipped brandy. A series of extinct bison was named
Platycerbison Geisti after Otto. He had excavated a Saint
Lawrence Island mound called Kukulik, collecting more than
50,000 artifacts for the University of Alaska and the Frick
Museum of New York.

I consciously sought the company of older Eskimo
women; they wore kerchiefs like my mother. They did not
speak English well. They were coping in an unfamiliar
environment with children who were growing away from
them, into schools and books — into another life, the life of
the dominant white culture. In the late forties, they had no
books, no written language of their own.

I became involved in the lives of people who lived in the
Arctic, unaware of how my interest would eventually change
my life forever. Few people hung Eskimo masks, paintings,
and carvings in their houses as we did, and few were aware
of it as great art. In the northern Eskimo village of Shismaref
lived Kivetoruk Moses with his wife Bessie. Her brother
George Ahgapuk made a living in Anchorage drawing in pen
and ink on caribou skins. George had tuberculosis, and while
in the hospital, a nurse encouraged him to begin drawing.

When Kivetoruk and Bessie moved to Nome, he began to
paint, using Marshalls colored photo pencils on small pieces
of paper, depicting hunting scenes, shamans, and whales. I
began to buy his small paintings when they filtered down to
Fairbanks. Without a single art lesson, he had the gift of a
true artist's eye.

The paintings had a veracity, a liveliness of color that only
someone who had lived the life could portray. Kivetoruk had
a strong sense of design and drama. Every drop of blood
from a speared polar bear could be seen on the ice, and every

stroke of the Eskimos' fur garments was painted accurately. His work reminded me of Grandma Moses's naive paintings, and they had the same last name. Museums and other collectors, including Vincent Price, discovered his work.

Eskimos were treated as second-class citizens, made to wait at counters, rarely invited into the homes of white people. Everyone knew they won dog races, and lived up north somewhere, but except for pilots, scientists, and some government workers, few people visited them in the Arctic.

Prejudice was strong. Indians and Eskimos were barred from theaters and hotels and were discouraged from sitting in restaurants. In Kotzebue, which was Eskimo country, white establishments had signs, "Eskimos not allowed in dining rooms and theaters except in segregated seats," and "Eskimos and dogs not allowed."

During World War II, Eskimo and Indian scouts had patrolled up and down the coast of Alaska to protect our country against invaders. Governor Ernest Gruening said, "I cannot call upon Eskimos and Indians to save our nation when they can't sit in the theater with us." He asked the mayor of Nome to introduce an anti-discrimination bill and was cheered by the presence of Frank Peratrovich and Andrew Hope, two newly elective "Native" legislators. The bill passed the House but was opposed in the Senate.

"The races should be kept further apart," said Allen Shattuck. "Who are these people, barely out of savagery, who want to associate with us whites with five thousand years of recorded civilization behind us?" Frank Whaley also opposed the bill, saying that he did not want to sit next to Eskimos in a theater; they smelled.

When the debate on the bill came in 1946, the packed gallery was tense with expectation. Clearly, passage of this bill would spell profound social change in Alaska. A young, well-dressed Southeastern Indian woman, Mrs. Roy Peratrovich, rose in the gallery and came to the floor. "I would not have expected," she said in a quiet, steady voice, "that I, who am barely out of savagery, would have had to remind the gentlemen with five thousand years of recorded civilization behind them of our Bill of Rights." She went on to give instances of discrimination against herself and her family. Her intelligence was obvious, her composure fault-less, and her plea could not have been more effective. When she finished, there was a burst of applause in the gallery, and the Senate passed the bill eleven to five.

One Fairbanks Indian seemed to sum it all up. "We bought Alaska for seven million dollars. What Indian get out of that? He didn't get nothing. All he gets is relief. Pension. Food stamps and hospital, the hospital we go to when we catch the white man's disease. White people came, they tried to trap, only they got no meat. We gave the meat. We fed them. We never let them starve. White people, he thinks Indian just like a dog. We didn't treat white people like that when they first come here."

I visited Margaret Hunter, who was making me a wolf fur ruff for my parka. Margaret was a white woman who had driven a dog team from Kotzebue to Nome to Fairbanks with her seven-year-old daughter. They had double sleeping bags and slept in snow banks or cabins along the trail. It seemed unbelievable that she could do this, this plain-spoken, forceful woman with a square face, in her fifties, who had lived most of her life with Eskimos. She wore a simple Eskimo parka. No makeup. The Diomede Island Eskimos had taken her from Kotzebue by skin boat all the way to Point Hope one summer where she bought ivory carvings from the Eskimos and sold them to tourists in her little store in Kotzebue. Her parkas and mukluks were sewn as well as an Eskimo woman's. The Eskimos respected and trusted her. She used to mine gold with her brother, but little else was known about her.

She was living in Fairbanks in a dark log cabin on Wendell Street. A large room with an uneven wooden floor led into the kitchen, where two old rocking chairs surrounded a huge, black woodstove. In the dim light I could make out old photographs, and a bookcase full of Eskimo relics, masks, whale bones, loon skin bags, animal claw bags, cartons of furs, wolf skins, bearskins, and sealskins hanging from the ceiling. She brought out a box of Russian blue trade beads, old ivory necklaces and carvings, all treasures.

She encouraged me to go North and invited me to visit her in Kotzebue. When she gave me the parka with the gray wolf ruff, she presented it with a gift of ivory beluga whale earrings. Margaret Hunter was the first white woman I had met who had left our community to live in a far northern Eskimo village.

Musher

✱

12
—

Frontier
Women

*In addition to my family, I love four things
— the wilderness, art, books, and people. Not
in that order. But what gives meaning to my
everyday life is being creative — visualizing
new paintings or new poems and creating
them with my hands and mind.*

From my journal

The women I met were remarkable for their stamina and
courage. The land had challenged their ingenuity, and they
gave their utmost, doing what was necessary to survive.

Many women worked at jobs that had been in the men's
domain: they chopped their own wood, hauled water,
installed electricity and plumbing, designed and built their
own houses. They hunted big game, flew cargo and mail
planes, and ran fishing boats. Women played extraordinary
roles in the legislature, owned gold mines, worked as nurses,
real estate agents, and teachers in the Bush.

Elmer recalled a woman who mined at Manley Hot
Springs. "She was strong as an ox, as good as a man on a
tractor. Tough. Many wives helped their husbands, put on
pants and gum boots and worked as hard as any man."

It was an education for me to realize what women could
do. It opened my eyes to the scope of choices that were

available. One woman homesteaded 160 acres in Fairbanks, then built her house from scrap lumber. Everything in the house was scrounged from the dump. She made her chairs and table of split logs, used a discarded washing machine wringer as a flower pot, grew her own vegetables, made her own bread, and shot her own moose.

Fannie Quigley was my idea of an independent woman. She died in 1944, but stories of Fannie were still told all over Fairbanks. How I wished I could have known her.

She managed to live very well by herself in the wilderness. When she married Joe Quigley, she was his equal partner in everything. When they hunted, she went one way and he another; she was a master hunter who felled her game with one shot. She didn't need him for assistance when she packed the carcass. Except for a few staples, she made, grew, fished, or hunted everything they ate. "No man could catch more grayling in a day," said one miner. "At day's end she would shoulder her heavy catch and tramp home as happy as a boy."

She had her own dog team, chopped her own wood, made her own moccasins, and was handy with tools. She never had a formal education. Born in 1871 in a Bohemian settlement in Nebraska, she didn't learn English until she was grown. Old photos showed Fannie in men's trousers, heavy wool shirts, and heavy boots. She was short, slim, and had a strong mind of her own. She loved the life of the wild with a passion.

Once she shot two bulls near Moose Creek. They dropped dead in the middle of the creek. Working in slush ice, she tied a rope to the carcasses, secured them to a tree, then pulled, cursed, and shoved until she had the meat ashore. It never occurred to her to go for help. She skinned and butchered the moose and took the meat home on her sled.

Another time she shot a moose with a single shot, gutting it in the fading light of evening. She was alone as usual, in the high country with few trees and no place to take shelter. If she left the carcass unattended overnight, the wolves would feast on her kill. She solved the problem by crawling inside the warm carcass. The meat froze while she slept and she had "a heckova time" cutting her way out!

Distinguished visitors came to Fannie's doorstep: Grant Pearson, superintendent of Mount McKinley National Park; Bishop Hudson Stuck; Harry Karstens, his partner and my landlord; survey crews; park rangers; big game hunters; geological crews; and climbers.

Belmore Browne, the artist-explorer who made the first painting of Mount McKinley and whose three attempts to climb the mountain were defeated by weather, visited Fannie. He compared her meals to Roman feasts — wild meat, garden vegetables, wild jellies, wild rhubarb sauce that beat any tame rhubarb Browne had eaten. All was washed down with ice cold potato beer Fannie had brewed!

Grant Pearson, in his book *My Life of High Adventure*, wrote of making a forced landing on the gravel bar near the Quigley cabin with Father Fitzgerald. They were invited to share her famous caribou stew and blueberry pie with crust of rendered bear fat. When they left after a two-day delay due to bad weather, Father Fitzgerald asked, "What kind of chocolates would you like me to send you?"

"Schlitz," Fannie answered, looking him in the eye.

The next day, the pilot returned with two cases of Schlitz and a quart of whiskey. Fannie liked homebrew, called it "Kantishna champagne," and often kept a bottle tucked inside her boot.

The story I heard over and over was about the time Joe Quigley crashed his plane. Fannie ran to see Joe crawling out, blood running from a gash in his nose. "It was split clean through lengthwise," she said. "I got out my needle and catgut, washed 'em, and sewed up his nose. That was the first time I ever sewed up a person, and I sewed him the way I do my moccasins, with a baseball stitch."

Fannie was a remarkable woman; she did everything expertly. She could embroider the finest stitches. She not

only grew the largest pansies, but she dried them and repro-
duced them in exact colors in her needlework. Pansies were
her favorite flower, and I think I know the reason. In the
wild soil it grows easily, lasting longer than any other flower,
blooming under the snow.

Joe Quigley eventually retired to the softer life of the
Lower 48, but Fannie, her face leathery from exposure, her
small body shrunken smaller with the years, refused to leave
her cabin in the wilderness. Once she broke her hip but after
a two-week stay in the Fairbanks hospital, she went home
with her walking stick in one hand and her rifle in the other.
She died in her sleep in 1944 at seventy-three.

Most of my neighbors had at one time or another lived in
the wilderness at mining camps or on hunting trips. One couple
took their baby on a sheep hunting trip, carrying her on their
backs Indian style. Another went glacier climbing. Changing
a baby's diaper on a glacier was doing it the hard way.

For sheer courage and endurance, I would nominate the
Bergland sisters, Evelyn and Hazel. I met them once on the
streets of Fairbanks. They were the kind of women who
could have made it to the moon. They lived near Fort Yukon
with their mother. When their father was crippled with
arthritis, they took over his job as trapper. They hunted and
trapped with twenty-five dogs, living off the land, subsisting
on game and fish. They chopped their own wood and
skinned and cut up their game. Money from the furs they
trapped fed their family.

As teenagers, they lived a hard, grinding life, cutting

wood, hunting meat, running traplines, and fishing. Their
mother baked and cooked, their younger sister chopped
wood; together they picked one hundred gallons of cranberries each year. Their diet was simple: meat, fish, beans, bread,
and cranberries.

They had a three-hundred-mile trapline with four hundred traps, six tents, and ten cabins. In autumn, they cut and
stacked eight cords of wood. They ran dogs in seventy
degrees below zero, setting and baiting traps and loading
frozen beaver, wolf, and wolverine onto their sleds. They
denied themselves every comfort, living without friends or
any social life, out on the trail in a harsh environment.

One year, returning from their trapline, they entered their
cabin and found a grizzly bear sitting on their bed. Evelyn
shot him, then she and Hazel rolled him off the bed. "We lit
the coal oil lamp and started a fire, pulled the blood-soaked
bedding off, and threw it to one side to freeze till we got
around to washing it. What a mess I made," said Evelyn,
"killing him on the bed."

"Why didn't you ask him to get off first?" retorted Hazel.

Hazel and Evelyn both married trappers. Ernie Pyle met
them and asked them to write a story of their lives, which
they did in *Born on Snowshoes*. When I met Evelyn in
Fairbanks, she had married a trapper and had five children.

"It was seventy-eight below one winter," she told me.
"Our cabin was filled with thick, white steam. The dogs were
white with frost — a five-gallon gasoline can on the stove to
melt snow water steamed instantly as though it were hot."
And I thought I had it tough in Fairbanks!

"Four of my five children were born, as I was born, on
snowshoes," said Evelyn. "It would not surprise me at all if
some of them spent most of their lives wrestling loaded
toboggans, lighting fires in the icy stoves of snowed-in
cabins, and making camp in the cold, dark of tents way out
in the timber, wolves howling far away. They will never get
rich, but they could do worse."

Fabian Carey the trapper once told me that when he was a young man trapping around Minchumina, they tried to get him to marry one of the Bergland girls. Word had spread to other trappers that here would be two wonderful, hardworking helpmeets. "They brought home lots of fur. They were tough, but too much competition for most men.

"They wore long Mother Hubbard dresses or overalls most of the time. Sometimes they dressed in boy's clothes, and wore their hair cropped short," Fabian said. "They were stronger than most men, lifting a 100-pound sack of flour over one shoulder and carrying another one uphill. Their hands were huge and work-hardened, and hung awkwardly, their ruddy faces were weather-beaten. The trappers who lived the same kind of life had tremendous respect for them."

They only came to Fort Yukon two weeks out of the year to sell their pelts and pick up winter supplies. They had to catch enough fish to feed their twenty-five dogs.

"As far as I was concerned, there was no *man's* work, just work," Evelyn said. "When we weren't trapping, tending dogs or chopping wood, we liked to knit or play checkers. Half the time we never even knew what day of the week it was."

Evelyn was almost blinded in one eye when she was on the trail with her dog team, but she continued her journey home. "Mom made a poultice of tea leaves. I suffered it out. We were 280 miles from the nearest doctor." She shot her first moose when she was twelve, and her first bear soon after. These girls were the Amazons of the North, the only white women who trapped then. They lived a harder life than the Indian women who usually had to tan and cut the meat their men hunted and trapped. But these women did both jobs well without a man's help.

In January, two women arrived in Fairbanks in a snow-storm, flying two surplus planes up from the states, a Stinson L-5 and a Gullwing Stinson AT-19. Celia Hunter and Ginny Wood, who had been pilots in the women's Air Force, had ferried planes in the United States and Canada during World War II, releasing men to fly combat missions.

It was generally thought then that women in the cockpit were socially inappropriate, even physically unable, but Marvel Crosson, Joe Crosson's sister, carried freight and passengers, setting a record climb of 23,996 feet. She crashed in San Bernadino at a women's competition in 1954. Virginia Clayton taught in the Top of the World Flying School. Ruth Hurst in Anchorage took over an air taxi service to deliver mail on a scheduled basis. Ingrid Peterson flew from Alaska over the North Pole to Russia. Joe said that during the Lend-Lease program, Russian women pilots flew to Fairbanks and back to Russia on a regular basis.

Ginny and Celia had been offered jobs flying two of Gene Jack's planes to his trading post in Kotzebue. "It was minus fifty degrees. It took us twenty-seven days to make thirty hours of flying time," said Celia. "Ginny's plane had no heat, and when we landed, we had to practically chip her out of the cockpit." They set up tours to Kotzebue, beginning tourism in Eskimo country.

"We loved Alaska," said Celia. "Whether you had money, whether your family was Boston society or raised on a stump ranch like mine, you had a chance. My father was a logger and jack-of-all-trades. My mother was a teacher, and she was my first passenger. She gave me a sense of my own worth. In Alaska, you were accepted for what you were able to do."

In 1952, they built a wilderness camp near Mount McKinley, after Ginny married Woody, a ranger at the national park. "We built the road in old Kantishna outside of Mount McKinley four miles from Fanny Quigley's cabin. The road was frozen tundra, a mudhole. We had to carry every nail, lumber, and food up that mountain. We didn't borrow any money. Put tents over a platform. Used a kitchen Primus stove," said Celia. "I never had goals. I just lived."

Nest Polenski was called "Laughing Woman" by the Indians because she made light of troubles, laughing at everything. I visited her in her cabin near the university, where she was "majoring in Library and Coffee Shop," hanging out with young students. A gray, wispy-haired, squat Polish woman, walking lightly in flat shoes, she was ageless. She loved to dance, and her figure was never restrained by a girdle.

The honey-colored log walls of her cabin had a heady fragrance from the spruce logs that burned in her woodstove. She lived without electricity or running water. At one end of the cabin was a greenhouse with tomato plants in the summer, mixed with seeds she brought from Hawaii, white, fragrant flowers that grew in tall profusion, called Nicotiana. A mouse lived there, as did bees and flies; she never killed anything. A treehouse held a bunkbed for visitors. She spent the winter traveling on a tramp steamer, but most of her money was spent on books. She cared nothing for clothes or adornments.

She spent only the summers in Fairbanks. In the winter, a letter would come from the Canary Islands or India in her round, slanted handwriting with her funny name, Nest Polenski, sharing her experiences of the places and people she met in her travels. Her children were grown, and she was free of all cares; she lived an unburdened life. "I'm ready to die anytime," she said.

She scoffed at pills and sickness. "I wouldn't eat the rotten, putrid flesh of an animal," she said, offering me peanuts to crack. A theosophist, she believed in reincarnation. Nest lived without conflict between her ideas and her life. She never seemed to want for anything, or pile up possessions; money and social position were not important to her. People from all walks of life visited her. She welcomed them, hands outstretched, laughing. She had no idle words; most of the time she listened. She was so rich in spirit, you could not give her anything less than the gift of your real self.

She refused to obey any time but her natural tempo, disdaining watches. Time spent with her seemed timeless. She showed you to yourself, and the things you said were deeper thoughts than you ever confided to anyone else. There I talked about my feelings, about painting and the desire to go into the Arctic to live with the Eskimos.

"Nest, I'd like to go visit the Eskimos, but I'm scared. What if I can't speak their language? What if they don't like me?"

Nest laughed. "Once I got off a plane in the middle of Mau Mau country. It was midnight and raining, and I didn't know a soul, but someone took me in and offered me shelter and food."

It seemed to me that if Nest could do it, I could also, and I became more confident.

There were all kinds of women who lived in our town in those early days; ordinary women like myself and Hildur, from every part of the United States, from every walk of life. Some of the women were not so fortunate. They did not have supportive husbands or families. Two of them stand out — unfortunate souls caught in the web of circumstances. One was Hulda Ford, and the other Irene Sherman.

Old Lady Ford was our town eccentric, our mystery

woman. It was said she had run a rooming house in Nome and married a good-looking man who took her money and disappeared, leaving her broken-hearted. She came to Fairbanks, and slowly began to buy up the old buildings on Second Avenue. In Nome she had collected canaries, but a fire killed her birds, so in Fairbanks she began to collect cats — all kinds of cats. We often passed her in the streets, a tiny, frail old woman dressed in dirty, black dresses, who blew her nose in an old scarf.

A miser, she kept her junk in her apartment over one of the stores on Second Avenue. She moved like a frightened rabbit around our back alleyways, in winter pulling a sled loaded with cartons and bags, or carrying two-by-fours, some sixteen feet long, which she dragged to her house. She was our town scavenger, our first bag lady.

I sat next to her one afternoon drinking coffee at the Model Cafe on Second Avenue. Two shopping bags were sprawled near her feet. She wore a dirty, black coat and a light blue, scroungy hat perched on top of her head. She pretended she did not see or hear me. The Model was the kind of eatery where they served corn, potatoes, or beans with every entree you ordered. As you ate, you stared at two large jars of strange fruit swimming in green liquid like embalmed fetuses. However, the Model was functional, it was warm, and their coffee was passable. When Mrs. Ford finished, she pulled up her skirt and reached into the top of her stockings to take out a wad of bills.

One day she left a paper shopping bag at the Model. The man who found it noted that it contained cash and rent checks amounting to $17,000.

Since she never bathed, some kind-hearted nurses from the hospital waylaid her and brought her forcibly, kicking and screaming, to the hospital for a bath and kerosene to wash her hair. I saw her going to the back of the grocery store where Mrs. Hall fed her a hot meal. No one knew much about her, and she had few friends, although she was said to have been a beautiful young woman.

When Joe worked as an electrician, he had to fix some wiring in the store next to her apartment over the Co-Op on Second Avenue. His ladder was at the level of her window. Mrs. Ford came to the window and opened it. "I never saw or smelled anything like it," Joe said. "The stench was terrible. About twenty-eight cats ran around on piles of old clothing, fouling everywhere. Pipes, lumber, junk, and garbage were spilled in confusion. She hoarded everything." In spite of her strange ways, most everyone felt compassion for her.

Irene Sherman made her way in life bumming beer off the tourists in the summer and the locals in the winter. We saw her grim, scarred face often, her dauntless eyes staring unblinkingly at us, as she poked her hand out from under three sweaters. Her faded, large-brimmed, dusty hat was covered with campaign buttons, a man's belt surrounded her waist, and she stamped around in heavy men's shoepacks, carrying a backpack. "Hi ya, baby," she would holler with a toothless grin. On St. Patrick's Day, she dressed up in her fancy hat with green feathers and wore a red boa over her ratty fur cape. Her big green pin read, "I've got my Irish up!" No hiding out for Irene. She was brazen, with a colorful vocabulary and a short temper. She wore her scars proudly.

Her father was a miner and trapper, away at the mine. Her mother, Agnes, was irresponsible and negligent with the children. In 1924, when Irene was about five years old, her mother left her with her baby brother and Dirty Face Porter's girl, Mary, in her Fifth Avenue cabin, and went out to drink beer.

Clara Rust's husband, Jesse, was at the Eagle's Hall when

a man ran in and yelled, "Call the fire department! Agnes's cabin is burning across the street, and the kids are in there."

The firemen saw two kids' faces pressed against the window. The door was locked, so they broke the window and got them out. Irene was hysterical. "I've set the house afire. My baby brother is in there." When they broke down the door, her baby brother fell out of his buggy, charred beyond recognition. The baby and Mary died. Irene was not expected to live, but she survived third-degree burns that melted layers of skin on her arms and chest. Her lungs were scarred, and she was in agony.

The children had been cold, so they revived the fire in the woodstove by filling it with paper, but the low ceiling made of pasted paper and stretched cheesecloth caught on fire. Irene and Mary pushed the baby in the carriage to the door, but couldn't open it, for Agnes had locked the children inside.

Poor Irene had to go to the burn hospital in Seattle for years. She worked in a convent, then at seventeen, wearing a black veil, was sent back to Fairbanks. Smooth, spidery lines crossed Irene's chin and neck, and her eyes had an open, surprised look.

Irene remembered her years at the convent. "When I was with the Catholics, it was the best years of my life. I wanted to raise hell, but as soon as I'd pull anything offbeat, I'd wind up sitting in a chair. I said to 'hell with you,' but they did turn me in the right direction."

When asked about the fire, Irene became agitated, and swore in a raspy voice about "that damn Porter brat who played with matches."

Irene reacted to the public with a back-slapping friendliness that was impossible to ignore. "I didn't hanker for being with people, but I didn't want to be a hermit, either," she told me, sipping a beer at the Pastime Bar.

Everyone admired her courage and defiance. Her dwelling at the dead-end edge of Noyes Slough was hidden by old refrigerators, stacks of lumber, garbage pails, wood, card-board, broken washing machines, and rusty bed springs, all stacked up like an impenetrable fort. Inside the fortress, a sprawl of tunnels and walkways connected the two structures. "I like to have stuff stored ahead, so that I know I can dive into it if I need it," Irene explained. Somehow the rotting junk barricading her house served a purpose for Irene — shielding her from a world of pain.

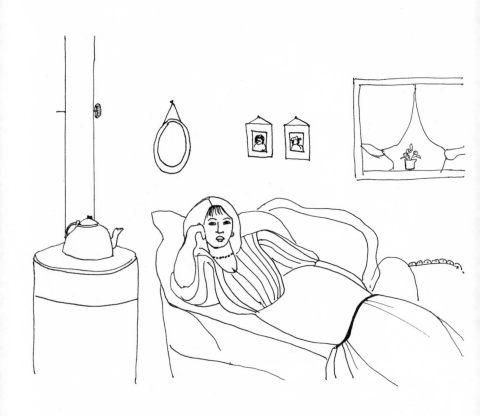

★

13

The
Line

*It's a silly question to ask a prostitute
why she does it . . . They are the highest
paid "professional" women in America.*

Gail Sheehy,
Hustling,
1971

Two kinds of women lived in our town in 1946: the
respectable kind, and the "girls" or "sporting women."
Whenever a woman said, "girls," or "pros-ti-tute," the taboo
word, she covered her mouth and looked around to see if
anyone had overheard. This piqued my curiosity. Prostitution
was considered a necessary evil in a town with so many
military, construction, and mining men and so few women.

Right in the middle of town, Fairbanks supported a row
of whorehouses called the Line. The log cabins on Fourth
Avenue were blocked off from Barnette Street by an eleven-
foot fence with a gate in it. As I walked to the N.C.
Company, I could see the fronts of the cabins, or cribs as
they were called, and their coal bins on the wooden walks.
Smoke poured out of the stacks of the pitched roofs. Respectable women did not go there.

On Second Avenue, there was always music and steam
billowing out of the cavern-like interiors of the bars. The
bartenders wore sleevebands as they dispensed alcohol, and
each kept a loaded pistol behind the counter. An undercurrent
of violence, mingled with a restlessness that drink could not
dispel, permeated the boozy air. Joe and Elmer would not
take us into a bar; it was off-limits to us. Too many lonely men.

Bootleg liquor was made on the other side of the river.
When the men bought one-hundred-pound sacks of sugar,
they told Mort Cass, the grocer, "We're just making fudge."

The Line opened in 1906, when the Flora Dora dance
halls closed, and wide-open gambling was outlawed. Thirty
girls were unemployed, and to survive they began to operate
out of small cribs, later joining a brothel operated by Panama
Hattie, one of the ladies of the night.

By 1919, there were about four thousand young miners
in Fairbanks, about half a dozen churches and 150 prostitutes, most of them illegal immigrants from France. An
investigator from Seattle found evidence of white slave
traffic, and arrested several prostitutes and four pimps. There
was an exodus of pimps to Valdez and several drifted down
the Chena River on rafts. Most of the French prostitutes
rushed to marry miners before they, too, were arrested as
immigrants and dragged into jail. One of the women,
Camille Leonard, had a standing offer of $5,000 to anyone
who would marry her.

The investigator also found twenty small shanties in the
outlying mining towns of Fox and Chatanika Camp. Nine
were houses of ill-repute, four operated as saloons, two were

churches and the remainder housed miners. "Fairbanks," wrote the investigator, "was the capital of all pimps and prostitutes in Alaska, with a red-light district in the middle of town. The three policemen were on intimate terms with the prostitutes."

In 1923, the girls were represented by Mr. Thompson, a bar owner who wore a black hat and long-tailed coat. He and his girl were later rumored to have been murdered in Mexico.

Prompted by the suicide of Marie La Fountane, who had killed herself when her pimp gambled away her savings, the city council clamped down on pimps who made a living soliciting customers in the bars.

In 1946, the city fathers still controlled the Fairbanks Line. They passed a law charging $250 a month for slot machines and juke boxes, and an amusement tax on cards and pan games. Each woman also paid the city for health inspections. The council rationalized that without the Line, there would be more rape and violence to respectable women.

Lonely men from the villages, soldiers, miners, construction workers, trappers, and homesteaders came into town on weekends. The F.E. Company's mining shift quit its seven-day work week at 5:30 P.M. on Saturday, and the men came into town. They came in from the creeks, did their serious window shopping on the Line, and plunked down their hard-earned money.

Red kerosene lanterns glowed as women smoked cigarettes, enticing customers inside. They sat looking provocatively out of the large windows into the alley. Some of the women had lap dogs who would bark and alert them that customers were coming. If the blinds were closed, that meant the women were indisposed.

There was an unspoken rule that they would not solicit outside of their cabins. They weren't allowed in a bar after 6 P.M. It was easy for the men to come to them under cover of winter. Since it was dark so much of the time, they were safe from scrutiny.

We townswomen could see only the fronts of the small,

one-story log cabins. Their cabins were built like ours, with wood piles and coal boxes outside, but some of them paid $900 a month rent while we paid $400 for the same space. Some of the women eventually owned their own cabins.

The Line was the source of social life for the lonely miners, a place where they could have a drink and enjoy female companionship. "Those women were real people," said one old-timer. "If you were sick, they made you chicken soup. You could trust them with your money.

"The girls had police protection. You could practically shoot a man and get away with it in those days, but if you kicked a prostitute's dog and she complained, you could go to jail."

I saw photographs taken in the cribs. The photos depicted elegantly dressed women sitting near their Victrolas. They played records; some played the piano. Their gowns were the newest fashions, shirred yokes with wide lace and pouffed balloon sleeves in the best fabrics. Their beds had embroidered satin and needlepoint pillows, and doilies covered the arms of stuffed chairs. Flouncy lace curtains hung at the windows. Dolls, photographs, stuffed toys, and china statuettes sat on their shelves. Kitchens had woodstoves or hot plates where they cooked omelets and other meals, but most often they sent out for meals from the Model Cafe.

Another photographer, Richard Geoghegan, an expert in Esperanto, and a Rhodes scholar who spoke Chinese and knew Sanskrit, was fascinated by the women, and spent a lot of time among them, eventually marrying Lola Belle Martin, of black and French descent from the West Indies.

Most of the men I knew would not admit to going to the Line, but they all knew the names of the girls. Black Bear, one of the girls, later married a gold miner. Her sister was called The Cub. Black Bear had lived on the Line at Iditarod before she came to Fairbanks. "She was built like a bear," a trapper said, "with a coat of hair like a black bear, and she measured an ax handle across the butt." We heard of Big

Babe, Finn Annie, Black Lena, Panama Hattie, Dynamite Red, Oregon Mare, Texas Rose, and one Italian beauty named the Spaghetti Queen. Beef Trust was big and fat. Two-Chin Sara had two chins, and Sweet Pea got her name because when a man was sentenced to be hung on the gallows at Iditarod, she brought him a bouquet of sweet peas.

Nosey Williams, a black woman who had dark spots like freckles all over her face, was named Nosey because a lover, in a fit, had bitten off the tip of her nose. Other black women were Jesse and Black Lena. Diamond-Toothed Lil, a blonde who came to Fairbanks when the strike was over in Dawson, had a diamond in her front tooth that sparkled when she smiled.

The women changed their nicknames when they traveled to other places and used their real names at the post office and when they did business in town. Some of the women were well-educated and good-looking.

They were often generous with their money and favors. If a man was down and out and turned down by the banks and his friends, they would lend him a grub stake for his next venture on the creeks. They might bail a man out of jail, or if they liked a handsome trapper, they would pay his fine when he was in trouble with the law. When a house burned down, the girls gave generous donations.

Some of the old whores came from other places to die in Fairbanks. They wore lots of makeup and kept the lights dim in their cribs.

The men were no bargains either. An old miner told me, "The men were a raunchy lot of bastards. There were two showers on the creek for twenty men and they all bunked in one room. They showered maybe once when they came into town and once when they left. They used the same blanket for years and their socks were changed about as often. They sweat cutting wood all day and when they walked into town they wanted action.

"The girls would sit in the big windows and rap as we walked by to get our attention. Sometimes we treated a youngster to one of the girls," he continued. "Then we'd all watch. They invited us into their living rooms for a drink, then we went to the back room. Sometimes they gave their customers a bath, and if they spent the night, breakfast. Every Monday they went for their physicals, which kept venereal disease down.

"We had other diversions too," he remembered. "Boxing, dances, and baseball. But we liked to sit and drink and horse around with those girls. On their days off, we went on outings, a picnic by the river maybe."

Texas Rose died in Fairbanks in 1942 at the age of seventy, and her obituary appeared on the front page of the Fairbanks newspaper. She had hustled all her life. The men had trusted her to keep their wallets. She sold them whiskey at a dollar a shot, a Coca-Cola cost the same, and they could take her into the back room for three dollars. When she died, every man in the vicinity who knew her came to the funeral. The men chipped in to buy her tombstone and buried her in the Clay Street Cemetery.

One man told me he had been about twenty-five when he met her. "I was lonely living out on the creeks. I cut wood all day in four-foot lengths, which came to about 79 cents an hour. I had drunk too much of Texas Rose's Ten High, and I was drunk. She fed me some of her spaghetti and I really got sick. I vomited all over." He chuckled as he remembered.

"After our bare camps and sweaty labor, we enjoyed the world of women. The perfume, the clothes. The girls favored the latest fashions and furs. They earned more in a few days than a dressmaker made in a month.

"I went to her funeral. She was one helluva gal."

Another well-known prostitute was Edith Neile, called the Oregon Mare. When younger, Edith was known as a lady of the night in Dawson where she did a pony act with a traveling troupe, wearing a horse's mask. An old-timer who had seen Edith in Dawson told me, "She could kick higher than her head. She galloped around the stage, whinnying like a horse in a low-cut outfit. During her act, men threw nuggets at her feet. I saw her at the faro table spending a thousand dollars one night, wearing a heavy gold nugget chain. A gift from some miner, no doubt." He winked and smiled. "She entertained a Mountie in her room one night wearing a pink silk night dress. Over that she wore his scarlet tunic, his Stetson, and his gauntlet gloves. She sat down on the bed flipping his riding whip. She was quite a gal."

Even the women liked Edith. "She was the best woman that ever lived," one of the townswomen told me. She was born in a mining town. "She was a soft touch for everyone. She was classy, had nice manners. They called her Oregon Mare because she could whinny like a horse. Once she sat down at the lunch counter at the Co-Op luncheonette and for a joke ordered, 'a bale of hay and a sack of oats!'"

"She was slightly deaf, and when she received a call she would ask the operator, 'What did he say? Is he coming over?'

"'Well, I don't know, I didn't listen in,' said the new telephone operator.

"'Next time, please listen and tell me what he said. I can't hear too well,' said Edith."

During the Fairbanks flu epidemic in 1918, she rolled up her sleeves and went to work as a nurse. She worked so hard the doctor cautioned her to take it easy or she would wind up sick.

"Don't worry about me," she answered. "I'm not worried about any flu bug!"

"Sporting girl, hell," said the doctor. "She was an angel during that nightmare; the best damn nurse I had."

She eventually bought the Palace Bathhouse on Third Avenue, where you could take a bath for fifty cents. She used to save special soap for the respectable ladies, so they would not use what the Line girls used.

I met her one day in the drugstore, a tall, well-groomed,

gray-haired woman with a pleasant smile. Though everyone
called her Oregon Mare, it made me angry that a woman
would be named after a horse.

Later, when she moved to the Nordale Hotel, Eva
McGown became her friend. Edith was made an honorary
member of the Pioneers of Alaska. "If you act like a lady,"
she said after that, "they'll treat you like one."

There were special movie showings after midnight for the
women of the Line, for it was considered improper for them
to mingle socially with the townspeople. The storekeepers
liked them, however, as they bought the most expensive
clothing. "I've got a hot one, bring over some dresses,"
called Dynamite Red, favoring the Hollywood Style Shop
where Mrs. Simpson sold negligees, even bathing suits, and
delivered them to their doors. When I worked at Gordon's
Department Store, one of the women came in to shop with
her fur coat and boots. Nothing underneath.

Dynamite Red, a popular prostitute, always wore a red
wig. She became bald from an illness when she was a child in
Nome. "I was married three times," she told me, "and I got
nothin' for it."

Panama Hattie, a madam who came from Panama City,
lived in a two-story building at the end of the compound.
She wore lots of makeup and had fluffy, dyed hair. As a sideline,
she raised and sold Pomeranians. Once, her building caught
on fire and one of the black girls who worked for her burned
to death, hanging onto the bar. Another girl died upstairs
and a john got out with a burned ear. Panama escaped with
her cache of silver dollars.

"Her stove was filthy with grease," said my Joe, who
repaired her electrical wiring after the fire. I never worried
about Joe's activity on the Line. I knew he was home with

me every night, and if he talked about Panama Hattie, it was her electrical wiring he was interested in.

Once, a group of schoolchildren — girls and boys on skates — saw the gate ajar at the Line and skated through the alley. They looked in and saw the women sitting there in chemises. They recognized a man coming in from the opposite gate who turned around and skedaddled out.

Ten-year-old Ray Keturi used to deliver newspapers to Panama Hattie. He also delivered milk shakes and peppermint candy to her from the store. She gave him big tips and patted his golden hair. She paid another boy eighty-five cents to shoot rabbits for her.

Soldiers from the base went in and out of the entrance gate. They tipped Ray to whistle if an M.P. came. When Hildur found out where he had been, she forbade him to go back. "But Mom, I have to deliver my papers there."

"Let them get someone else to take that route," she firmly ordered.

Clara Rust lived in an apartment overlooking the Line. She said women came out into the streets and danced naked at night. But Hildur and I never saw any forbidden sights, although in our hearts we wanted to.

Hildur told me that when they lived in Flat in 1937, mining in the summers, the sporting girls lived in tiny cabins with a boardwalk in front, built by the miners. The rest of the town of two hundred sprawled beyond without a wooden walk, so when it rained, it was a mud hole for the other ladies.

"When a respectable woman went into the store to trade, she never looked at the cabins or made out that she saw the other women," said Hildur. "If they passed them on the street, they looked the other way, and if they met at the store, the sporting women waited to one side."

The men caused a lot of trouble. During the day they would butter up their wives and talk against the girls, and at night they would sneak over. After a few drinks they would loosen up and complain about their wives, keeping trouble stirred between them!

The girls rarely went out. "Those girls didn't get any exercise except on their backs," said Hildur. "In Ophir the madam delivered every child born there, as she was the only nurse."

When President Warren G. Harding came to Alaska to drive the golden spike in the railroad ceremony at Nenana, Mayor Thomas Marquam of Fairbanks was supposed to accompany him. Marquam, of a socially prominent Oregon family, was living with one of the Line women at the time. The respectable women of the town made a point of going to Marquam's house in an outrage. They insisted, "He has to marry her whose bed he shares!" He married her in time for President Harding's ceremony at Nenana.

The Episcopal priest used to oversee the Line to make sure the girls had weekly checkups by the doctors.

The Line was supposedly off-limits to the military during World War II, but the servicemen had one day when they were invited in at special prices.

Joe and I used to visit a nice couple in their forties at their small cabin. The husband was a handsome man who worked in Waechter's meat store. His dark-haired, vivacious wife, formerly on the Line, was a chubby woman with round cheeks, sparkling eyes, and an olive complexion, content to be a housewife.

In Alaska, most people were tolerant when a prostitute married and gave up her old way of life. As long as she behaved like a proper wife and mother, she was treated as one. There were simply too few women in Alaska.

It was the Presbyterian Church and the Fairbanks Women's Club that were influential in getting the Line shut down. The Women's Club had a meeting and protested the location of the Line right in the middle of town. "It is a disgrace," a member said. Another woman stood up and commented, "Now you women, you think you know where your husband is tonight, but you don't know!" That threw everyone into a panic.

The Women's Club got a court order to close the Line, with the military backing them. The Line hired a lawyer to fight the court order. Most of the town attended the public meeting at the Eagle's Hall; the Women's Club, the representatives from various churches, the Salvation Army, and the military.

Dr. Paul Haggland got up at the meeting and said, "If the Line was gone, you women wouldn't be safe on the streets. I examine every one of those girls and give them a clean bill of health."

One of the club women objected, and Dr. Haggland said, "I don't care what you think, you old biddy."

Colonel Gaffney, the Army commander, threatened, "Close down the Line or I'll put the whole town off limits." The Line was not two miles from the post and was against military regulations.

So, in 1952, the Line was finished. The fences were taken down, the dilapidated cabins were razed; the land was sold, the women scattered all over town.

On bulldozed ground, a new Safeway store eventually went up, and later, when it moved, a post office rose in its place.

Before the Line was razed, I painted a watercolor of the

old shacks with their slanting roofs and chimney pipes askew. "By Order of the Police" was nailed to the boarded-up front doors. Glimpses of purple-flowered wallpaper lined one wall. Broken wood, pink and purple peeled wallpaper, small rooms with boarded outhouses in back. Old shoes, whiskey bottles, three-legged tables, and stained mattresses were left to decay in the yard. Part of a toilet lay among the weeds, a cup, some old, dried-up potatoes, bottles of Lysol. An era of legalized prostitution was gone.

Maybe to outsiders, there was a mystery and intrigue about the Line. I could only guess what the lives of the women were like. What could we townswomen know of their degradation, their depression, and their sufferings at the hands of men, who, for a few dollars, could do anything they pleased. These women were virtual slaves, cooped up in a segregated area in the middle of town. Some of them were addicted to alcohol and drugs. It was rumored that one of the drug-addicted women tried to kill herself, and was shipped out.

Edith Neile finally left for Seattle. When news filtered up to Alaska that she was down and out, a group of men who had known her kindness chipped in to send her a monthly check. When she died, her obituary was on the *News-Miner's* editorial page, recounting her brave work during the flu epidemic.

Eva McGown told me, "There are few women here. The other kind of women here are the prostitutes, and they are pioneers too. They are independent, on their own, no husband, no family, with no other training."

Some of the women bought land and stayed in new houses. Some, like High Pockets, married respectable businessmen. And the others? Who knows where they have gone.

Picking Cranberries

★

14

Wild Cranberries

*"The prisoners were starving . . . with holes in
their ragged foot gear . . . miracle of nature,
1/2 a sprig of cranberries, red so deep that it
almost looked black and so tender that it
broke one's heart to look at them . . . If you
tried to pick them, they burst in your fingers;
but you could lie on the earth and suck them
off the branch with dried, chapped lips,
crushing each one separately against your
palate and savoring its flavor. Their taste
was indescribable, like that of old wine . . .
its sweetness and heady flavor were those of
victory over suffering and winter.*

> *Semyonovna Ginzburg*
> Journey Into
> the Whirlwind

The radio reported frost. I gathered all the flowers to stay
their execution. One day the flowers were brilliant, the next
day withered blobs hanging their heads; our four-foot
sunflowers died without having bloomed. Everyone was
pulling carrots and beets, preparing their gardens for next
year, putting potatoes into root cellars. The rain water that I

used to wash my hair had turned to ice in the barrel.

The days were passing quickly. I ordered four dozen diapers from Sears, went for my regular doctor's appointment, shopped for groceries, cooked, baked bread, and constantly fought the woodstove.

Hildur did not accompany me to the woods. She'd had her fill of living at remote mining camps. "But Hildur, why stay in the house when there's space to move about in the woods?"

"Trouble is, I don't feel much like moving out in that space," she answered. "In the summer there's the mosquitoes and bears, and in the winter it's too cold. Don't feel like freezing my fingers."

But Joe and I loved to pick berries on weekends. We squatted, picking handfuls of cranberries, filling our buckets, taking a picnic lunch and a thermos of coffee. We had eaten our way through wild raspberries and blueberry patches, but not so with cranberries; they were to bitter to eat raw, but delicious in breads and sauces. They grew in thick, wine-red clumps in peat near rotted stumps, mushrooms, mosses, and wild rhubarb. Their odor was wild and rank, especially the high bush cranberries. Low bush cranberries, or "lingonberries" as Hildur called them, were darker red and sweeter after the first frost, so we picked the last batch and put them to freeze on our back porch.

Autumn slowly revealed itself, first a glimpse of yellow among the birches, then overnight the whole forest seemed golden. The white birches and golden leaves were startling against the dark spruces; in a week or so the gold leaves dulled, faded, and began to fall, covering the forest floor. Leaves trembling in the wind were reflected in the lake waters and flowed down the rivers.

We watched a moose, her long, dour face feeding from the bottom of a pond; a magnificent two-year-old cow moose in prime condition, a thick, black brush of stiff hair along her head and spine.

Some of the men went hunting during the open season and reported they saw a caribou herd run eighty-two miles up on Eagle Summit on the Steese Highway. "It looked like a living, moving mountain," one hunter said.

Our neighbor brought us some caribou meat and two spruce grouse. He had shot the grouse near the willows and alders. They had eaten well of cranberries, rosehip seeds, and dogwood berries. They were tiny, but delicious, especially roasted with potatoes. The caribou was tougher than moose meat, and I had grown accustomed to the gamey taste. Mooseburger was wonderful baked with onions and spices, very low in fat, and delicious with cranberry sauce.

Lolla Hudson, who lived down the street, made the best cranberry sauce; she had a recipe for everything. She read the weather like an expert. If the weather was dark and cold, she would say, "My arthritis is acting up. It's going to rain." If it turned warm suddenly in the winter, she would say, "Watch out, it's flu weather."

"Lolla," I asked, "what's the proportion of cranberries to sugar for sauce?" I leaned over the sink, defrosting a batch of frozen berries.

"About four cups of berries, two cups of sugar and one cup of water," her bubbling midwestern voice answered. "My, it sure sounds good to hear about berries when it's so cold out."

"The juices are running out of these frozen berries. Do I have to wash them again?"

"Wash them," her voice went up a pitch. "Wash them?" she giggled, "I should say not! Once is enough. They're clean from the woods, and a little lichen or leaf won't hurt a thing. Makes it taste better in fact." She refused my offer of a jarful. "Couldn't get another one in my cupboard. I always put away gallons of berries along with my fish and moose."

I met Lolla in Livengood, about seventy-two miles north of Fairbanks, where she lived all summer with her husband, Albert, and two adopted Indian children. In the winter, she moved to Fairbanks when the mining season was over.

I had gone to Livengood to paint for a day. In 1914, when gold was struck, Livengood had about three thousand people. The town had boardwalks, restaurants, bars, pool hall, barber shop, and a boarding house. But in the late forties, Livengood was like a ghost town. Dog team trails led in all directions like the spokes of a wheel, but there were only a few cabins left, a few miners and trappers. The main street was only one block long.

However, there was a small post office, and Lolla was the post mistress. It was a cold autumn day when she invited me to come up by her fire and warm up. I followed her to one of the old cabins clustered on a slight hill. Violet iris, or "flags," as Lolla called them, were in full bloom around her doorstep, and white daisies dotted the roadside. Dandelions had gone to fluff and wild rhubarb to seed, their green knobs tasselling.

We climbed her worn wooden, silvered steps to her storm porch and then went into her kitchen. Huge Hills Brothers coffee cans held geraniums on her window sills. Flowered curtains framed her deep-set windows. Caribou soup simmered in a kettle on her black woodstove. I sidestepped a big, scruffy, black husky as he barked weakly at me. A bird twittered in his cage.

Lolla offered me her rocking chair. "Make yourself

comfortable." She filled the kettle with water and measured out coffee. Lolla's kitchen, the main room of the house, contained everything necessary for Bush living. The black woodstove, the welcoming hearth, heated the room and cooked the many moose mulligans, countless cups of coffee, all of the cakes and berry pies.

"Pretty tat," Lolla said. The "cat" was a baby lynx with peculiar hind legs, a stump of a tail, his rear end up in the air. When Lolla picked him up, he purred against her face. "Pretty tat," she murmured in his ear. He put his paws on her face, purred, then rolled over. "He was a few weeks old when I found him. Some bird of prey must have dropped him. He would have died if I hadn't taken him in, fed him with warm milk." She set down two cups of coffee on the chipped yellow oilcloth.

The lynx had silky, dark brown coloring on the back of his legs and tail, with white markings under his stomach and immense paws that did not seem to fit his body. Looking at me with large, friendly eyes, he straddled an imaginary fence as he walked. Lolla set down some milk and crooned, "Are you hungry, pretty tat?" The lynx drank his milk with his chin in the saucer, then played like a kitten with some yarn.

"How did you get to Livengood?" I asked, leaning back in the rocking chair.

Lolla explained. "Albert's brother Ted was mining in Alaska, but drinking up what was in the ground. It was Albert's father and Jay Livengood who first discovered gold. Albert came up to work at the mine with his father.

"When I came, there were only about twenty-five respectable married women and a few children. The cooks were all men. After the mining season, the men spent the winter trapping lynx, mink, fox, and wolverine."

I sat motionless, lulled by her soft voice and the heat of her wood fire. Lolla got up to add more wood and stirred her pot of caribou meat. She reminisced as she sat down. "I was brought up in Montana. My father, who was part

Indian, died when I was a baby. My mother took in laundry.

"My sister-in-law was a missionary from China, very ladylike," she continued, smoothing down her skirt. "She never bent to the country till the end. Polite and dainty. When her husband Ted drank, she ignored it."

The lynx played with the dog — putting his head into the dog's mouth. "He loves our dog," grinned Lolla, pouring coffee. "He used to be my lead dog — pretty old now. I used to hunt a lot. Shot a moose last spring not far from the river. I love the winters.

"When the men were working, I went hunting — had seven dogs. I packed a thirty-ought-six and a sleeping bag. If the terrain was too rough I'd sit in the sled, but mostly I ran behind the sled or on the runners. It felt so free and wonderful." Lolla's tiny wrinkles at the corners of her eyes gave her face a softness that was appealing.

"Weren't you afraid of bears?" I asked.

"Not with my dogs," said Lolla as she stirred the sugar into her coffee. "They would protect me. At night I tied the dogs to the sled in a circle and tied the sled to a tree. I curled up in my sleeping bag on the sled, safe and warm. Sometimes I'd stay in a cabin on the trail."

"What did you take with you on those trips?"

"I took potatoes to roast, matches, tea, sugar, an ax, a can for tea." She leaned forward and took a sip of her coffee. "I'd shoot a ptarmigan and run a stick through it over a fire for supper." Lolla stood up over her counter and peeled rutabagas, then cut up carrots and potatoes to add to her stew.

"The worst I had to fear was the moose in rutting season in late September after the first full moon. The trees were bare then. The bears would be hibernating.

"If I was on a sled and the team going well, I'd watch to see if something crossed the flats. Sometimes I'd stop to see if it was a black stump or a moose. I'd take aim at his head." Lolla walked to the woodstove and took the lid off the stew. "I'd cut the moose lengthwise down the stomach, guiding the knife between two fingers underneath the hide, so it wouldn't go too deep and cut the entrails and spoil the meat.

"I cut the penis off and threw it away, but saved the moose testicles to cook for Albert. He likes it fried and sliced in bacon grease, but first I soak it in salt water. The jaw makes good head cheese." She pulled the kettle to the back of the stove, as the stew was boiling too fast. "I'd save the legs and ears to make jelly. I could pack a quarter of meat and the head on my sled. The neck makes a beautiful boil.

"Took the fat, heart, and liver, left the guts. Never eat raw meat or it will act like a physic, Clara," she cautioned me, sitting down and petting her husky, who had laid his head on her lap. The lynx went over to his milk dish and lapped the last bit, falling asleep with his head in the saucer.

With her turned-up nose and sturdy body, Lolla was an inspiration. I had never hooked a fish or held a gun or shot anything in my life. I had hit the bull's eye the first time I held a bow and arrow at Bear Mountain, but it was a fluke shot as I tried all day to repeat it without success.

I could imagine Lolla bundled up in a fur parka with a wolverine ruff. "Whoa!" she would holler and "Mush!", commanding the dogs, who obeyed her without a whimper. The dogs knew my ilk. For me, they lunged and bared their fangs, displaying purple gums dripping with saliva as they strained at their chains.

Lolla petted her old lead dog's head. "First extra money, I bought a washing machine. Albert wanted to spend every cent for mining equipment, but then I begged for a sewing machine and got it. They brought it in by plane."

I refused a third cup of coffee, "Thanks, but I'm going to try to paint the Pioneer Bar." Lolla waved as I left and ambled down to the bar.

The old Pioneer Bar sagged. The floors were uneven, the stovepipe crooked, the bar sloped, and the pool tables were dirty green. Eighty-year-old Moose John, an old miner, sat in the sun in front of the building. I painted his portrait in his battered old hat sitting there like a king leaning on his cane. Then I painted the Pioneer Bar and the block-long Main Street.

In the evening, I sauntered over to the Livengood Inn for a party where two Indian boys twanged a guitar and sang cowboy songs in Athabascan. A few locals did a freestyle dance, part polka and part whatever they felt like dancing. Soon I was dancing with a lanky miner in patched overalls short enough to show his socks and shoepacks. The place was jumping. What fun! Later, the cook invited me for a bear steak dinner. He explained, "They used to have a roller player piano, and Zackarias, the barber, used to play it. Now we have live music."

The bear steak was delicious, smothered in onions and served with mashed potatoes.

Lolla admired my painting of Moose John.

"How did he get his name?" I asked.

"Moose John cut wood, worked for the mine. Don't know how he got his name," giggled Lolla. "He never shot a moose in his life. He did like to fish."

When I visited Lolla in Fairbanks, she told me stories of the old-timers at the mine. She settled back in her chair. "One old miner I knew used his old blanket until he died. He never took a bath or washed his blanket."

"Never washed his own blanket?" I said, my eyebrows lifted.

"No sir! He kept all his grease cans full of lard in assorted buckets in one corner of his small cabin. When he was sick, I'd bring him some moose soup. He would never go to the doctor, or worse, the hospital. No sir, he would rather die first!" It wasn't funny, but we both laughed.

"What on earth did he use all that grease for?" I said, laughing harder.

"He fried everything in bacon grease," Lolla giggled. "Coulda put it on his hair, too, for all I know!

"When the road to Livengood was built from Fairbanks, they all felt angry. They were used to their ways and didn't want outsiders. The road opened up the area to hunters and soon the GIs were shooting all over the place and looting the old cabins." Lolla shook her head. "Before that, no one stole, and if a miner made a stake, he hid it in a can in a corner of his cabin all winter and never locked his door at night."

Albert and Lolla's house in Livengood used to belong to a Mr. Van Stone, who left behind some medical books. Lolla had been a nurse's aide, so when the miners were hurt, she began taking care of them. Old trappers alone on the creek died a terrible death of prostate malfunction. They were said to have had "blocked pissers."

The miners at Livengood had many accidents. Two prospectors, Freddy and Carl, were building fires in a hole to thaw the frozen ground, unaware that there were explosives in the hole. "When Carl went down the hole to light a fire, it exploded," related Lolla. "His whole body was burned: his testicles were real bad. I wrapped him in olive oil. He flew to Fairbanks, stayed in the hospital for three months.

"Another time, a swinging cable split open a miner's head. I had to sew it up to stop the blood.

"Charlie Ulsh's hand got caught on the cable of a drill and four of his fingers were cut off. The men used cotton to stop the flow. I put on a tourniquet to stop the blood, and worked four hours to clean off the cotton and smashed bone splinters.

"Dr. Haggland usually trusted me with morphine to administer, but I was out of morphine. Charlie sat holding his hand up. Never said a word. After Charlie flew to the Fairbanks hospital, Dr. Haggland said I did a beautiful job sewing his hand up. I put a cloth with olive oil wrapped between his fingers and bandaged it all with gauze."

I looked at Lolla as she talked, amazed that such a tiny,

ordinary woman was capable of such extraordinary feats. She suffered with arthritis, but she was tough and strong-willed. In addition to the two Indian children she and Albert had adopted, they were foster parents to other Indian and Eskimo children. She was a stern but fair mother, and taught them all how to work and take care of themselves.

The Livengood mining camp attracted women who had been ordered off the streets in Fairbanks. Six prostitutes came in a chartered plane, setting up business in the small cabins. The men cut wood for their stoves. "At night the girls strutted in their pretty clothes to the bars," said Lolla. "Bud and Georgie Lee visited me sometimes, but I could never visit them because it would keep the men away.

"Georgie Lee and two of the red-light girls had a man with them who opened a bottle and skinned his knuckle to the bone. They came running up to our cabin. Georgie was screaming her head off. I told them to sit down and shut up. 'Put your hand up. I'll be right back,' I said. I ran out to the woodpile and got an ax, cut some flat wood pieces, made a sling, taped it together so he couldn't move his hand.

"Blanche Cascaden, who leased gold mines, was a big woman, a real hard worker who did all her own assessment work," said Lolla, handing me a piece of cake. "She was filing an ax one day and got some metal in her eye. I ran to the drawer and got out my magnet and took all the pieces out of her eye."

"What did you do in your spare time?" I asked, shaking my head in admiration.

"In the winter I liked to sew. Saved fifty-pound sugar sacks to make a dress with hemstitching around the neck. Dyed it rose pink. I baked a lot. Bread, cake, cookies."

Lolla gave me another recipe for wild cranberries. "Put

on one pair of rubber boots. Pick cranberries. Buy one whole orange. Add the juice of one lemon, sugar to taste. Grind together. Freeze on the back porch."

"Did you ever eat lynx?"

"Sure, not that I'd ever eat my lynx. It tastes just like chicken; coat it in flour and fry. And Clara, don't forget the salt and pepper."

I finished pouring the paraffin over the cranberries. The electricity had gone out; there was a power outage at the N.C. Company power plant. I was reading by kerosene light in the kitchen, with my feet in the woodstove oven, time forgotten, supper not started, when Joe came home from work. Ten jars of burgundy-colored cranberries and two cranberry breads decorated the sideboard.

The next day I brought one of the jars and a cranberry bread to the Keturis. Hildur had made Finnish "Vispipuuro" for dessert. It consisted of cranberry juice cooked with farina. Her recipe read, "Cool farina and mix with cranberries until it turns frothy pink. Eat. Good with strawberries." What strawberries?

I gave Lolla my painting of the Pioneer Bar. Lolla complained about the pain in her joints. I had a rare headache, and Hildur had a cough. Her predictions true, Lolla nodded direfully, "Flu weather."

CHAPTER

15
─────

First
Snowfall

We will watch the Northern Lights
Playing their game of ball
In the cold, glistening country.

Abanaki Indian

Joe banked leaves close to the house for warmth, fixed the rain spouts, and did last minute chores before the cold set in. Still, when the first snow came, we were not ready; the hose was outdoors and the storm windows not up.

The first snow in September melted away. Early in October, a thick fluffy snow descended on the dried grasses and roads. By noon, only the tips of the grasses showed. The potato fields had white snow on the brown furrows.

I put some soup on to boil, cut an onion, carrots, new potatoes, parsnips, parsley. I put it on the back of the stove to simmer and fell asleep listening to the fire crackle. When I awoke it was still snowing, the road was covered with white, and a yellow light shone on the mountains. Then the sky changed to a sodden gray. Tree branches stood out in their bareness, their twistings black against the snow.

When the temperature dropped to fifteen degrees below a week later, the landscape became misty, and soon nothing was seen or heard except two flies trapped in our house. Joe named the flies Herman and Millie. The freeloaders knew a good warm house; they knew how to survive.

"Working as an electrician has its moments," Joe said, coming home hungry. "I had one dilly of a day. I was sent out to do some work in the home of Honest John Brennan." Of course his name alone was suspect, since we assumed everyone was honest. Honest John owned and operated the local army surplus store, well supplied with army and air force cast-offs.

"His house is fairly new," said Joe. "I climbed through the access door into his attic, dragging a length of Romax and a tool belt. Boy, what a mess met my eyes.

"Honest John had the most unique and cheap insulation I ever ran across," Joe said, taking off his parka. "He had spread out and layered all through his attic, hundreds of olive drab GI overcoats — belts, buttons, and all — at least ten coats thick. Real wool, too. Maybe Honest John figured that some day the coats would be back in style, and he'd make a killing." I had heard about olive drab army quilts being used for insulation and for covering cars, but army coats? Alaskan homes had to be insulated well, so ingenious materials were used, like sawdust, moss, cardboard, and, if you had the money, commercial insulation.

Joe's job as an electrician paid the rent and fed us. Joe did all the tough jobs, like killing the rat that wandered into our basement. He lifted heavy loads of wood, repaired the furnace, did the electrical work, the plumbing, the carpentry and helped around the house. All this, besides playing the violin.

Joe had to take joshing from the construction stiffs he worked with because he played the violin. Joe was a shop steward, defending their rights, and together they lifted electrical conduits, worked their guts out, broke their backs, and froze their lungs. The men shared common working conditions in below-zero weather, breathing in kerosene smoke from the Herman Nelson heaters, which stole oxygen out of the air and made them dizzy and light-headed. The men could not understand anyone who carried a fiddle case.

They wore hard hats, and a violinist was a "longhair," a dirty word in those days.

Joe played his violin every free chance, sometimes before breakfast on Sundays. I usually made a hearty sourdough pancake breakfast on Sundays from a yeast starter that was supposedly old enough to have come up the Chilkoot Trail (walking by itself, I suppose).

Drinking his coffee in the morning after ten hot cakes smothered in syrup, Joe remarked, "Tastes like you ground up a lead pencil in this coffee, Claire." I had used that new glass coffee pot, too. Automatic coffee makers had not been invented yet.

We were excited about the invitation for Thanksgiving dinner at the Keturis with Mary and Ray Woolford. As I rolled out pie crust, I thought of my family. My sister Elaine's letters were full of the latest plays, concerts, the art galleries and museums, their trip to Europe and news of our close friends. My sisters and their husbands had bought houses in Yonkers, New York, and saw each other often. They attended painting classes. Their husbands were artists who made their living in the commercial art world. Their world was not my reality — we were living in a remote white world of our own. I missed my family and their laughter.

By Thanksgiving, snowfall blanketed the housetops and clung to every twig. Wood smoke rose from every stack in town. Huge flakes floated softly against the darkness of trees.

For Thanksgiving dinner, Hildur served her famous baked ham, a cranberry fruit gelatin salad with pink whipped cream, and Elmer's favorite boiled onions. Mary Woolford, a fabulous cook, had stuffed a huge turkey with wild rice. I had made scalloped potatoes and a sweet potato dish, and we finished with whipped Avoset cream (a whipping cream that came in glass bottles) over my pumpkin pies. I had poured some brandy into the pumpkin filling according to Lolla's recipe, and everyone enjoyed it.

Mary's husband, Ray Woolford, handsomely tanned, was a man at home in the wilderness. He could have played the Lone Ranger or a Canadian Mountie in a movie. He was head of the Fairbanks office of the U.S. Fish and Wildlife Service. In the summer his float plane, a Cessna, took off from the Chena River to the Arctic villages where he enforced game and fish laws. I was fascinated by his stories of northern villages. He had promised to take Joe and me moose hunting next year in the fall.

He had invited a Yugoslavian trapper friend, Steve, who worked as a blacksmith in the summer; a lanky, thin man. "So good to smell turkey again," he said, his wide grin revealing his missing side teeth. He wore a wide-brimmed hat, which he took off when he sat down.

After dinner, Steve crossed his legs and cracked a walnut. "Last year a wolverine tore up all of my winter's catch. Boy, was I mad! I swore to kill him.

"I had cached about a thousand pounds of moose. That night I was walking back to my camp when I saw this wolverine running across the flat near my moose meat. Five days later the wolverine had all the meat from the cache on the ground, just bones laying around, cleaned up slick. All my meat gone. Y'know."

Along with bears, the wolverine was considered the most ferocious beast. He was treacherous, preyed on caches, fought like a tiger, and was believed by the Indians to have supernatural powers.

"Next week my dogs woke me up at four in the morning," Steve continued. "There were a lot of moose around so I figured one wandered into my camp. Next morning I got up, started a fire, and went out to get water from the creek. I heard a noise so I looked in the willows for moose, and there was this son-of-a-bitch wolverine backing down a tree."

I refilled his cup and watched Steve put three lumps of sugar into it. "What happened that night was that the wolverine came toward my cabin and walked right between the dogs. When they started barking, he ran up a tree. By the time I got my rifle out of the cabin he was headed into the brush. I touched one off, but missed him. God, I hated that creature." Steve stuck a spoon in his coffee and churned up the sugar on the bottom. "Besides eating the moose meat he had wiped out my winter's catch of marten and mink skins. I tied a chunk of hide and meat to a tree and set a bunch of traps all around. I was going to get the son-of-a-bitch if it was the last thing I ever did. Y'know, y'know, y'know." Steve had a disconcerting habit of saying, "Y'know," with a Yugoslavian accent.

We were all listening intently. "I was gone for a week checking my trapline, and it snowed a foot. The wolverine came to the cabin and packed off some marten carcasses I had piled outside to freeze. I figured if I ran out of dog feed I could cook them up with cornmeal for the dogs." Steve crossed his long legs. "Damned if he didn't pack all those carcasses off. That made me so mad I could have spit.

"When I pulled up to the cabin, I saw his tracks went right past my door. He was headed up the creek following my trail. I unhooked my dogs, put on snowshoes, and headed up after him. That wolverine had walked right into a big number four trap I had set on the trail. I finally got him!

"I took that frozen bastard out of the trap and threw him on the woodpile behind the stove while I set about warming up a chunk of beans and bacon. I was drinking my coffee when I noticed that the wolverine was not on the woodpile." Steve leaned forward and looked at us. "I looked under the bed and there was that bastard backed up in the corner. I grabbed the broom handle and went after him. When I jammed it at him he hung on to it with his teeth. I was so mad I grabbed a heavy chunk of firewood and clubbed him. Damned if he didn't run around the room, blood and all. I finally did him in, y'know."

"Course there were not that many wolverines around," added Ray lighting his pipe. "Trappers get only seven dollars apiece for them. A good lynx fetches fifty and marten is worth forty."

"Talking about the wolverine," said Elmer, "one of the miners was having trouble with wolverines getting into his cabin so he rigged up an anvil over his cabin door. The trouble was a friend came to visit and he almost got killed. He didn't get hurt but he was madder than hell."

"Some trappers put ten-penny nails through the bottom of their doors to keep wolverines out," said Joe. "A pilot, Bob Jacobs, told me that a wolverine chewed a hole through the door and scattered beans and flour in a cabin belonging to Champagne Kid on Iron Creek."

Wolves were the big topic then, and no one ever agreed on what to do about them. If you wanted to get people steamed up, you could talk about wolves. The *Fairbanks News-Miner* often printed letters to the editor for and against the hunting of wolves. The hunters blamed the wolves for cutting down the moose population. The miners didn't care one way or another. The Fish and Wildlife people paid a man to lay down poisoned wolf bait and encouraged hunters with planes to shoot the wolves on sight. Trappers got a $15 bounty for hunting them and their pelts brought money. The opponents argued that wolves killed only the crippled moose and caribou who could not keep up with the herd. I agreed with people who wanted wolves left alone, but we were the small minority.

On one of Steve's visits to town for supplies, he talked about trapping as he sat on the rocker near our stove and filled his pipe.

"You never went around another trapper's line. It was a

gentleman's agreement," began Steve. "It was the worst kind of business to move in to someone else's territory. Old Murphy moved in once . . . everyone knew who he was. You couldn't make a move without people knowing in the woods . . . well, I moved him out in a hurry."

"What did you do?" I interrupted.

"I ran him out. Grabbed him by the collar one day and shook him up a bit, y'know, y'know, y'know.

"You have to leave matches and cut wood in the cabin for the next guy. Leave a bit of grub, coffee, tea, maybe some rice. If someone used my cabin and burned all the wood, left without replacing my woodpile, well he wouldn't last long, I tell ya." Steve accepted a piece of lemon pie.

"Just a tetch," he said as I offered coffee. "The dogs always got you home if you were lost. If you broke the sled, you just hewed out another piece of wood and tied it with babiche."

Fabian Carey, the trapper, became a good friend in later years. He loved flowers, operas, and paintings. An avid reader, he surprised me with his choice of Edmund Wilson as his favorite writer. Fabian loved the wilderness for its harshness. He viewed it as a place to get fur, and prided himself on his skills of survival. He was a fighter, interested in liberal politics, speaking out his mind at council meetings.

He said that his best friends in the woods were "fire, water, and my ax, yet they were also my worst enemies." Always accompanied by his Dalmatian, he worked in construction in the summer, and trapped alone in the shadow of Mount McKinley in the winter. He recalled the early years while in his twenties. "I had hired a pilot to drop me off at the trapping cabin, about fifty miles from Lake Minchumina. He was supposed to come and get me in the spring. I waited a week, and he didn't show up. My arm felt paralyzed. I couldn't move it. I was afraid that I would perish there. I was lonely, out of food, anxious to get home to my family. He did show up eventually. When I got into town, my arm functioned; it was psychological. I went out and put a deposit on a small plane, and learned how to fly. Never again would I depend on someone else to pick me up. Once I knew I had the means to get in and out, that I wasn't helpless, I had no more trouble."

After Elmer quit mining that year, he gave permission to Joe Stuver, The Cowboy, to trap out of his Moore Creek cabin. Elmer said the Moore Creek Mine just did not pay enough, and he was quitting. He moved the whole outfit, thirteen units including the dragline and Cats, on sleds to Taylor Creek in the Holitna River country.

The Cowboy and his brother, Jul, who had a degree in geology, were hired by the Department of Mines to prospect cinnabar, which is quicksilver ore, in the Moore Creek valley.

They had trapped all winter, living in Elmer's cabin. It got so tense that they hated the sight of each other. They could not stand each other's cooking so they arrived at a solution. Separating the wood stove down the middle, one cooked on one side and the other slammed his fry pan down on the other side.

They were looking for cinnabar when they accidentally found gold in the creek bed. By that time, they could not stand to be in the same room with each other.

Finally The Cowboy said, "The hell with this. You buy me out and I'll quit."

"Okay," said Jul. They agreed on the price and split. Joe took his outfit, packed and saddled his dogs, and took off, mad as hell.

We heard later that Jul went to the nearest town of

Ophir, and asked the first man he met if he wanted to be his partner in a gold mine. The guy was in his early twenties, and owned an airplane handy for mining. He got a terrific deal because the next gold cleanup was about eighteen thousand dollars, and he owned half of it.

Jul was the one reputed to have said to Elmer, "What, me marry? Hell, no! First thing you know they'll be wanting a washing machine." (He did marry later, and sure enough she wanted a washing machine.)

"The hell with gold mining," said The Cowboy. He found a cabin and went trapping. The snow was about six feet deep when he came upon a young cow moose, stuck in the deep snow. The Cowboy slipped off his snowshoes and got behind the moose, jumped on her back as if she were a bucking bronco.

"That darn critter pert nigh tromped me to death," he said. "I figured I could harness her like a horse and get me some work out of her, but it didn't work."

The Cowboy's prowess with a gun and a lasso were well known. Elmer said he witnessed The Cowboy shoot a bear with his revolver. The bear ran and fell in the ditch behind him. The Cowboy jumped in and pulled it out of the water.

The Cowboy also encountered bears while trapping at Moore Creek. One day he noticed a window missing from the messhouse. He whistled, and to his astonishment, a black bear jumped out of the window. He shot it with his six-shot pistol. At the shot, another bear jumped out and he shot it also. They had been feasting on Elmer's sugar, molasses, oatmeal, flour, and beans. In a few minutes he had shot six bears.

At 3 P.M. the sun glowed and spread crimson. The snow cover in the woods gave the whole landscape a moonscape aura. The townspeople went to work each day at shops and offices; the soldiers on maneuvers held mock wars in the snow. Women stayed home tending the fires. The children walked home from school in the darkness.

Our house was filled with the scent of cabbage leaves stuffed with meat and spices, Hungarian style. Joe was famished when he came home from work; he was thin, but I grew heavier each day. Our child quickened within me; I felt a faint throb, a pulse moving in my belly like undulating waves. The monthly checkups with Dr. Schaible were pronounced normal. I took vitamins to offset the shortage of fresh food and lack of sunshine. Hildur introduced me to "klim" (milk spelled backwards). It was named by a farm woman in Ohio. We bought the white powder by the gallon and mixed it with water.

In the evenings after supper, Joe played the violin while I sewed baby clothes. When our baby's little feet and arms poked me, I smiled, patting my belly with satisfaction. "Joe," I called, "come and feel the baby."

★

16

Woodstove

Winter scatters
A gray dawn
Obdurate and cold,

Stony silences
Shape the trees
Laden with snow,

Puffed birds
Softly stir
Frozen to the bone.

They plumb
The snowy depths
For seed

Desolate waste
They will find
Snow on eternal snow.

From my journal

Inside our house, our window panes steamed. Outside,
snow flew thickly, no space between the flakes, an endless
outpouring of goose down fluff.

Joe worked on the army base as an electrician. Until the
building was closed in, the workers did their jobs out-of-
doors in sub-zero weather. Joe got up at six to start the

wood fire in the furnace and in the kitchen woodstove. I got up awkwardly in my flannel nightgown, threw on a robe, and set about cracking eggs and making breakfast. My eyes were half closed and I was silent; food was the last thing I wanted. I crawled back into our warm bed and watched him pile on three pairs of pants over his long woolen underwear, two pairs of socks, two sweaters, a fur-lined vest, fur-lined jacket, and fur hat. When he put on his work coveralls, my thin Joe swelled to an extra-large.

There was a boat strike in Seattle, so we had no fresh foods for three months. We switched to dried fruits, banana flakes, canned peaches. I had made his lunch and wrapped a slice of apple pie made of dried apples for his coffee break. Carrying his black lunch bucket, he disappeared into the snowfall, swallowed up in a whiteout. In town, heavily furred figures moved like pale shadows in the haze that fused land and sky.

Joe usually came home from work tired and cold. He added logs to our wood furnace, washed up, put the news on the radio, then settled down with the *News-Miner* while I rolled out biscuits and prepared dinner on the woodstove. Joe was the listening type while I was the talker. I told him about the stove, how the fire kept going out, what Hildur and I had said, small happenings, while he nodded. He was the pessimist and I was the optimist. We balanced each other. Sometimes after his long silences, I would say, exasperated, "Joe, talk to me."

"Well, what do you want me to say?"

"Anything. What did you do today?"

"Oh, the same ole thing," was his infuriating reply. Gary Cooper was my favorite actor. He, too, grunted and was a man of few words. Joe was like many men, macho — he would not talk about his feelings. When he was angry he clammed up. It took me a long time to figure him out. I would not go to sleep if we'd had a disagreement. I wanted to have it out, and it was hell getting him to talk. It finally dawned on him that we were not going to get any sleep until we straightened things out. It hurt me a lot to put up with his long silences, especially since I came from such a talkative family. With my three sisters, usually it was difficult to get in a word.

Elmer, on the other hand, loved to talk, and held forth at great length on any topic, mostly to do with mining, mechanics or people he had met. Hildur was the perfect listener. Even though she had heard his stories a hundred times, she always acted as if it were the first time. We four were the perfect foils for one another. We had found our true companions: Joe listened to Elmer and Hildur listened to me, then we all listened to Elmer, who held us spellbound, fulfilling a need in us all. Joe learned a lot about mining; I enjoyed a master storyteller and learned about the ways of the North, and Hildur got a lot of knitting and crocheting done. She often said that Elmer talked about every little thing that happened to him at work. "I get more detail about welding than I'll ever need to know," she said.

"If only Joe would talk more," I complained.

No wonder we enjoyed the Keturis. Hildur would poke Elmer in the ribs, tell him "Not so loud," and soon she and I would huddle together at the other end of the room, talking about books, clothes, sewing, and whatever interested us, while Elmer's strident voice would ring out about the time his Cat fell into the icy river and the operator jumped out just in time, or when a bear chased one of the Finn miners up a spruce tree.

"You have that long-distance journey and far-out spacey look again, Claire," said Hildur. I was dreaming again. I looked out the window at the darkness, at the absence of leaves on the birches, and thought about the birth of our child. I missed my mother's sweet smile and comforting presence terribly. I was homesick for my family. When I called home, the connection was choppy. When I heard my mother's voice calling me "Clarala!" I broke down and sobbed. After the third crying call, Joe said, "It's no use spending money to call home if you're going to cry the whole time." Little did he realize how I needed to cry, to hear her voice and tell her that I loved her.

My mother was losing her memory. Doctors called it arteriosclerosis, but now they suspect it may have been Alzheimer's. No wonder I often had felt as if I were her mother. When I was a child, she was well, and I remembered how she used to carry us all on her back piggy-back style after a bath. She used to go down on her knees to bathe us, wrap us in a towel and then dry and put powder on us, then we'd climb up on the toilet seat onto her back. She tucked us into a clean bed, then sat and sang, "Oyfn pripetshok brent afayerl . . ." (On the hearth a little fire is burning.) Or, "Shlof mayn kind, shlof." (Sleep, my child, sleep.)

I read constantly, going to the library often. How important books were to me in the North. I lived in them. They helped me through the monotony of the dark winter days. I found Alfred Kazin's *Walker in the City*. His nostalgia brought back memories of my childhood. Kazin wrote of his mother, "It was loneliness. Some endless bitter brooding over all those left behind, dead or dying, or soon to die; a continent locked up in her kitchen that dwelt every day on the hazardousness of life." I added another log to the wood fire, wiped away the tears. It was mother's uprooted life. Was it mine, too?

I rarely cried when Joe was in the service for three years and I lived alone in New York. I still had my sisters and my work then, but now, being pregnant, I shared a link with my mother that I had never felt before. I could sympathize with her, for she had also lived far away from her Polish mother when her children were born in America. Soon I, too, would be a mother and I needed her comfort. I cried because I knew she couldn't help me even if I could fly to New York. Would she even recognize me?

I found myself looking at the one road leading "outside" with a fierce hopeless longing. It was our only connection with the rest of the world. At that time it was an eighteen-hour flight to New York, usually taking two days. Impossible. We had no money.

I missed my family, my friends, the museums, the fruit stands, the excitement of Broadway and the East Side, the tumult, the pace, the high energy of exchange, the cultural life — all of the life of the city that I had been born into and had wanted to escape from.

Loneliness lodged deep within me like a bone that I could not digest or pass out. I longed for my family with a terrible passion that I could not express to anyone, for surely every one of our friends shared that loss.

Our door was always open to friends. It was an unwritten Alaskan law of hospitality. Anyone who ventured out in forty-below-zero weather had to be desperately in need of company. Many women were living in dark basements with small children while their houses were being built around them by their husbands, usually amateur carpenters — a volatile situation.

One morning I sat reading in my bathrobe, which did not quite cover my bulging belly, when Mrs. Karstens knocked on the door. Her Cheshire-cat grin so early in the morning was startling. "How's everything?" she inquired. She had been the matron at the jail, and she still carried keys in her hand. She worried about the pipes freezing; I worried about my feet freezing even with two pairs of wool socks and my feet stuck in the oven door.

A blast of cold air entered with her as she stepped in the doorway, clumps of snow sticking to her galoshes. I knew she was just interested in her house, not me. She hadn't even noticed that I was pregnant.

"How's the stove?" she asked.

"Oh, the stove. Something's wrong, it's not working right. My feet are frozen," I muttered.

"You say the pipes are frozen?" a look of terror came over her face.

"No, my feet are frozen!" I shouted.

"Well, I'll send my husband over right away."

"No, no." All I wanted to do was read. I didn't want the door opening and closing and snow puddles all over my freshly washed kitchen floor. Her husband had already looked at the stove. "Just be sure and bang the pipes once in a while for creosote," he had advised, banging the pipes so hard that a lot of whatever it was hiding in the stovepipe fell like scared mice.

"It's creosote?" I repeated.

"You say they're soaked?"

"No, it's fine," I yelled.

They were always checking on their poorly insulated house, afraid of fire with that old furnace and woodstove.

My life seemed glued between the radio and the woodstove. Either I was inexperienced, or the wood was too green, for it was a continual battle between me and the old stove. The ritual kept me busy most of the day, chopping the kindling, wadding the paper, setting the drafts, banging on the pipe to cause the creosote to fall — then the damn stove would go out and the process would begin all over again.

The stove had a maniacal life of its own, taking off willfully without reason, burning wildly, and at other times refusing to catch a spark.

A kettle of water steaming on the stove put some badly needed moisture into the dry air. Inside the kettle was orange sediment from the iron in the water. The water had to settle out overnight before I could use it for cooking. Two marbles in the kettle helped to bump off the encrustation, but the sediment in the water turned clothes orange and whiskey black.

One evening the stove fired up and roared merrily; water boiled in the kettle. "What a waste," I thought as I sat and read the paper. With a burst of energy, I cut onions, put up a bean soup, rolled out a pie crust, boiled some dried apples and raisins and put a pie in the oven. In went four potatoes to bake, and some left-over rice became a pudding. Then I decided to use the hot water to wash my hair. It was midnight when I was through scurrying around. Even though I was exhausted, I used the soapy water to mop the kitchen floor, and put the pie to cool before I collapsed in bed.

That damn stove was my boss, whether I liked it or not. When company came, the moose roast would be raw inside and burnt outside. My cakes would fall as if a hex were on them, or they would bubble on top or come out hard as a rock. (This was before cake mix.)

We invited Dave and Benje Adler, owners of Adler's Book Store, to dinner. Dave, born in England, was distinguished by his gentle manners. He kept a calendar of events for the town. If a club wanted to have a dance on the second of December, it would check with Adler's so there would be no conflict. The Adlers brought us a baby book and a beautiful Hiroshige book of colored woodcuts.

For the occasion, I used a table centerpiece of an Eskimo ivory bird carving set on dried moss. As my lamb roast cooked, the wood fire went out and no amount of stoking would keep it going. Even with new kindling and kerosene poured on paper — at the risk of burning the house down — it would not burn. Joe excused himself, went out to the kitchen and added his magic touch, shoveling ashes, talking to the woodstove, adding more kindling, everything but kicking it. Finally, in desperation, at nine o'clock I served up the roast. It was bloody!

Dave, ever the gentleman, said politely, "This 'beef' roast is rare, just the way I like it." I gave Joe a wifely look, but he refused to meet my eyes. The roast was tough and bloody; no one could chew it. My chocolate cake, made the day before, redeemed my culinary reputation.

When it dropped to sixty-nine degrees below zero in town and seventy-two degrees below on Badger Road, Joe lent me his sheepskin parka, the one he had worn in the Air Force, called the "Gaffney coat" after General Gaffney, in charge of the Alaska Air Command. It kept my stomach warm and was long enough to cover my rear. It made me look almost as wide as I was tall, but the hood and sheepskin lining kept me warm. At three in the afternoon, it was dark as night, so no one recognized me as I crunched carefully down the icy streets like a fat, furry barrel.

Awkward and afraid of falling on the ice, I was exhausted before I had walked three blocks. After the errands, I rewarded myself with coffee and a bun at the Peerless Cafe with Kathy Rogers, who worked nearby.

Liza, sitting on a stool drinking coffee, confirmed what my mother had told me about childbirth. "Having a baby is as easy as a sneeze," she said. Liza and I both knew Indian women who walked out during the winter, squatted in the snow to deliver their babies, then walked back with their newborn wrapped in rabbit fur.

Viola, my Eskimo friend from Point Hope, had walked out to the seashore, cut her own cord, and walked back with her baby. These women endured natural childbirth because their culture demanded it. Our culture did not ask anything from us except that we submit our bodies to the doctors. I refused to believe I could not handle it.

I had always had my teeth drilled without anesthetic while the dentist and the nurse cringed. No Novocain for me! I chopped kindling and walked a lot, but did no special exercises.

After examining me, Dr. Schaible said I was coming along well. Taking out a chart with a wheel on it, he twirled it and said, "Your baby will be born about February 22." That was just nine months from the first day I had arrived at Moore Creek!

"Aren't Eskimo and Indian women built the same as me?" I asked Dr. Schaible.

"Yes, they are."

"If they have natural childbirth, why can't I? I don't want an anesthetic."

"Oh," chuckled Dr. Schaible, "Oh, you'll be screaming for a shot."

"Oh, no, I won't."

He responded by shaking his head. "You'll change your mind."

"No, I won't," I answered. "I want a natural baby, not a drugged one. I want to feel everything, to be awake to see my baby." I believed in the old adage, in having good thoughts while pregnant, to influence the baby. I talked to the baby often, patting my belly, reading poetry out loud as if the baby could hear me. Hildur and I pored over the Sears catalog, carefully ordering baby blankets and nightgowns.

Joe and I were now the same weight. Even though he held my arm to steady me across the icy streets, I envisioned us sliding down together on slick ice. At night, sleeping together spoon fashion, Joe would put his hand over my belly to feel the baby kick. We did not fear birth defects then. We wanted a baby very much and were confident that all would be normal.

The brightest spot all month was the Beta Sigma Phi shower given by Hildur and Mary. The gifts included knitted and hand-sewn blankets, a high chair, and a smaller-sized crib given by a friend who asked me to pass it on when I was through with it. It had already mothered six babies. Boxes arrived from family and friends in New York with all kinds of new apparel, and I was thankful for their remembrances.

We heard the fire sirens wailing all over town. My neighbor, Minnie, ran in out of breath, "Come, let's go downtown. The telephone building is burning. Hurry!"

Shooting flames and dark smoke billowed as we came closer. People stood clustered around us, mesmerized. Panama Hattie and Big Babe stood behind me, wearing fur coats. The flames warmed us as we watched our small fire crew desperately trying to put out the fire with water that froze soon after it hit the icy temperatures. In the frigid, brittle air, we could hear the crunch of the firemen's footsteps on the crusty snow as they struggled with their long hoses. The rancid smoke billowed in the gray sky. Orange-amber sparks flickered like fireworks against the snow. The warm crackle of flames contrasted with the below-zero temperature.

While the telephone building burned, the whole town turned out to help and watch, carrying out charred furniture, doing what they could to protect the surrounding area.

It was a forty-below day; ice formed in strange shapes, a pairing of flame and ice.

We dreaded fire, for our flimsy buildings were full of sawdust insulation. We worried that this fire could spread and destroy the whole town as had happened once before. Luckily, the winter snow kept the fire from spreading.

The fire died down, and the next day the whole area was a mass of iced lumber and debris. We had no phone service but our homes were safe.

After the fire, people were extra careful with their oil and woodstoves. High school boys were let out of school to deliver messages. Taxis toured the area in case anyone needed a cab. Clinic-to-hospital communications were set up by walkie-talkies, which were given to pregnant women who lived out of town.

No more telephones. I could not call the doctor or the hospital. Mothers with sick babies could not call the doctor. I would not be able to get to the hospital. "Don't worry," said Elmer. "Joe can come and get me and I'll come with the car to take you to the hospital. I'll take the battery out of the car every night, bring it in the house to warm up." Few people had garages for their cars so they took out the batteries at night or put firepots under the engines in the morning. Hildur volunteered her help, as usual. "I'll come with you to the hospital when it's time. Don't worry."

✶

CHAPTER

17

Cabin Fever

Unrest of spirit is a mark of life.

Karl Menninger

Constant snow fell on each tree limb, the rooftops, the roads and mountain passes. The snow fell like a benediction, covering up the ugly cans and shacks, unifying the town. The countryside, seen through the swirling flakes, sparkled by sunlight and by moonlight. We lost all sense of time. Our pace slowed; the daylight hours became shorter and colder. The telephone wires accumulated thick layers of snowfall. Within a month, the rooftops and every resting object had a foot-high white cap.

As soon as the snow became yellow with dog urine and black with car exhaust and chimney soot, new snow fell, making all clean and white again.

The delicious scent of wood smoke filled the air. I sat at my easel near the window and sketched the man across the road chopping wood. I painted the houses up the street, then a dog team that went around the corner.

I had difficulty painting the snow; the pristine fluff had too great a familiarity, a fault of my own vision. The snowy spruce branches were too white, the sky too blue, its commonness reminiscent of a thousand banal paintings. It seemed a painted set that would disappear in the next act, a fantasy.

Icicles formed on the roof's edge, and hung like daggers. When I opened the door to sweep out the front porch, I knocked them off with a broom. If only the warmth of my hand could melt the cold as it did the icicle; but nothing in the world would dispel the winter cold.

The darkness deepened each day, grayed to blackness, and with each darker shade I mourned, helpless against the loss of color.

The outside world was a frozen place, and we were locked in lonely isolation with few people or ideas filtering in. The one thin highway leading from the rest of the world to Fairbanks was kept open and a trickle of cars ventured through.

Gradually, oh so gradually, so that we were not aware of it, except in imperceptible ways, the closed-in feeling began. Friends did not venture out to visit as often; we were alone day after day. Time dragged. Our skins began to dry and itch from the constant heat of the woodstove. The teapot continually bubbled on the kitchen stove.

The sun set earlier and rose later in the morning, becoming a monstrous ball which barely moved along the horizon. It was seen covered by mist, sinking out of sight in the south. I found myself watching it, glued to its color as the only bright spot in my life. When it departed, its absence left me feeling bleak and stripped of light.

Some days were clear, with a temperature of forty-five below zero. Even a slight wind set fire to the skin. The sun barely lifted over the horizon; then a red incandescence spread an unearthly twilight over the sky.

Snow that fell had a shadow. The Eskimos used over forty words for snow: "snow on the roof," "snow ready to fall off," "the thickness of snow," "snow with a crust," "snow that is dangerous," and more. Snow had many meanings to Eskimos and also to me. I noticed that it was harder for sparrows to plumb the snowy depths for seeds, but on the other hand it gave protection to our plants, and provided insulation around our house. I loved and hated the snow; it comforted and plagued me. Some days, I felt restless, irritable, brooding, pacing like a wolf in a cage.

During my daily walk, my eyes would become blinded by wet snowflakes, my lashes frosted. Sometimes their soft, white, flaky wetness touched and caressed my cheeks, but other days the force of the flakes was icy, cutting and biting my face until I pulled the hood tighter. Snow was my master, hurrying me along, bending my head to its force.

One day, the neighbor's child set her tongue to the metal railing and the skin was ripped off, bleeding. Wet hands froze to an iron gate. I learned never to feed a dog out of a tin pan — his tongue would stick to the plate. A boot not tightly seamed or too thinly padded let in the cold, and mittens too loosely woven were useless, as were gloves. Two pairs of mittens or fur-lined mittens were best.

We could dress against the cold, but there was no defense against the darkness; against darkness we had nothing but our will and what inner light we possessed.

As the winter progressed, walking to the grocery store became an exhausting torture. I stumbled on errands, arriving so numbed that I could not remember what it was I wanted. I knew that I had to get out of the house. The walls were closing in more each day.

The house had become a jail and the door a way out of prison. Below-zero temperatures froze my bare hand to the knob. Joe came home from work, gray with fatigue and numb with cold. It seemed pointless to plan things away from home in the evenings. Where could one go? We could hardly afford restaurants. Was it worth venturing out in such weather? Better to stay home by the warm fire and read.

Early in the morning I drew the curtains tightly against the outer darkness and lived within the circle of lamp light. The snow gave me a feeling of nothingness which only emphasized my isolation and loneliness. The street lights glowed at noon with a milky haze, their light the only color in the sooty dark dullness, the only sound that of the huskies howling. It was so cold and dreary that I lost all desire to paint.

On his days off, Joe dressed in his favorite winter gear, an old, heavy, red wool-checked Canadian jacket, his floppy fur-lined boots and his favorite beaver fur hat with flaps tied under his chin. He rushed out of the house, mumbling when he climbed the icy roof to shovel off the snow; he stamped down to the furnace muttering oaths about "green wood." He could fix anything.

Joe and Elmer sat in the kitchen in their bulky clothes, drinking coffee, and talking about sewers, frozen water drains, frozen tires, sump pumps, two by fours, carburetors, furnaces, and basements.

I caught snatches of their conversation as I made coffee in the kitchen. "Copper tubing right in the elbow sprung a leak." "It dripped every half minute. You ought to cut the whole goldarn chunk out." "The damn thing kept backing up." It was another language, and they were superior with their knowledge. Hildur and I exchanged resigned looks, then laughed. We knew better.

The homesteaders' children had to walk from the school bus in the below-zero temperatures; their figures could be dimly made out in the dark. What kind of a place was this that would not close the school unless it registers fifty below zero? The few people downtown, in heavy furs and woolen scarves that covered their mouths and noses as they went from store to store, assumed a cheerful boisterousness. Steam from their breath hung in the air and frost formed on their scarves. They puffed for breath as if they had run a mile. We said hello to everyone in the streets because there might be a friend under all the mufflers, hoods, and furs.

We listened to the weather report at night and groaned when it was down to forty below. At twenty below, it felt warm by comparison. High pressure from Siberia made temperatures drop and the radio announced that the weather "would turn to fifty-six below zero with no let up in sight." The announcer always mentioned the hours of daylight, saying, "Tomorrow there will be four hours and three minutes of daylight."

With the continued lower temperature, cabin fever set in. My spirits sank further. Lassitude overcame me, and life seemed barren, without action. I read until I felt blind. My eyes heavy, I fell asleep. Work was at a standstill; it took the greatest effort to do the simplest chores. My peace was shattered; I longed for what I did not have, and that longing was a one-edged blade pointing at me.

I dreamed of elegant women in furs and perfume walking down the theater aisles in New York; of my sisters laughing, their warmth enveloping me; or of oranges on a tree in Spain, their globes burning my fingers and the juices running out. Or else I dreamed of a hot beach somewhere where the tide lapped my sides as I lay sweating and soaking up the sun like a ripe grape. I imagined fragrant blossoms on the trees in exotic places where it was hot all the time and women wearing bare-armed dresses and wide-brimmed, flowered seductive hats laughed, showing pearly teeth as they accepted icy drinks.

In the dreary, dark winter days, I sought an inward peace and exhilaration. At rare moments, I sensed how little I needed to be happy, and then all the trappings I thought necessary in my dreams seemed unnecessary here.

Sometimes I was filled with a contentment so deep, giving and taking everything in a day and savoring it to the fullest. I thought then that the act of living was the only creation needed, that I need not paint or write, that the deep longings inside of me would subside in sheer happiness of being and living. Sometimes I listened to music, and it seemed to be beyond the pale of everyday life, an art richer and deeper to my senses; I wanted to live more intensely on that plane forever.

But those rare moments came and passed, and I could not hold on to my ecstasy. I had to let it go for the fragmented demands that made up an ordinary day. I visited our friends and did the shopping and housework, on the surface a woman like any other.

When I opened the door in the morning, the whole house would creak and thump. I tried to shake off lethargy and keep warm by drinking hot coffee. I wrote poetry and long letters home to dispel my cabin fever.

The isolated days gave me time to meditate and to read everything from Jacob Boehme and St. Theresa to D.H. Lawrence and the books of women — George Sand, Isadora Duncan, Mary Webb — taking out six books at a time from the library. I read a lot of poetry and daydreamed. Joe and I read avidly every evening until after midnight.

The books spoke to me like friends out of the silence of the winter mornings and struck a responsive chord, some nostalgia, some reminder of another time. A tear would fall to the page. Wiping my cheek, ashamed of my loneliness and weakness, I drank hot tea. "Why, this is our life. What am I crying about?" My pregnancy made me feel so vulnerable.

As I read about Albert Schweitzer, his life in Africa, I discovered his kinship with Goethe, my father's literary hero. Schweitzer and Goethe believed that life itself was the greatest thing, far greater than poetry, prose, music, and art. Life itself was the greatest epic, and to create a life was to create beauty. Life to them was written in deeds. They followed their natural instincts, opposing anything foreign to their own natures.

Goethe wrote:

> *To self be true, and true to others*
> *Let thy search be in love*
> *And thy living be the deed.*

If only I could live these words. They would sustain me through the pregnancy, the bitter cold winter, and thereafter.

60° below zero!

CHAPTER

18
___

Sixty Below
Zero

This silent day
Cold beyond fear
Pierces my marrow;
Ice hangs from my roof
In threatening spears;
Fog, hoar frosted
Oppresses
The bitter air.

From my journal

The end of 1946 brought some of the coldest weather
Fairbanks had ever seen, a siege of four weeks that broke all
records. When the little town of Snag, on the Canadian
border, reported ninety below zero, we, in Fairbanks, felt
relatively warm with only sixty-nine below zero.

The nailheads on the wall turned white with frost, and
thick ice encrusted the bottom of the doors. We stuffed old
towels under the doors to keep the ice from seeping in.
When I clumsily opened the door to get more wood or coal,
wafts of ice fog enveloped me.

The heavy ice fog made it impossible to see out of the
window; all was dark, dreary, and horribly gray. I felt sick
from imprisonment, numbly stumbling around in baggy
slacks and old fur slippers, getting fat on homemade bread

oozing with butter. Ravenous most of the time, I leaned on the refrigerator door, gazing into its meager contents as if the answer to the world's problems lay within. It was easy to freeze things by just setting them on a shelf on the back porch. When spring came, there would be a pot of beans or a stew, months old, forgotten.

The trees stooped wearily from their snow burden, frozen into obeisance, bending until they broke. Shoppers let their cars run while they lingered in the warm stores, and the car exhaust added to the ice fog.

The cold pushed against us like a hard wall. At sixty below, the terror of the cold night froze something within me as I huddled closer to the stove.

We all listened keenly to Maury Smith, the radio news commentator who reported the six o'clock news. We had an abnormal obsession with the weather. After the weather report, Maury said, "No news tonight, folks, nothing happened."

Many women living in the Bush flew to Fairbanks to give birth, but delayed too long and the pilots had to deliver their babies. Often the pilot contacted Dr. Schaible and was told what to do, but sometimes Dr. Schaible would rush to the airport to find that the pilot had already delivered the baby.

Hildur had a thirty-three-year-old Polish friend, a miner's wife, who flew to Fairbanks to have her baby at the hospital. Her first baby had died of diphtheria out on the creeks near Flat.

Hildur told me that when Dr. Schaible told her that her second baby had died the day before of a tumor, she jumped into the air from her bed, as weak as she was. How sad to lose two babies.

The Keturis were her only friends in Fairbanks, so Joe

and I offered to visit her. Stella's slavic face was beautiful, with high cheekbones, surrounded by dark, braided hair. She moved her graceful hands. "Why this happen to me? I can't understand." Her voice in its broken accent dropped and choked. "I see the baby only once, they take it away from me right after it's born. A nice boy, too. Seven and one-half pounds. Nothing wrong with him, only something presses on his neck. I'd like to take a picture of him so I can show my husband what a nice boy he was." So Joe went to the funeral parlor to take photographs of the baby in the coffin. I could not.

Dr. Schaible checked my blood pressure again. "Watch that weight," he cautioned. "How do you feel?"

"Doctor, I feel low, depressed. It's so dark out," I murmured.

"It's tough," he said as he listened to the baby's heartbeat. "This time of year, more divorces, depressions, drunkenness, sickness, real and imaginary. You're fine. Won't be long now and you'll have a baby to take care of. It's just the darkness and the cold. Imagine it as a long tunnel. You'll soon see the light at the end of it."

As a teenager, I heard pregnant women talk to my mother. She had closed the door so I would not hear, but I listened anyway. Women told her of their fears. I remember my mother saying, "Don't worry, it comes out like a big laugh." She was not afraid to have her babies, and so I was not. Besides, Joe would be with me.

We had no classes then. Dr. Schaible had never heard of Dick Read's book on natural childbirth. I read the book in my seventh month and tried to absorb the message of breathing and relaxation. I did one exercise Read suggested, squatting to stretch the birth canal.

Hildur, Mary, and other women had told me horror stories. They would never have a baby without anesthetic or a spinal block.

The last weeks, Joe held me carefully as we crossed the icy streets, protecting me from slipping. He would not let me lift anything heavy. He cut all the kindling and took care of the stove as much as he could. Once when I had a yen for sour pickles — something sour to eat — he walked to the store in the cold to buy them for me.

I decided to have my baby without an anesthetic even though I was not as tough as the Indian women our friend, Sam White the bush pilot, told me about. "It was forty-eight below zero. I was traveling by dog team on the winter trail near Kokuyuk. I caught up with these Indian women who had stopped for tea. The women piled up bunches of brush and built a fire to one side so the heat would rise up through the lattice work and warm their babies. One woman had just delivered her own baby. At night they piled logs high, four feet wide. They stayed warm. Logs held fire all night.

"If they were caught without a sleeping bag, they swept the hot coals away, then slept on spruce boughs. Sometimes they wrapped themselves in fresh moose hide. If it rained, they slept under sheltering spruce with tarp over sleeping bag, spruce boughs underneath."

I was making the house cheerful for the baby's arrival, sewing new bedroom curtains and a baby quilt for the small crib. I made a pillow from some Hungarian embroidery Joe's mother had sent. Our baby would see his grandmother's handiwork when he came home. I painted a small landscape, and painted bright flowers on our kitchen cupboards.

We visited the Keturis often. Hildur was teaching me to crochet one day when her sink stopped up. "Oh, you darn women," said Elmer coming home from work. "I'll have to take the whole trap apart." He fumbled with "the dang thing," then stomped down to the basement mumbling under this breath.

In the meantime, Hildur got a bobby pin and string, bent the pin into a hook and fished out her dishcloth. Elmer came up with a handful of tools and when she dangled the rag in front of him, he acted astonished, dropping the tools all over the kitchen floor, pretending to faint.

Hildur believed in the "free and easy school" of bringing up children. Little Hilda had her mouth full of something so I went over and squeezed her cheeks. Out popped a marble.

"Come quickly," I shouted. "She's eating marbles!" The little mouth fell open and four more marbles fell out. Hildur only laughed.

Out of doors there was no differentiation of grays, making an unearthly frame of reference. A stillness prevailed as if someone had died. It was so silent, the sound of my voice startled me.

Some process seemed to decay the mind, to slow up normal responses. I had a longing to hibernate like a bear in a cave. It was hard to crawl out of the warm nest-like bed in the morning, for sleep was all I wanted. I yawned constantly, huddling near the woodstove.

At night, though, I sometimes lay awake listening to the rhythm of the stove. The wooden house contracted from the cold; the wooden cupboards would not close due to the permanent heaving of permafrost. I wondered what would happen if the fire went out and we froze to death. I turned and put my arms around Joe's warm, comforting body.

The countryside was silent, held supine under the weight of constant snowfall. We lived for days in the netherworld, in cold twilight looking out past the icicles hanging from our windows to the gray-white landscape between light and darkness. We lived under incandescent light from the moment we awoke. The fog world outside floated through space in frozen time.

It took all my energy to walk in the cold, but I could not stay locked indoors all day, my feet in the oven to keep warm. I hated my long, itchy underwear, but it was necessary in the battle against frostbite. My big stomach stretched my coat to the last button, and a wool muffler covered my mouth as if I were a child. My eyelashes were coated with ice and even my eyeballs hurt. My breath came in quick vapors as if I were already in labor. I could not get warm.

The sky seemed to hang low, and from every cabin, blasts of smoke poured steadily. I could hear the sap pop in the trees. The only other sound was the occasional scrunch of my boots on dry snow. I put my arms around my protruding belly to comfort myself. It won't be too long now, I whispered.

★

CHAPTER

19

Winter Solstice

Today the sun barely lifted over the horizon; its incandescence spread an unearthly twilight over the sky, briefly covering the mountains with a bloody red flame. Each day the light dies and darkness comes in its place.

When I opened the curtains at three in the afternoon, it was dark as night.

It is sixty-five degrees below zero today. My first winter in Alaska is the coldest Fairbanks has ever seen; a siege of four weeks that has broken all records. I sit with my feet stuck in the oven door of our woodstove, trying to keep warm in two sweaters, long underwear under wool pants, two pairs of wool socks, and Joe's old fur slippers. It is so cold the nailheads and the trim around the inside door are frosted with ice in spite of old towels stuffed in front of the door jamb. I feel the ice advancing.

Our radio reports eighty-two degrees below zero in Snag, a town on the Canadian border. Eight-two degrees below! How fortunate they imply we are — with only

*sixty-five degrees below in Fairbanks! I make
a cup of hot tea.*

*What am I doing here, alone in this small
house? When I gathered wood from the back
porch for the stove, wafts of ice fog enveloped
me. It is numbing. I feel so drowsy. Lonely.
My toes feel cold. Is this the way explorers felt
when their feet froze, then gradually turned
black until they had to amputate their own
toes with a pocket knife? I must stop this, but
as I have been out only for a short walk to the
store, the walls are closing in on me: this
house is becoming my jail.*

*Today is my birthday. I will be twenty-five! Oh,
for an apple, a New York Macintosh apple
with its juice squirting down my chin as I
bite into it. It has been three months since the
boat strike and I haven't tasted any fresh
fruit. Never again will I take apples, running
water, or a warm house for granted!*

*My belly bulges with new life. In two months
I will give birth. Oh, how I miss my mother!
When I put my arms around my body, rocking
back and forth, I feel strong kicks. Dear unborn
child of my heart, perhaps this land is a frozen
wilderness which only the strong, capable of
bearing great loneliness, can endure.*

> *From my journal*
> *December 14, 1946*

The landscape had a pearly, opalescent harmony unrelieved
by any other color. A vast emptiness of snow, like the desert,
stretched out from our window. Huge drifts lay on the back
porch; the door could not open because it was iced up. I put

on an orange robe to brighten up the dark, grim day, pulling it tight around me and retying the sash.

My mind seemed to be shriveling, my ideas for work going down a frozen drain. I experienced a blocking and insensitivity to art that was deadening. The neighbors looked askance at the paintings on the walls and avoided looking at the drawings of nudes. I was an alien from another world, New York, the place where they "might like to visit someday, but wouldn't want to live." My ideas were novel, my goals unheard of. "To be creative" was not necessary, not needed in a pioneering country. It would have been better had I been able to hunt, fish, or cut wood, instead of paint and write poetry.

Creative work, where my feelings and imagination and intelligence worked together, was the most important thing I did. Sometimes I felt like William Blake, who said that when his energies were diverted from his drawing and writing, he was "being devoured by jackals and hyenas." Blake's love of art, expressed in painting or poetry, was so great that he would see nothing but art in everything he loved. He thought creative power should be kept alive in all people for all of their lives because he felt it to be life itself. Oh, yes. Yes.

At four o'clock in the afternoon, with stars overhead, the circle of the moon was the brightest shape in the landscape. I walked faster, burying my nose deeper in my fur ruff, trying to keep warm. The moonlight encrusted each limb with jewel-like feathered particles. My knees felt transparent, bones frigid, ice penetrated to my essence. My cumbersome clothes heated up in the steamy stores and I began to sweat.

Walking home from the grocery, my breathing was labored, my back ached, and my movements slowed as I carried the groceries. It was a relief to be home, slipping my feet into moose hide slippers. In the evenings after dinner, Joe and I listened to the radio while he read the paper and I baked cookies and finished the small watercolors I had made for gifts.

Each day we had a little less daylight, until the winter solstice on December 21 — the shortest, darkest day of the year. The radio reported: "There will be three hours, forty-three minutes of daylight."

The Beta Sigma Phi Christmas party was coming near and I had nothing to wear over my prominent stomach. In desperation, I selected a pattern and found a dressmaker to make a dress out of gray wool. An extravagance we could ill afford, but I rationalized that I could make it over after the baby was born. I wore it the last few months for every occasion. When I arrived someplace, I had to take off the long underwear and ski pants I wore underneath. After the birth, I was so sick of that dress that I never wanted to see it again. I gave it away to another pregnant woman. One size fits all.

At the Betas' Christmas dance, we had a tinseled tree full of glass balls, plus popcorn and cranberry garlands. A large table was laden with sandwiches and homemade cakes. When the door opened, white clouds of frost rolled into the warm room.

On our first Alaskan Christmas, our windows were frost-etched, and the tree limbs carried six inches of fresh snowfall, gleaming with crystal reflections. Tiny lights twinkled from spruce trees inside and outside the cabins. All manner of decorations and lights were on the roofs and around the windows, little crèches were placed in windows, and big wreaths with red bows decorated some of the doors. Santa and his reindeer team had been carved out of plywood and put on top of the N.C. Company building, framed with red lights that blinked in the darkness. Inside the store were candy boxes, heady perfumes, silken underwear — impractical, tempting things our womanly hearts cherished. We bought practical presents: wool shirts, underwear, and socks.

The townspeople were determined to make the town bright and homey to withstand the cold and darkness, and merry greetings flew from person to person. The children of the town were as excited as children everywhere.

My swaying walk had given way to a rolling gait; I had gained twenty-six pounds. My emotional balance became unpredictable. I was frequently tearful, depending more and more on Joe's stability. He never failed me, his arms were around me, comforting me. There was no doubt about it, our baby was going to have a wonderful father.

We celebrated Christmas Day at the Keturis with the Woolfords and Gus and Aina Uotilla, Elmer's uncle and aunt. The Keturis had a huge tree lit with bulbs, tinsel, and popcorn. We had all drawn names and brought little gifts for each other. The Uotillas brought a box of tangerines for everyone to enjoy. After a huge dinner, we exchanged gifts. Ray and Hilda Keturi and Larry Woolford played with their new toys. Joe played the fiddle, and we all sang "Silent Night" and other songs, feeling mellow and nostalgic.

While the children played, Gus began reminiscing about his early mining days at Ophir. At eighty, Gus loved gambling and spent a lot of time in the back room of the old Pastime Cafe playing Pan. He did not own a car, and all winter he walked around in an Indian sweater and knitted cap; of course he wore wool underwear underneath. Aina had cut his hair and one gray wing hung over his eye and high cheek bone. Gus leaned back in his chair and in his Finnish accent began, "While skiing up from Valdez with a change of socks and clothes, I stopped at the roadhouse. That place was dirty with filthy blankets and sheets. Men slept on bunks or on the floor in sleeping bags.

"While skiing, I met a trapper who invited me into his cabin. I admired two fox skins hanging on the wall. The trapper said I could have them for ten dollars apiece. I thought they were probably worth twenty-five dollars apiece, so I bought them. At Iditarod, I asked the storekeeper if he'd price them. The trader said, 'I'll give you two dollars apiece. They're not prime fox.' Boy, was I mad. I threw them under my bed.

"Two years later, one of the miners was going outside and said, 'Gee, I'd like to give something nice to my nieces. Do you know where I could get some nice fox skins?'

"'Fox skins,' I said, 'Wait a minute,' digging out the furs from under my bed.

"'What do you want for them?'

"'You make me an offer.'

"'Twenty dollars apiece.'

"'Sold.'

"When the miner came back that spring, I didn't have the heart to ask him how the nieces liked the fox skins. I was too embarrassed. Finally a year passed, and one day I casually said, 'By the way, how did your nieces like the fox furs?'

"'By golly, my nieces never got them.'

"'What happened then?'

"'I got on the steamer down the Yukon and some tourist on the boat offered me fifty dollars apiece for them!'"

One story led to another and Elmer told how one night at the Savoy Hotel lobby in Seattle, he showed his biggest gold nugget to a friendly fellow, who passed it around. When it was time for the nugget to come back, it didn't.

The Christmas parties, the tree lights, the gay store windows and charisma of the holiday season lasted until after New Year's Day.

Then the blues set in, and I wrote to my sister, Elaine:

> *It's fifty-eight below zero today. Miserable.*
> *About to blow my top. Can't go out except by*
> *cab and we have to wait an hour to get one.*

*No cars start in this weather unless one has a
garage. It's so hard to keep warm. Tired all
the time. Joe went to work in this frozen
atmosphere. Fairbanks has been declared a
semi-emergency condition. The brakes freeze
and the car wheels feel square and bump
terribly. Planes haven't been able to fly or
land out of the airport due to ice fog. We are
in an icy grip. Terrifying. Sewer facilities
have been breaking down and some people
have been forced to move out of homes that
weren't warm. We are lucky.*

*I look at our wooden chairs and think if we
can't get wood, I'd burn them first. I'm
wearing Joe's big wool socks over my fur slippers.*

*Everyone downtown is wearing mufflers over
their noses and mouths. From the back you
can't tell a woman from a man walking
down the street.*

All of my defenses were down. Just combing my hair was
an effort, my hands felt so heavy. Some days I felt like a
trapped animal, chewing on its own leg.

January plunged us all into a twilight of blues and grays;
the earth, the sky, the houses, and each tree limb were white.
Icicles hung in long daggers from many rooftops, and we
judged heat loss by the length of icicles. Icicles always
reminded me of the perfect murder mystery: *He stabbed her
in the heart and it left no trace.* My bird-watching friend
Brina would make a pot of coffee and stir it with an icicle she
plucked from the eaves of her roof. When the icicle melted
completely in her coffee, she felt it was just right!

The bird watchers went out Christmas morning. When
they left at five in the morning, it was forty-five below. Such
dedication. You wouldn't get me up that early. It was my loss

— they saw fifteen varieties of birds, 150 hoary redpolls, one raven, one snowy owl, a hawk owl, and lots of ptarmigan.

Joe bought a yellow canary and taught him to peck at his mustache. He took the canary out of his cage and talked to it. Mary Woolford was afraid to come into the room with the canary, but Hildur ignored him.

Joe slapped on his beaver hat with the flaps hanging down over his ears, and grabbed a shovel and gloves. "The roof has over four feet of snow again. It's going to cave in if I don't go up and shovel it." The fence was completely covered; everyone had to dig out their cars.

"Be careful, Joe. Don't slip on the roof." I stood watching him as I held my big stomach, one hand shading my eyes. Then I went inside to begin supper.

I was peeling potatoes for the moose stew when Joe came in, kissed my neck, and warmed his hands on my backside. "I'm going to haul garbage with Elmer later," he chuckled, removing his shabby, old parka. "You ought to come, Claire. You haven't lived till you go."

Elmer came in the back door, stomping his snowy boots. "Got any coffee, Claire?" He pulled up a chair and took the cup I handed him. "I got tired of teaching Hildur the garbage trade." He pointed at Joe. "I got a new apprentice. I'm breaking him in." He gave an appreciative grin, which spread all over his face like slick molasses.

Elmer and Joe disappeared down the cellar steps. Joe was going to adjust the furnace. I asked him if he needed help. "I can hold it for you." I meant the tools, but Joe gave a ribald laugh and chuckled all the way down the steps.

"Can I hold it for you? Ha, ha," repeated Elmer. "Ha, ha, ha." What a team. Laughing friends, the Indians called them.

★

20

——

Birth

Dance as did your ancestors
Arms outstretched in measured beat,
Awake, arise, affirm:
Mark this day of birth.

From my journal

When I put my arm around my stomach, it was immense, a huge, sculptured shape. When I awoke on February 22, the light came faintly from the window pane, with only a bit of blue sky visible through two-foot-long icicles.

It was thirty-eight degrees below zero when the pains began. No way to call the doctor or the hospital. Joe dressed and ran all the way to the Keturis while I waited impatiently. I had packed my bag a month ago. The pains were about twenty-five minutes apart when the Keturis arrived.

"What's the rush?" Hildur said. "Let's have some coffee." Finns, in any emergency, had to have coffee.

Surprisingly, the contrary woodstove took off in a hurry and we had hot coffee. Joe nervously rushed around the small kitchen trying to find the can of Borden's. Hildur sat on Elmer's lap saying, "Relax, Claire." Joe found the milk and brought the can opener instead of the can puncture. Finally, Elmer took a nail from his overall pocket and punctured the can. Hildur and I put lots of milk into our coffee, but I was so nervous I couldn't drink it.

Joe put my boots on since I could hardly bend over. As the pains were speeding up, we all piled into the car and drove to the hospital. Dr. Schaible was out of town and Dr. Haggland, good for plane crash victims and people who needed bone reconstruction, could not be located. A Catholic nun came in to check on my contractions and then disappeared. I was grateful that Hildur was with me. When I was born, my mother would not go to the hospital, so a midwife delivered me at home.

At the hospital, I was prepped and given an enema, but had none of the tests that women undergo today. We did not have the overflow of information that women have nowadays — nor all of the attendant fears and worries of what could go wrong. I believed I would have a normal baby and my attitude was, I'm healthy, why fuss? It's a normal part of life that generations of women have gone through before me.

The pains were coming closer, and the sweat poured from my face as I gripped the bed railing. Finally, I cried out in the understatement of the year to Hildur, "My mother was wrong! She told me it was easy as a laugh!"

After eleven hours of straining and pushing, with a nurse running in every once in awhile, I was exhausted. I braced myself, holding Hildur's hands and then the bedpost. When I was dilated to the nurse's satisfaction, Dr. Haggland finally appeared. I was wheeled into the operating room and strapped to the stirrups. Twelve hours from the time I entered the hospital, Dr. Haggland delivered a baby boy. Without anesthetic!

Joe, pacing outside the delivery room, heard me say, "Are you sure it's a boy?" He could not believe it.

"Seven pounds, nine ounces," said the nurse as she showed me our son swaddled in a blanket, his tiny face with his newborn flattened nose, wet black hair and blue eyes. How happy my father would be to hear his first grandchild was a boy!

Just as Dr. Schaible had predicted, our son was born

February 22, nine months from the first day I arrived at
Moore Creek. It was George Washington's birthday too! Joe
had been pacing outside the door the whole time. The nurse
would not let him in, which was the rule in those days, but
Dr. Haggland brought our son to show Joe and Hildur.

We were so proud and exhilarated. It seemed so tremendous a feat to give birth; it felt like the most creative act of
my life! I was glad that I experienced every phase of it
without anesthetic. I was prouder of that than anything that
had happened in my life.

I felt a unity with all women. It was not exactly like the
Eskimo or Indian women, having their babies alone or with
a midwife, but at least it was not like some women, who
would never have a baby without drugs.

Dr. Schaible, who had missed my delivery, wrote in my
baby book, "With apologies to Dick Read."

In a week, Mark Steven was ready to go home. It was a
sunny, frosty day. Elmer drove the three of us carefully over
the Chena River bridge.

We were glad Mark was born close to spring when he
could have the advantage of sun all summer instead of being
born in the fall, stuck in the house through the winter
darkness.

How tiny he was, and how frightened I was at first to
give him a bath. The home nurse came to the house and
showed me how to bathe him in a dishpan in the sink. She
recommended water, canned Borden's milk, and Karo syrup
in his bottle, and also some orange-flavored "Homecebrin,"
a vitamin.

My belly was flat; no stretch marks after the birth. My
mother was wrong, though — having a baby was more than
a good laugh. It hurt, but it was small discomfort to pay for
such a great treasure. Later, I learned from Eskimos how
they viewed pain, conquering it by will power.

When I came home from the hospital, my neighbor
Minnie made me a complete dinner on a tray — liver and

onions, mashed potatoes, delicious lemon meringue pie, and a loaf of her special pink bread made with tomato juice.

We looked at our baby's features to see where he resembled us. Did he have Joe's nose? My eyes and eyebrows? He burped lazily when I patted his back and held his head up strongly.

I asked the doctor at what temperature we could put him out-of-doors in his buggy in the sunshine, and he answered, "Down to twenty degrees below zero!" Minnie had made his white rabbit parka with a hood, and also his first pair of Indian moose hide moccasins with fur and bead trim. He wore them until he was nine months old, when we bought him his first pair of shoes.

Joe's virtues were patience and perseverance. He was a modern father for his day, always taking equal responsibility for Mark when he was home. From the first day, Joe would get up at night to hold Mark when he cried. The Keturis became his grandparents, his uncle and aunt and his extended family.

Our son was well and growing stronger every day. I held him close as I fed him, watching his smiles, burps, and facial nuances. He held on to my fingers with tenacity and stared at me in deep contentment when he awoke from sleep. We marveled at both his strength and fragility as we played with him.

My strength returned with renewed energy. I wrapped Mark in furs, with a big scarf around his nose and mouth, and set him in the little box on top of a small sled and away we went to town. Some mothers had elaborate sleds that they pushed instead of pulled. Some had enclosed tops; often two children rode in the sled with a third child trudging along. Some of the sleds were painted brilliant colors with flowers and folk designs.

Diapers were a major project, and washing them was an operation that took all afternoon, even with our new wringer-washing machine. Hating drudgery, I invented a way to save time. The custom was to accumulate smelly diapers in a pail in the bathroom, but I took each soaked diaper and immediately threw it into a box on the back porch where it froze instantly. No germs could accumulate. Once a week, I heated water on the woodstove, dumped the load of frozen diapers into the machine, then added the hot water. After putting the diapers through the wringer and rinsing them, I hung them to dry on racks over the grate. The diapers came out stiff and orange from the iron-rich content of the water, no matter what bleaching agent I used.

Every day, I bathed Mark in a basin in the kitchen near the woodstove, heating water in the kettle and putting my elbow in, as my mother did before me, to test the temperature.

Dr. Spock's book was our generation's baby bible, a best seller at twenty-five cents in paperback. Our doctors were busy, and rarely made house calls, so the health nurse checked Mark every month. When he ran a temperature of one hundred four degrees, we called the hospital in the middle of the night and they said to bring him right in. But it was thirty below zero and we would have had to wrap a feverish child in blankets and call a cab. Instead, the hospital nurse said, "Put him in cold water to bring down the fever and give him lots of aspirin." I could not bring myself to dunk him in the cold water, but we put cold towels around him and gave him aspirin. Joe and I worked all night, and by morning his fever was down.

The snow cover over the tundra gave the landscape a moonscape aura. The hours of daylight had begun to increase since the winter solstice, but it would be a long time before Mark could nap in the sun.

★

21

——

Dancing in
the Dark

*You see a bit of Fred Astaire in
everybody's dancing.*

George Balanchine
Time *Magazine*

Rosy-cheeked children in warm, colorful winter garb
rolled like puppies, coming up with patches of snow on their
red, blue, and green parkas. They skated on the rink under
the Cushman Street bridge, or skied, or took up dog racing.
For winter recreation, adults used an indoor curling rink
where players swept the ice with a broom to move the
granite stone. People played whist, bridge, pinochle, and
pan. Women had sewing and quilting parties. The Empress
Theatre on Second Avenue showed Roy Rogers and John
Wayne movies.

When the boat strike was over I could hardly wait; I ate
an apple right in the store. I never wanted to see dried apples
again as long as I lived. The hospital was short of medicine
and there was no toilet paper in town. The first supply boat
that landed in Juneau, however, was full of liquor, evidently
a commercial priority.

We sat around the Keturis' kitchen table drinking coffee
and eating Hildur's cinnamon buns, hot from the oven and
dripping with white frosting.

"Back on the farm in Spencer, New York," said Elmer, "we danced all night at the Grange — me, Hildur, her sister Hulda, and her boyfriend Sula. Four in the morning we boosted the girls up to their window. Got home in time to milk the cows." Elmer took a big bite of bun and chuckled.

Hildur poked him. "Finns love to dance."

"Hungarians love to dance, too," said Joe.

"Why don't we go dancing?" I said.

"But where?" said Hildur as she looked at me. We found baby-sitters and asked Eva Larimore, who used her large living room to give dancing lessons to children, if we could use it for a dance. We collected records of polkas and other folk dances, then we invited other couples. Joe and I had first met at a dance in New York City. We knew how to waltz, fox-trot, lindy hop, and even tango. Now we learned how to folk dance.

We gathered a young, enthusiastic bunch of dancers. One man was short, another fat, and another too tall — my chin hit his buttons. One wobbled and another hopped. I laughed all the way through the dances. I jumped on the wrong foot at the wrong time; he jumped on my foot; I hopped up and hit his chin. It was hilarious, but gradually I learned to folk dance well. I loved to dance so much that I could not sit one out. We whirled, we dipped, we dosie-doed.

Before we knew it, everyone wanted to join, so we hired the Odd Fellows Hall and named our group the Fairbanks Folk Dance Club. Joe or one of the other men fired up the big barrel stove and put on a huge urn of coffee. Women took turns bringing sandwiches or cakes. We sat on wooden benches the length of the hall, never missing a dance unless we had a high fever.

Women wore long johns under their skirts and carried low-heeled dancing shoes. We wore frilly blouses and long, gathered skirts with pantaloons and petticoats underneath. I made a violet voile dress with ruffles twirling along the edge. The men wore cowboy-type shirts with string bolo ties.

Some women sewed matching men's and women's shirts. Our babies slept on top of our parkas and fur coats. One evening was set aside for the older children to come and dance with their parents.

One of the best dancers was tiny Mom Carter, who had eight grandchildren. She and her husband used to run the trading post at Fort Yukon, an Indian village, where Mom learned to dance jigs and Virginia reels.

Charlotte Ames played the piano, George Rayburn played the drums, and Joe fiddled. Not many men could do my favorite dance, the Hambo, as one had to be strong and skillful to lift the woman, then swing her around, but Joe put down his fiddle and we twirled and leaped. Walt Schuette, the caller, taught us new square and circle dances. The broom dance was fun — whenever the music stopped, we switched partners; the one left out had to dance with the broom.

Joe and I did a triple-turn-polka all around the room with everyone twirling the same way. The Varsouvienne was romantic; I leaned back in Joe's arms facing outward, my head on his shoulder, feeling like Ginger with Fred, gracefully turning round and round. We polkaed, waltzed, did the Black Hawk, the Lily Marlene, and the Swedish Waltz. Then all the dancers did a fast Schottische, which Elmer danced with me. We always had plenty of partners, Hildur, Mary, and I.

After midnight, we went out into the frosty night exhilarated. The moon glowed and the stars were clear in the dark sky. The men had rushed out beforehand to start the cars so the seats were not icy. The night air was full of gas fumes from running truck motors, and was so cold and brittle it took my breath away.

Once, we were all invited out to dance at Ester, about fifteen miles away. We drove in groups, bundled up in the forty-below weather, the wheels crunching on the snowy road. The Ester dancers outdid themselves with refreshments, and we heard their new records and learned new dances.

The stars were brightly hung in that frigid sky, and on the drive home our breath froze. The snow was piled high on either side of the narrow road. We did not have four-wheel drive then; if we slipped into the snowbanks, the men got out and pushed, rocking the car.

On the road or trail you could always depend upon help. It was the rule, because your car could be next to break down. No one locked their doors in fear. They might own a gun in case of bears, but they did not fear their fellow man.

Beta Sigma Phi was having a formal dance, and I had to find an evening gown. I dragged out eight yards of gray jersey that I had brought from New York, and with Hildur and Mary's help, I draped it over one shoulder and around my waist. Mary basted the jersey together as I wore it. I thought to use it again someday, and did not cut into it. A belt covered the seam at the waist. My mother told me to chew thread when someone sewed right on my body or the stitches would sew my brains together — an old Polish folk saying. I did not believe it, but I chewed thread.

The dress held together, and I had a good time dancing with Joe. I wore a crown of braids on my head like a coronet, and earrings. At home, when the dance was over, Joe cut the threads of my gown apart at the seams. Unfortunately, clinging jersey formal gowns were not in demand in Fairbanks. The fabric was not suitable for sheets, tablecloths, or curtains, so back it went in a box under the bed. I don't know what happened to it.

The clothes we needed were slacks, long underwear, and sweaters. Everything else was fluff. My craving for beautiful clothes just festered and spent itself over the occasional *Vogue* magazine.

We were invited to the Electricians Union's annual dance with free dinner and drinks — of course we went. The ladies room at the Club Eleven Restaurant had a green fluorescent light, giving every woman a haggard look with dark circles under her eyes. I wore a daringly cut, black velvet evening dress my sister Elaine had sent from New York. I had worn it to the Elks' Purple Bubble Ball, where Joe and I had danced until three in the morning to music by Billy Stroker and Band.

"Say, honey," said a blonde woman in a swinging green dress and long fake eyelashes, one of the electricians' date. "I bet you didn't get that dress here, did you?" I asked her name and she said, "Don't you know me? I'm Bunny, the worst bitch in town." Obviously she had had too much to drink.

There are not too many women who would be that candid. I blinked, smiled, and put out my hand, "I'm Claire. My sister sent me the dress from New York."

Most of the electricians knew each other. It was not like the university dances where the men had to watch their deans and their p's and q's. The working men here all had union cards and were freer and more outspoken than the academicians. There were a lot of hale "Goddamn-son-of-a-bitches!"

After the delicious steak dinner, the dancing began. Phil Haluptzok, a young electrician, danced with his hand out-stretched and his nose buried in my neck like a sniffing bunny, breathing deep into my ear. We did a lot of swirls and dips. I was unused to liquor and felt dizzy with one glass of wine. Phil and I were improvising new steps as he swung me out in the Lindy Hop.

One of the electrical contractors who fancied himself a lady's man danced with a woman, not his wife, who wore a dress tight as a sausage casing. He held her around the waist, then slid his hand down until he was frankly caressing her buttocks while his wife, sitting at our table, looked on.

One of the old "narrowbacks" came toward us, but he asked the contractor's wife to dance instead of me. When they returned, he was tipsy, and with his usual blarney said, "You look beautiful," as he kissed my hand. "When I first met you, you were skinny," he said, "but now you are beautiful." I wanted to believe him.

Then his wife came over, highly charged with drink and said, "Why don't you stay with me, who you brought?"

He told her, "Go-wan, go-wan, before I get mad." So she took off, carrying her drink and muttering under her breath.

Joe wanted to go home, and was sending me eye signals. I was giggling about everything, enjoying our rare outing and my new dress. I tried to delay him, but when he came back wearing his beaver-fur hat and carrying my coat, I knew it was time to go. I begged for one last dance with Phil, and we did a splendid rendition of the Lindy with improvised steps, everything but Phil swinging me over his head. Outdoors, I was sweaty in a light coat, silk stockings, and high heels. I steamed in the cold, but, oh, it had been fun! Now it was back to the chores, the woodstove, and keeping warm in the cold darkness.

Harding Lake

✷

22

―――

Harding
Lake

For the children's delight
For warmth near our fire
For comfort at night
Rest your weariness;

For haven in storms
For shelter in rain
Come closer dear friends
Rest your weariness.

> *Written by me*
> *on the door of our*
> *Harding Lake cabin*

The winter passed and spring came when a butterfly with white-tipped wings fluttered on a birch limb. The water ran strong and brackish-brown between the river banks. We were greeted by the hoarse cries of the sandhill cranes, and the ravens called out from the topmost branches. A mosquito bit right through my heavy sweater.

Phalaropes in the dense weeds mucked about near the cattails. A muskrat left his silver trail, busy at work. Pintails dipped down to get juicy waterbugs, and mallards, widgeons, and teals skimmed the weeds. Joe picked up a tadpole and I felt its soft throbbing body until I flipped it back into the water.

Along our windowsill at home, a pan of zucchini seeds grew in strong, spiraling shapes toward the light and sun. Chokecherry trees were the earliest blossoming trees. An engineer had first brought them to Fairbanks from Norway. They survived the winters, a tough transplant like the settlers who had planted them. Their snowy white flowers hung in massed profusion, scenting the streets. They bloomed and left suddenly before anyone had their fill of looking, and then hard, sour green berries appeared, which turned black in the fall, to the birds' delight.

Joe turned over a garden plot on the side of the house. He did all the heavy digging, while I pulled weeds and hoed. It was a joy to dig in the earth with bare hands to sift the lumps with my fingers.

"Your rows are all crooked," complained Joe. Of course, his were straight; he aligned them with string. We hauled peat from the woods and crushed moose droppings to enrich the soil. We planted our first seeds — lettuce, carrots, radishes, and turnips. We bought cabbage, broccoli, and cauliflower plants and put sweet peas along the fence. We carried rocks to make a border around our garden. Whenever we went into the woods, we brought home plants — cinquefoil, yellow daisies, fireweed, and wild poppies. In a week, little green plants were poking up with the weeds.

Joe bought a second-hand 1936 International pickup, and on Sundays, his day off, we put Mark between us and drove out on a dirt road, breathing dust from the car ahead. We drove out to see Koontz's Hog Ranch on Badger Road where he raised over three hundred hogs.

Rabbits crouched by the sides of the roads. Some of the poor creatures had leaped out in front of cars, and lay crushed. "Look before you leap," I wanted to shout, "you rabbits of the world. Wise up!"

The next week we visited Edith and John Holm, home-steaders on Chena Hot Springs Road, who lived in a tent without electricity or water. They had planted potatoes and cabbages. Later on they bought plants from Norway and Canada and began to grow other varieties of vegetables, selling tons of their produce to the military. Edith, originally from Los Angeles, was a fine soprano. She baked bread in their woodstove in addition to helping John with the garden.

We talked about Dr. Gasser, from the university's experimental farm, who was trying to raise wheat at Rampart on the Yukon River. Gasser had to put chicken wire around his garden or the rabbits and moose would eat it. He also raised strawberries. The Indians would invite Gasser to their potlatches where they served bear fat cut in slabs, boiled mountain sheep, beaver tail, moose, king salmon, and a feast of doughnuts fried in bear or moose grease. "The Indians won't farm," John Holm said. They didn't want to grow greens with a shovel and rake!

Leaving the homesteaders, Joe drove on the bumpy dirt road, passing an abandoned trapper's cabin with mosses and six-foot spruce trees growing out of the sod roof. We picnicked on a sandbar along the Chena River, where the wind swept the mosquitoes away. The river dashed against the shore in whirlpools, dragonflies skimming the surface. I picked buttercups and Jacob's ladder for Mark.

When the weather was warmer, we camped overnight near a lake or a river. We roasted hot dogs or hamburgers, opened a can of beans, and made a pot of coffee in an old Hills Brothers can. I watched for bears as Joe fished for trout. We often saw a moose drinking, his head searching for greens at the bottom of the lake.

Mark slept in a large basket covered with a mosquito netting. We wanted him to feel at home in the wilderness — to feel the Great Spirit, the land's richest heritage.

Joe and I stood with our arms around each other, watching four white moving specks on the hillsides. Dall sheep.

We listened to the running river water, smelled the wood smoke, and looked at our peaceful, sleeping son.

We were expelled into the sun by its magnetic force. Sun became a justification for living; our bodies craved its healing force. It gave energy instead of taking it away. None of us could bear to come indoors.

The color of green should be celebrated and glorified. The ancients understood that in their spring rites. Grass and leaves should be drunk like elixir.

On June 21, the longest day of the year, the sun remained near the horizon, leaving a twilight glow even at midnight. People read their newspapers without lamps all night long. Fairbanks had its traditional midnight sun baseball game.

I yearned to live out in the woods, to have a view like our friends, Kathy and Les Rogers, who lived on Chena Ridge, but Kathy said, "We go to work in the dark and come back in the dark. We don't see much of the view. You have to make the choice, to live in town with the conveniences, or struggle without water and plumbing in return for view." Kathy and Les had hauled peat, broke virgin ground, and planted a garden in their rocky soil.

Joe chuckled, "I can see Claire living without water!"

I would have lived without running water! I dreamed of a log cabin in a clearing, but it seemed that as soon as a house was built the wilderness disappeared. Trees were cut for firewood, new trails made and soon the countryside looked tame. Perhaps it was better to come upon a wilderness place unexpectedly, to savor its beauty, to remember it and then leave it untouched.

If only people could live in these places like the Indians. They had respect for the land and did not leave it scorched, poisoned, and defiled when they left. Indians had lived for hundreds of years in Alaska and their land is the same now as when they came.

I remember the first time I sat with my back against a spruce tree, facing Harding Lake, unable to move or talk, completely mesmerized by the sound of the water, the moving shadows and motion of the waves. The spongy earth held me like a magnet.

The lake was a forty-minute drive from town. The cabin was two unfinished rooms, a summer shack with bunk beds and a small iron stove to cook on. No running water, insulation, electricity, or plumbing, but the terms were right. We bought it.

The lake shore resembled a Japanese watercolor. The terrain was covered with spongy moss, cranberries, and spindly black spruce. Around the cabin grew sphagnum moss, startling white, star-petaled flowers, and salmonberries.

We visited our cabin every weekend. As we walked down the path to the cabin, Joe carried a backpack of groceries and a chain-like pulley contraption over one shoulder, which he called a "coffin hoist" or a "come-along."

"A what?" I asked.

"A 'coffin hoist'," he said grumpily. Things that just astounded me, he took for granted.

"How come it's called that?" I asked.

"I dunno," he answered.

Because of permafrost, we had to steady the cabin underneath, leveling it with logs. Our friends the Kornfiends had given us some thirty-foot telephone poles. Joe tied them behind his canoe and towed them across the lake. We used the "coffin hoist" to pull them uphill from the lake. I helped manipulate this pulley-contraption slowly. With Joe guiding it on the other end, we maneuvered the logs up the hill to use them as pilings.

On the trail to the cabin were tracks and moose droppings, small droppings for such a big animal. I knew a woman who used the hard, egg-shaped pellets to make earrings for the tourist trade!

Small sandpipers danced their jerky rumba line on the beach. Mosquitoes, flies, gnats, bees, butterflies, and dragonflies were thick.

The first thing we noticed near our cabin was bear tracks in the mud near the water's edge. I was glad we did not meet the mother bear as we hurried inside. That bear must have been hungry to come so close, nosing around our old garbage can. A storm was brewing; trees swayed and the water churned white. After settling the baby, I began to cook lentil soup. From the window I could see the small red-orange bunchberries among the Labrador tea bushes — locally called Hudson's Bay tea. It was spicy and pungent, used as a cathartic. I heard the buzzing insects, but I was listening for the crash of underbrush. I felt safe in the cabin, but I knew that the bears would not hesitate to go through a wall, as they did out at Keturis' mine.

Joe built up a good wood fire in the stove. Within the warmth and safety of our cabin, we watched the darkened, speckled lake and the hard rain that fell on the green mosses. The trees shook violently as if to tear up their roots.

When the storm died, it was silent except for the baby's sucking noises in his sleep. I was uneasy at every crack of the trees, until I fell asleep. Joe's gun was right under the bed, and the bear was out wandering in the storm.

I awoke at the sound of the wind pushing smoke down the stove pipe. Rain came down the pipe, sizzling on the hot stove top. Joe was not in bed or in the cabin. I ran out in the rain with only my nightgown and was soon drenched.

White caps rode the waves and a yellow light silhouetted the hills. Joe was not anywhere, neither by the shore nor in the canoe. He had been ill with pleurisy and I was worried. I hollered, "Joe, Joe!" then ran back to the outhouse to see if he was there.

Finally, I saw him walking up the path from the neighbors. He had gone there to tie up their boat, which had torn loose from its mooring and was battering itself on the rocks at shore. Instead of hugging him, I scolded. "You scared me half to death," I kept saying, with a pounding heart. I crawled back into bed still scolding, worried he had made his pleurisy worse.

"You're all emotion," he said angrily. "I had to fix their boat. They're not here today. It's all a neighbor can do. I didn't want to wake you."

On the moss sat a bird nest with three newborn, mousy-colored shore birds. My thumb seemed monstrous near them. Their absurd, ivory-colored beaks turned towards me as to their mother. When I went to see them the next day, I thought they were gone or that the dog had eaten them, so cleverly were they hidden in the indentation covered by the grasses. Lifting the spruce boughs that hid them, I heard a tiny rustling, and from their dark nest I saw their orange-pink naked throats and open beaks, all three squirming for better position. When they sensed no food was coming, they burrowed into the deep hole until they could be seen no more.

In the cabin, I fed the baby, washed my hair in lake water and mopped the floor with soapy suds. Dipping the mop into the lake, I carried it aloft like a flag. I would have been a good homesteader's wife, frugal with water.

Joe put tar on the leaky roof while I painted a large blue

rug with fringe on the knotty pine boards of the wood floor. Then I made up a welcome poem and painted it on the door with a brush and red paint.

The clouds turned black and threatening; the spruces whispered ominously, their spindly trunks swaying violently. Yellow streaks of lightning flashed. I called out to Joe to come in.

It rained all night long, noisy on the tin roof. We lolled in bed, playing with Mark and listening to Bach on our battery-powered radio. In the morning, Joe hopped out of bed and built a good fire while I made sourdough hotcakes, eggs, and coffee. Joe hauled up more lumber, and I helped to carry the heavy plywood for our new deck.

Joe put a yellow strap over his shoulder and carried the gas-powered saw on his hip. It made a screeching sound that could be heard miles away, enough to frighten any bear — zzziss, zzziss and crash. Trees fell one after the other.

"Stop it, Joe. That's enough," I pleaded, hating to cut down any tree. My request fell on deaf ears. We needed the wood for our stove, but did he have to clear so many trees from one place?

The scrawny black spruce were seventy-five years old and only four inches in diameter. Their roots could not grow very deep in permafrost. They poked up everywhere; knobs bunched together like some spiny animal. Jays, squirrels, and robins nested under their cover. Ravens used them for survey posts.

"If we cut them out, the birch will have a chance to grow," reasoned Joe, sawing the spruce stumps down where they protruded through the moss.

I lay on the earth looking up at the trees. I felt as if I were spinning round and round. The tree tops waved and the clouds moved swiftly over the mountains. My thoughts spun round and round through a void to far-off places. I closed my eyes and dreamed of a canoe trip down the rapids, sleeping on hard, stony ground near a campfire, the wind howling. The thought of climbing mountains through snowstorms and braving the elements excited me. But Joe had little desire for wilderness adventure; he liked the home fires.

The temperature rose to a hot eighty-five degrees in August. The baby and Joe loved it. Sheepishly, I complained about the heat, saying that I was better able to withstand the cold. I got the sudden impulse to leap into the water, clothes and all. I did it, then seeing no one on the lake, neighbors gone, I stripped and enjoyed a swim. The water was about seventy degrees. Joe never went into the water unless he had to. He watched disapprovingly from the shore.

The lake water was clear, reminding me of Walden Pond as it must have looked to Thoreau. I could clearly see each grain of sand and my footprints along the bottom of the lake. A pike leaped out of the water.

Hildur and Elmer came to visit only once at our lake cabin, and I couldn't understand why they wouldn't come again. Finally Elmer confessed. "I just hate those goldarned mosquitoes."

"But Elmer, after all those years of freighting through the mountains to the mine during the worst of the mosquito season? And what about Moore Creek?"

"Well, that was different. All those years I *had* to rough it. It was part of the work and I had to do it. I don't have to now."

Hildur added, "If there is one mosquito in the bedroom, he won't sleep all night. He has to get up and hunt it down."

"I've swatted a thousand if I've killed one," Elmer chuckled. "Boy, I chinked all the cracks between the logs at Moore Creek and tightened all the doors, but they used to creep in."

I absorbed every nuance like a sponge, following D.H. Lawrence's adage that it was a great art to do nothing well. On the lake in our canoe, I paddled lazily, hat shading my face. The sun reflected all the colors in the lake. Tasseled wild rhubarb grew against the dark peat and verdant ferns. Water lapped the edge of the land with a gentle sucking sound. I filled the jugs with spring water and paddled home. We used spring water only for cooking and drinking and lake water for everything else.

Later, I poured water into a pot on the stove and then ran down to hand Joe the jug to refill with lake water.

"You poured out the gas; didn't you smell it?" said Joe as he handed me the jug.

"No," I answered. "Oh yes, it did smell a bit funny!"

Then it hit me, the jugs looked the same. I had been heating the gas instead of the water on the stove. Oh, God, the baby! I dashed madly for the cabin. Luckily our wood stove was slow and I got there in time!

In the afternoon, we put Mark in the canoe and paddled close to a young moose who stood fifty yards away, pulling at his mother's teats, braced with both feet in the marshy water. The mother ate the succulent weeds, chomping the stringy clumps, water dripping from her homely face. The baby moose looked at us from time to time; probably her first glimpse of humans. We sat in the canoe until darkness fell on the marsh grasses. It began to drizzle softly so we headed back.

In the cabin the fire sparked. Three tin pans to catch the rain went plop, plop, plop and Joe's chest went up and down, snore, snore, snore. The rain on the tin roof spat like a cat.

The next day I awoke feeling uncontrollably happy; everything was harmonious. How changeable my nature was, and how my moods changed with it. Even the pink bluebells had turned blue. I never knew a flower did that.

The lake cabin was good for me. No running water, just a slop bucket. It kept me humble, hauling water from the lake, heating it on the woodstove, and using the outhouse. It felt good to know that in an emergency, we could rely on ourselves and the land to keep warm and have something to eat. There were plenty of berries, mushrooms, and wild plants to eat, good soil for a garden, clean lake water supporting animals and fish. If we had to, we felt we could survive.

Here were abundant trees for fuel and plenty of water and fish. This was new thinking for a born New Yorker.

In the lake a family of loons swam, one ducking after the other, then popping up in a row. We paddled quietly to them. They were silhouetted with that distinctly long throat and arched back of head. How beautiful their white markings and perfect symmetry. I whispered an incantation, "Come, come, come to me." When they ducked, we paddled closer without dripping water. I looked into their red eyes. A passing boat made the loons take flight, their wings flapping against the sky, blending bird wing, wind, sky, and water.

Our neighbor shot the three-year-old black bear who had been nosing around our place. Back in town, Lena Phipps told about a bear who scratched his back on her door, broke the latch open, and fell back into her cabin. "He chomped on my tea kettle and coffee pot. I found them down the trail a little way," said Lena. "He was trying to get out more than trying to hurt me. I hollered bloody murder. He looked bigger than the house."

✳

23

Going
Within

I love to wander in the wilderness,
Into the dense, weedy wilderness
With my thoughts all alone,
To see the sun on the smallest leaf.

From my journal

If spring was a release from winter's ice and snow, and
summer was a glorious festival of sun worship, then autumn
was a heightening of all the senses, the most beautiful, sensuous
time of year. Our only complaint was that the days passed so
quickly, gone before we could savor them fully. Best of all, in
autumn, Mark could crawl and play free of mosquitoes.

After heavy rains, the woods were full of mushrooms. On
weekends or in the evening light, Joe and I picked berries
and mushrooms. The mallards flew low over the pond at our
favorite mushroom-picking place. The marsh grasses were
yellow-tipped and the path was dotted with wedge-shaped
moose tracks and hard pellet spoor. The ground cover was a
mosaic of reindeer mosses, dwarf willow, russet-colored
Labrador tea, bunchberry, crowberry, and lingonberry. We
picked wild blueberries, eating as many as we put in our bucket.

The scent of rotting mushrooms and high bush cranberries was rich and sensual, like fermenting wine. We picked
large orange delicious mushrooms, leaving the spongy,

wormy ones. Filling our bags with shaggy manes and puff-balls, we lingered over the odd tawny mushrooms that we could not identify, the ones with creamy underbellies, soft as a woman's skin, or the poisonous red amanitas.

We sat on the mosses watching spider webs, small gnats and bits of seed filling the air with floating stuff. Foxtails blew across the tundra like live birds.

As we picked mushrooms, gnarled branches and wild rose thorns scratched our hands. We sat on a stack of logs a homesteader had left to season for his cabin. They were peeled as clean as hard-boiled eggs. We ate our snack with Thermos coffee, backs against the logs, chewing rosehips for dessert, spewing out the seeds between our teeth, gazing at the flawless sky.

I made spore paintings, leaving the mushrooms face-down overnight on paper. In the morning there were spores in beautiful colored designs.

Joe didn't mind the picking, but he was nervous about the eating. I prepared a batch of orange delicious mush-rooms for an omelet, wiping them gently with a soft towel. Butter sizzled in the frying pan while I sliced the mushrooms with sharp knife, enjoying their tender softness. We ate the omelet with toasted bread and butter and fresh coffee. A satisfying meal of mushrooms, from woods to pan to stomach.

"I'm still alive," said Joe after our meal.

In September Joe and I packed our tent, baby food, supplies, and camping gear and drove north to Eagle Sum-mit, about 110 miles north of Fairbanks.

We stopped at Sixty-Eight Mile, where an old-timer, sans teeth, sold coffee and doughnuts from his shack. He told us about the caribou hunters. "They tell of the caribou they shot in the belly, who had escaped in the woods. Disgusting," he said, shaking his gray head. "Hunters nowadays expect caribou to jump into the backs of their trucks and commit suicide."

We stopped at Miller House at Mile One Hundred Fifteen. Mrs. Miller, a sweet-faced woman in a dark dress with a lace collar and white buckskin slippers, sold us maple syrup. In the main room was an old kitchen pump, barrel stove, rocking chair, and polished wooden table. Indian baskets were piled beneath a Lambert painting of an old trapper. Basic groceries, canned beans, and tomatoes lined the shelves.

At the top of Eagle Summit, above treeline, we got out of the car to look for caribou, but there were none. The countryside was rocky, bald, and barren-looking except for low mosses and lichen. It was hard to see how anything could survive the wind on top of the summit, yet we saw a large variety of flowers and shrubs. Infinitesimal blue crocus, tiny blueberries, Jacob's ladder, poppies, lousewort mountain avens, yellow daisies, and white curled lichen lay beneath snow patches like white snow writing. Most of the flowers grew in short clusters due to the high winds and abrasive blowing snow.

Great varieties of birds nested at Eagle Summit, including the golden eagle, horned lark, and yeagers. The rarest was a six-inch bird with a white head and breast, the wheatear, who flew eleven thousand miles across the Bering Strait from equatorial Africa to Alaska.

After a picnic lunch, we picked the last of the blueberries. The fruit was bittersweet, turning darker blue violet when our fingers touched them, their leaves deep red. The squalling and babbling overhead marked the early migration of geese. They flew in formation, their underbellies a dark blue, their cranky, hoarse voices high in the wind.

Leaving Eagle Summit, we continued north. Finally, we pulled up to a dusty halt in front of Circle Hot Springs. Legend said that an Indian, the first discoverer of the hot springs, had shot a moose and washed his hands in the hot water. The hotel, a three-story building, was a welcome sight. We quickly put on our bathing suits and headed through the picturesque old bar to the hot springs pool to soak our sore bones. We immersed ourselves up to our necks in the hot, steamy, sulfurous water. The cold night air gave the whole room a strange mystical aura. It felt like awakening from anesthesia and finding everything musty and unreal. I floated, smiling like a Cheshire cat. A man swam near me like an inflated walrus, his heavy jowls bullfrogging along.

Miners from Circle City and Central came to soak their tired backs in the hot water. The spring heated the hotel, the small cabins, and the garden, which produced early lettuce, rutabagas, cabbages, beets, cauliflower. The greenhouses were stuffed full of tomatoes and cucumbers. Some of the cabbages would be fifty-pounders.

Mrs. Lynch, wife of the hotel owner, was mangling sheets and linens for the hotel. She told me they grew twelve tons of potatoes that year. They also shot their own moose, caribou, and rabbit. Grouse and wild fowl were plentiful. We treated ourselves to the family-style meal of king salmon and garden vegetables. It was one of the best meals we had ever eaten.

Afterward, we walked around the area inspecting an unused, sod-covered well house with a dead muskrat in the bottom. There was a general store and old cabins every-where; the logs still had the old bark on them. We camped the night near the springs.

Then we drove farther along the dirt road to the banks of the Yukon River. Circle City had been a historic gold mining community. Now a few Indians lived around the trading post. I sat on the bank of the wide river, in the grasses, painting a watercolor of the gray, silty water, mud sandbars, and a lone fisherman.

Later, we picked wild raspberries and stopped at an Indian cemetery where gray fences with small crosses on top surrounded each grave. As we turned a bend, we saw a large black bear standing in the road, then disappearing into the brush.

Indians used to live off the land along the Yukon, mainly on salmon, moose, bear, small animals, berries, ducks and their eggs, wild plants, mushrooms. They did very well before the trading post introduced them to sugar, pop, white flour, and booze.

The last camping trip of the year, Joe and I drove south to Summit Glacier. We had packed our camping gear and piled it into our truck, driving down the Richardson Highway. Mark slept soundly. It was our last chance to camp before the zero weather. We slept the night in our tent near a river so we could make camp coffee in the morning. The tent — canvas hung over poles, one end of it tied to a tree — was makeshift, and in the morning, the center pole fell on my head. Ouch!

Every turn of the road revealed shadowy and bleak mountains without sign of human habitation. The rivers were empty of spawning salmon; the wind ripped through chasms, pushing our truck along by its force. The birches were a winy, colored haze of bare limbs with a few stubborn, clinging leaves.

At Summit Lake Lodge, a severed, mangled moosehead lay by the roadside where some hunter had carelessly left it. The destruction of such huge beasts repelled me, and I drew away from the smell of carnage. The hunters sat drinking beer, puffed up, eyes shining, ready for more bloodletting. They leered boldly at the women in the bar.

Summit Glacier looked withdrawn, its cold head hidden in the sky, remote and inaccessible. While I was frying hotcakes on a two-burner camp stove near the tent, the first snowflakes fell, and a golden light flooded the sky. The earth was frozen and cracked as we walked, every minuscule plant encased in ice. We shivered over hot coffee mugs while six-month-old Mark slept blissfully wrapped in his rabbit skin bunting.

Flowers glittered with the brilliance of diamonds making crystal halos. Layers of wet leaves were slippery with ice, and piles of moose droppings were everywhere. We turned our reddened cheeks away from the wind and headed towards home. Soon the passes would be packed full of snow, and our main artery to Anchorage closed until the road commission plowed it open. Winter was fast behind us, biting at our heels.

In Fairbanks, the valley was warmer. The trees were still golden. The camping trip fueled my desire for more. I needed a simplification of life away from nurturing the family and the everlasting chores. I needed to wander alone. A friend lent me an old trappers shack, nine miles out of town up an old trail on Chena Hot Springs Road. Joe took care of Mark for the weekend.

It was a sunken log cabin full of history. No electricity or running water. An old shed behind the cabin had a sagging sod roof with five-foot spruce growing from it; beyond that was the outhouse, slightly tipped. A moose trail led uphill over fresh droppings. Birch and spruce logs were piled outside the door. A moose skull and horns hung over the doorway, nails hammered right through the empty eye sockets. Two pairs of snowshoes and six traps hung from the side of the cabin.

Inside was a log pole ceiling, a Yukon stove, a kerosene lamp, and a bed. A wild, prickly rose bush grew to one side of the wooden door. Was it a subtle reminder of life's thorns in one's path? I gathered broken branches from the forest for kindling. Coming back, I slammed the top of my head on the door's low threshold.

The original homesteader and trapper, long dead, was named Ackerman. He raised potatoes in the summer and trapped all winter. Did he sleep in the bunk, losing track of days, or did he mark it on a calendar? Did he let his beard go, dreaming and reading on blizzard days?

I made up the bunk bed with clean sheets, threw an old patchwork coverlet over it, then covered the rude wooden table with an embroidered tablecloth, and heated tea water on the woodstove. Soon the cabin vibrations began, the snap of the fire, the squirrel scampering in the attic.

I boiled a few potatoes a homesteader had given me. The potato plants had never flowered. The sun had baked their roots dry, then the rain had almost rotted them, then the frost hit them just as they were about to bloom. I boiled the potatoes for the longest time, but they remained hard as rocks. Then I cooked dried apples, the homesteader's mainstay, mixing them with dried apricots, cranberries, and cinnamon. They bubbled on the stove, filling the room with fragrance.

When I swept the wooden cabin floor, I found a horrible concoction under the bunk bed. Carpenter ants were slowly making sawdust of the old logs. Squirrels had taken mattress stuffing, mixed it with bark, and left their droppings. All this work going on, undermining the cabin while I slept. I put a chair in front of the door as there was no latch. I wasn't afraid of people coming in but of a wild beastie. I slept fitfully, hearing mouse noises and the squirrel scampering in the attic, finally falling asleep with the covers over my head. The stove hiccuped, and the bed squeaked.

Wind blew down the stovepipe all night, and I had to get up several times to stir and replenish the fire. When I opened the door in the morning, what a shock. The browned fields were covered in white fluff — each flowerlet held flakes of snow. The reindeer moss sparkled with snowy flakes between curly fronds.

My weekend over, I headed home. The snow melted away completely.

A week later, on an Indian autumnal day, I went to the cabin again to gather mushrooms and high bush cranberries. I was looking for a spot that I had visited before, an enchanting spot with mosses and miniature flowers growing in a circle, like an imaginary fairy dell.

Walking deeper and deeper into the woods, I enjoyed the soft, wet carpet of yellow leaves. When I turned back, I realized there should have been a trail, but no landmarks seemed familiar.

The wilderness had always been a welcoming place, but now it turned unfriendly. Stumps set out to trip me and branches caught at my sweater and held me. Hoping I would not have to spend the night in the woods, I walked, trying not to panic. Luckily, out of habit, I had dressed properly, with sturdy walking boots, socks, jeans, and my warm Cochican Indian sweater. No matches.

Heading for the tallest birch in a clearing, I fought through a scratchy thicket of alder. Piling dead brush and a log under the birch, I hoisted myself as high as I could climb. Strange hills and another tall birch poked up.

In answer to my shouts, I heard the faint bark of a dog. Preferring to be bitten rather than to be lost, I picked up a stout branch and advanced out of the thicket into a clearing. I followed deep grass growing waist high along a deeply rutted moose path. I saw a tractor and a house. Two dogs barked at me. I shouted, "Anyone home?" A young woman in an orange dress, her hair pulled back by a ribbon, came out. I was four miles from the road, completely opposite to the direction I thought I was going.

I asked her how she liked living out there without anyone else nearby, and she said they had been there four years and she was getting a job in town for the winter to be with other people.

I kept returning to the cabin — it became my retreat. In September, the hills were bathed in yellow light like a Blakelock landscape. I felt like the first Indian seeing the land. Near the cabin I followed the hoof prints of a large bull moose through the fields.

The rose hips by the cabin door dried and shriveled. The forest turned burnt umber, sienna, ocher, and a touch of olive green. In the dark evenings, the northern lights appeared. They reached down and spoke to me in a powerful voice. "Claire, are you there? Don't just stand there. Do something. Tell the world. We are all one . . . one . . ."

An awareness of my purpose in life was gradually taking form. A search for integrity, the desire to live as one with nature, no duplicities. I needed to find myself, to work as an artist — to paint what was within. I read somewhere that as wheat fell to the earth and died, the husk must perish before the seed could generate. The seed of an idea was beginning to form in my subconscious. I began to think longingly of the North where Eskimos lived together on land without a tree; where everyone had to depend on the land and each other. Would my restless spirit find what I was longing for in the Arctic?

★

24
_____

Twilight

Ice blanketed the city
The truck wheels were flat,
The steering wheel frozen
And the clutch sounded like a tin can.

From my journal

It was our second winter in Alaska. The oblique rays from
the arctic sun and long shadows in the twilight shed little
warmth. The barren twigs in front of our house were encased in glittering ice crystals. During the darkest December
days, the moon acted as a sun when it was full and high.
Some days, it appeared bright enough to illuminate the
distant mountain peaks, so bright that Indians could take
aim with their rifles and run traplines in the light of the full
moon.

Joe gave me a bouquet of red roses for my birthday and
our wedding anniversary, which fell in the same week. The
fragile fragrance of roses in December was a rare gift. They
came by plane from Seattle, bringing with them an aura of
exotic warm places. They gradually died, a red petal at a time
falling to the table, all the sweeter for having so short a life.

Several years later, I thought of those roses when I took
Mark to New York to meet his grandparents. My hunger for
beautiful things proved too much for me. Instead of buying
the practical coat I had saved for, I spent all of my savings on

a black angora coat I bought at Bergdorf Goodman's. The reversible coat had a Persian brocade lining made with real gold thread. It was a fairy-tale coat, lustrous on the inside with reds, violets, blue, and gold woven threads. No buttons, it just swung elegantly to one side. I wore it inside out to the Metropolitan Opera with my hair up in a braided crown. I had never felt so elegant.

When I returned to Alaska hugging the brocade to my body, content in its brilliant, glowing warmth as I trudged through the snow, Joe complained, "You're an electrician's wife, fergodsake!"

But I was an artist, I needed some bright color in the white fog. Even if no one could see that beautiful lining, I knew it was there!

When the second Christmas in Alaska rolled around, Mark was ten months old. For months before Christmas, our family thought how to humor the Keturis with our gifts. Both families agreed our gifts could not be bought, but had to be made, and the letter accompanying them had to be funny.

On Christmas Day, after an enormous dinner, the Keturis, Woolfords, Fejeses, and Aina and Gus, Elmer's aunt and uncle, sat around watching the children opening their new toys. The highlight of the evening was the reading of Elmer's and Joe's letters and opening of their gifts. Joe sometimes borrowed Elmer's tools, so Elmer's letter involved an exaggerated claim about a plumber's helper that had languished in Joe's basement for a year.

Joe gave Elmer a large box with string poking out. Attached to the string were rusty tools, railroad nails, old socks, an oil can, and at the end an old hot dog. His accompanying letter, which he read aloud ceremoniously, recommended their qualities as aids to long life, etc., etc.

After the singing and gifts, Joe brought out his fiddle and played "Silent Night," the rest of us joining in the carols. Hildur and I passed the coffee and desserts around before story time began.

Hildur told of a Christmas at the Moore Creek mine. "One year we made an eighty-mile round trip by Cat and 'go-devil' sled from Moore Creek to Flat for the Christmas dance," she said. "Tony and Liza Gularte went with us. The men loaded the go-devil with grub and supplies, nailing a Yukon stove on the floor. Elmer rigged up a tent on it, and hitched the tractor to the sled.

"The going was rough down Camelback Summit. The Cat kept jerking and sliding while we were heating up the moose meat mulligan. The sled hit a log, and the sudden lurch pitched the kettle to the floor, spilling all the stew.

"Liza and I hurriedly scooped up the leftovers, added more snow water, and reheated it. The stew tasted thin but the hungry men lapped it up. Elmer was so hungry that he didn't notice Liza covering her mouth so she wouldn't burst out laughing.

"It took us all day to reach Flat down the Bonanza and Otter Creek, but we made it. We primped, put on our best dresses and shoes, and went to the dance. It was forty degrees below. The Moose Hall in Flat was decked out with a huge Christmas tree. The miners were all spruced up in their checked wool shirts and heavy shoepacks, hair slicked back with Brilliantine. The wind-up phonograph played records of schottisches and polkas. We women were in constant demand, never had a chance to sit down, especially when the Swedish men danced the Hambo. There were about twenty prostitutes on the Flat line, but they never came to the Christmas dances."

Elmer interrupted to tell the end of the story. "At the bar, John Ogriz and Fritz Awe, who weighed 280 pounds of muscle, were having an argument. John told Fritz he could drink him under the table.

"'Ha, drink me under? That'll be the day,' said Fritz.

"John told the bartender to bring four shot glasses. They began to slug whiskey, one drink after the other. I quit watching and went back to dance. Later that evening, we saw Fritz with his arms hugging a birch tree to hold him up. John had disappeared. As for us, we danced until four in the morning. Never did find out who won the drinking bet."

With the passing of the years, the competition to have the funniest gift has remained the highlight of the year for our families. One Christmas eleven years later, Mark built a still out of old pipes and an oil drum to give to Elmer. The best gift of all was an old vintage radio. In the spring we had casually mentioned to the Keturis that Mark had no radio in his room. The next week, Elmer and Hildur came over, carrying a huge monstrosity of a radio. It could hardly fit through the back door.

Joe protested when he saw them coming. "Get away from here with that old thing." He braced his foot against the door jamb. But Elmer firmly pushed him aside declaring, "This has a great antique radio and cabinet, it works beautifully! Gus and Aina gave it to us and we've used it for years. Think how happy Mark will be to have this twelve-tube Super Hetrodyne Howard radio!"

The thing didn't work too well and took up too much room, but Mark had a radio. When Christmas came around, Joe and Mark and I conspired and decided to return the radio. Our family grinned in anticipation as I wrapped up a huge carton with red ribbon. Everyone laughed good-naturedly at the joke, but that was not the end of the Howard radio episode.

A few months later, Joe met Elmer driving his old pickup and asked him where he was going. "Just got back from the dump," said Elmer. "Finally decided to get rid of that old radio."

Joe and I just happened to be going to the dump with our garbage. We drove around until we spotted the radio and gleefully hoisted it into the back of our old pickup.

The next Christmas, we were all excited as we helped Joe draft his annual letter, giggling over it for days. We hid the large box containing the Howard radio in a snowdrift outside so that the Keturis could not guess the contents. With great glee and anticipation on our faces, we listened to Joe reading his letter praising Elmer "as a humanitarian, a man of the world, that only he, the greatest mechanic in the world, would appreciate this great gift, this electronic marvel, etc. etc." Then he and Mark left the room and lugged in the heavy box, setting it in front of Elmer.

Elmer untied all the ribbons and opened the box to find the old familiar Howard again. "Hooooly Mackinaw! I thought it was smashed and burned to bits at the dump," he shook his head in disbelief.

A few days later the Keturis drove to the dump to give Howard his final resting place. To this day we have continued the tradition, only now it is our children who make the gifts and compose the letters.

The New Year began with the sun appearing for a few minutes each day, casting long, pink shadows under the branches heavily laden with snow. The four-foot snow drift reached the top of our fence. Three black ravens on a birch tree gave my eyes relief from the numbing landscape. Fifty below! I broke two glasses with my fumbling. Ice fog lingered and made me irritable. In desperation, I called Hildur. "How are you today?"

"Gloomy," she reported.

"Can you see across the street?"

"Of course not."

We had acquired Kathy Rogers' Siamese cat. "The cat is horny," I told Hildur. "He's driving me nuts. We could be living on the planet Mars, imprisoned by frozen boundaries. I feel like shooting out of here like a comet on flame! Oh, for some glitter, high heels, museums, fashionable clothes. I miss the theater. A change. I'm so damn natural, my hair hangs down my back like a gypsy. I'd like it up for a change with long earrings!"

I chased the cat with my broom. He had begun to spray the curtains again.

Finally I could stand being cooped up no longer. "I'm going to the library," I announced to the cat, who stuck his tail up at me. After donning my arctic gear, I slammed the door in protest. It took a snowstorm to snap me back to reality. It exploded into a blizzard, fifty-mile-per-hour winds, blowing four feet of snow off our rooftop into the streets. Drifts piled up, making traffic impossible.

The cat and I kept feuding. I sneezed when he came near and jumped every time he dug his claws into my leg. Joe loved him and I tolerated him, but when he began sleeping between us at night, I protested. When Joe came home from work and kissed the cat before me, that was the end. I took a heroic stance, pointing my finger out the door. "Either he goes or I do." He went back to the Rogers.

We perked up a bit for the New Year's parties of eggnog and whiskey, cake and sweets, but then came the letdown. The gray-white snow, pallid gray sky, and snowy branches were still there. Ice fog blanketed the city. The truck's steering was frozen and the clutch about to go, sounding like a tin can. Tire pressure had to be checked daily because the tires went flat overnight. The brake pedals almost froze, the accelerator stuck, the door handles would snap in two if we were not careful.

Sometimes the land was a place of peace, sometimes I thought it had a moral order that was lacking elsewhere. The land could be calm, it could be cruel, it could cure, and it could kill. "I stand here on this high frozen bit of earth and take sensual note of the universe." Who was it who said that?

KLIM

Elmer Sharinghis
Clam Chowder

★

25

Winter
Hysteria

*It is forty-five below. An Eskimo woman,
twenty-two years old, a night club dancer, was
beaten and left half-naked. She froze to death.*

From the Fairbanks Daily
News-Miner

The doctors' offices were full, and so were the bars.
Illness developed; backaches, headaches, depression, and
stomach troubles. Suicide notices appeared often in the
newspapers. Women and men gave vent to rages, throwing
things, saying things they did not mean, slapping the children for minor infractions, giving way to nerves due to
winter's confinement.

Winter discontent aroused dormant conflicts between
couples. Wives left their husbands and returned when the
sun came back again. One woman could not wait; she ran
out into the storm and was gone for three days. There were
ads in the paper stating, "I will not be responsible for any
debts contracted by anyone except myself . . ."

The shock of the darkness and cold reacted on humans in
abnormal ways. Some people ate constantly or would not go
out of the house, or they slept all the time, or became closet
drinkers. When it was dark and lonely, alcohol filled a need
for them. Drunks froze to death on their own doorsteps.

Under our snowy exterior, our town fermented like yeast, and in many cases the yeast in the alcohol kept it fermenting.

What upset me was the ordinary question Joe asked when he came home from work. His coveralls dirty, he walked in cold and hungry, glad to be home.

He asked me the wrong question: "What did you do all day?" Innocent words — fighting words.

"What did I do all day?" My voice went up in decibels. "Nothing. I just walked to the store; it was fifty below. I packed and dressed Mark as if we were going on an expedition to the Pole. He screamed when I put on his parka, refused to put on his booties. I lugged the groceries home, fixed lunch. The fire went out. I went to the basement and tore off a fingernail carrying wood up. Mark cried all day. His teeth are coming in."

I was too ashamed to admit that I felt incompetent. I was having difficulty coping. I hadn't had a chance to paint or think of myself as a woman for months. It was too dark to care about clothes; I was tired of the same slacks and sweaters. I had not looked in the mirror for a long, long time. Who could see in the dark? Lipstick, no! Vaseline, yes.

I wanted the luxury of feeling sorry for myself, but I was ashamed. I had not worked as an electrician in fifty degrees below zero all day. We both knew it was the winter blues, commonly known as cabin fever, which turned us all into monsters. Joe knew it would blow over.

Every time I thought my life was a struggle, I called Hildur, my unpaid psychologist. She often got antsy herself, as did most of the women. Old Jesse Bloom, though, walked every day all bundled up in all weather. "How do you fight cabin fever?" I asked her.

"I never get it," she said. "My advice is to get out and walk every day. Get out and do something!" She was a remarkable woman. Sensible. Irish combined with devout Jewish prayers. She was the founder of the first Alaska Girl Scouts chapter. Her husband, Bob, a gruff, dour man, came from Ireland via the Klondike in '98. He walked the Chilkoot Trail. He mined and experimented with strains of Siberian wheat. He was on the Board of Regents of the University of Alaska. Their three daughters were educated in Ireland. One is a psychologist, one a lawyer, and the other an educator.

"Never ride if you can walk," Mrs. Bloom told me in her thick Irish brogue. "Stop sitting around feeling sorry for yourself, get involved."

We read in the *News-Miner* about a customer who, in a fit of anger, bit off the bartender's nose. The police picked up his nose and rushed him to the hospital, where Dr. Haggland sewed it back on again. On the Line, one of the women bit off a nose (in a fit of passion?) and spat it out in the toilet! "Please don't flush, don't flush!" begged her John.

We learned from *Jessen's Weekly* that a man had accidentally shot his wife by firing through a log wall; he pleaded guilty and was sentenced to a year and a day in prison. Shortly afterwards, an item appeared in *Jessen's* about a Swede, who, in a fit of anger over pancakes, hacked his partner to death with an ax.

A woman opened a window, and with her shotgun, blew the back of a taxi apart. The cab driver had not been true to her, she claimed. In court she testified, "If I had really wanted to kill him, I would have." Her lawyer brought a footlocker filled with her trophies. Court adjourned and they went out to the Chena River, where she gave a shooting exhibition rarely seen. She was let go with a fine of $150.

Stories from the North filtered down about Native women who ran out into the snow. Doctors called it Arctic Hysteria.

One day I met an old woman at a routine checkup at Dr. Schaible's office. She was not really as old as she looked, I discovered later, only in her forties. She admired Mark's sweater, hand-knitted of cream wool with a cap to match that our Hungarian friend had sent us from New York.

"Why are you here?" I asked.

"I just went out to get more wood for the fire from the wood pile. It wasn't far, but I guess I didn't realize how cold it was. I just wore my shoes and stockings and ran out. But in that short time I froze my feet. One year later I still have trouble with them; I feel the cold so terribly, they hurt. I will suffer all my life."

I was having my hair cut at the beauty parlor, a rare event. A heavy woman — a country woman even by Fairbanks standards, in crude men's boots, heavy woolen stockings, and baggy pants — was having her hair washed. The look on her worn face was one I shall never forget.

I could tell she hadn't had anyone to care for her or do anything for her in a long time. Living in the Bush, she had come to town, not just to visit, probably not enough money for that, but a necessary trip, like going to the doctor's for a checkup because she felt sick. She had forgotten how it was to look in the mirror. But now she was submitting to the luxury of having someone care for her, of having her hair washed with soft water from a tap, and curled in a beauty parlor. A soft smile lit her face. I smiled at her and thought I would never be like that. Or would I?

When Joe came home from work and asked what I did all day, I realized that I had been busy every minute, but I couldn't remember one thing I had actually accomplished. Mark was teething again and it was too cold to take him out.

When the days grew longer and the sun shone brightly

on our window, Joe played his ultimate trick. On the dust of one of the big windows he had inscribed with his fingers: "Last washed — 1876." The irony of it was that it had been so dark I hadn't even noticed it. Besides, what was the use of washing one side when the snowdrift on the other side was four feet deep outside. That was the last straw. I broke down and laughed until I cried.

The Keturis had problems, too. Hildur had sent Elmer out with a list to buy some groceries. He met a mining buddy so they stopped in at the Pastime Bar to warm up on a cold day. They had one drink — just to warm up. Elmer told his famous stories; they had another drink.

About eight in the evening, all sense of time lost, Elmer decided he had better go on his errand and get home. He stopped at the market, but forgot where he put the "dang slip." It had been pitch dark when he left home, and it was pitch dark when he returned. All he could remember of the list was hot dogs.

At the door was an anxious, hungry Hildur, arms akimbo. Elmer grinned foolishly as he handed her the bag. "I lost the list."

She peered into the bag and took out the limp hot dogs, then stepped back into the house to let him enter. Taking aim, she flung the hot dogs one by one at his head, until Elmer collapsed on the floor in helpless laughter. "I'll hot-dog you!" She launched another one, and then she, too, collapsed with laughter.

At least they had a sense of humor about the whole thing. Another time Elmer, who had joined the Moose Lodge, came home looped after the meeting. Hildur's patience gave out and she declared, "Nothing makes me madder than a drunken Moose."

Joe and I had no serious fights, just the usual married couples' petty quarrels. After a heated argument one day —

I don't even remember what started it, something petty —
I felt I had to get away from Joe and the house. But where
was I to go? I gave myself the luxury of slamming the door
as I left. Let him worry about me freezing to death. Where
should I go? I could go to the Keturis, but for how long?
Our other friends had small places, and even if I could sleep
on the couch, would I want to ask? I was too proud to admit
to anyone that we had quarreled. I did not have a cent of my
own. My folks lived five thousand miles away. I crouched
down in the snow in my boots and winter coat, crying my
heart out, huddled against the heat of the house. I stood it as
long as I could, until I was cried out and my toes felt numb.

In the end, I slunk back into the house. There was
nothing else to do. We had to work out our differences;
there was no escape. Joe had been worried. He gave me a
sheepish look, and we made up.

The affair of the "dishrag" grew to exaggerated heights
in the winter darkness. One day I ran to Hildur's house in
tears over Joe. "He comes home and finds fault with everything I do," I cried. "He criticizes me constantly."

"What did he say?"

"He said, 'What's that dishrag doing in the sink?'" I
sobbed childishly.

"Well, we've got to stop that," she replied. "Next time he
says that to you I'll tell you what to say."

So I went home giggling, and the next time I was ready.
When Joe said, "What's that dishrag doing in the sink?" I
calmly replied, "I'm growing mold on it!" His bewildered
expression gave me satisfaction. He never mentioned a
dishrag in the sink again.

Finally, I had learned how to defend my sensitive ego.
"Growing mold on it" became a landmark joke. I learned
other funny remarks, and a great series of Italian finger
expressions, disrespectful but useful.

★

26
—

Ice
Carnival

Come out and play, let's join the carnival
Come out and play, we're pleasure bound
Winter's gone and spring is on the way.

Carnival Song —
Ray Hufman

In March, the mayor proclaimed a week-long holiday for
the Ice Carnival, which had been canceled during the war.
The celebration was a needed stimulus. Pietro Vigana, a local
engineer, built a fifteen-foot throne and an aurora display
out of ice. Our town resembled an icy fairyland with twin-
kling, colored lights shining on the ice throne. Ice sculptures
lined the streets, and a colonnade of ice totems faced the
square.

The carnival began with a parade. Leonhard Seppala, one
of the mushers who delivered diphtheria serum to Nome in
1925, led fourteen teams of Pioneers of Alaska members
dressed in parkas and mukluks.

The Royal Canadian Mounted Police from Dawson, in
town for the curling Bonspiel, dressed in red jackets and
black pants and rode horses in the parade, after which came
floats featuring the beauty contestants. The winning float
depicted Snow White and the seven dwarfs.

Blanche Cascaden, gold miner of Livengood, was selected

as the Pioneer queen, and a miner from Central was the king. Decked in robes and beaded mukluks, they were escorted to the throne wearing ivory crowns studded with gold nuggets.

In the evening, beautiful girls from Anchorage and Nenana competed with our hometown girls for the Miss Alaska title, parading on the runway in the center aisle of the Moose Hall in fur parkas, ski suits, swim suits, and evening gowns.

Wearing his beaver hat, Joe pulled Mark's sled. Mark was resplendent in his white rabbit parka as we watched the children's mutt parade.

Joe invited Harry Havrilik, marshal of the Yukon River village of Rampart, home to dinner to talk about gold mining. Dapper Harry, a thin, short man who was born in Brooklyn, was called the "Hollywood Kid" by the Indians because he had a slick mustache and wore a Stetson. He dug out his latest find, an eight-ounce gold nugget, and informed Joe that old Pete Larkin was trying to sell his mining claims. Then he began a nostalgic conversation with me about the merits of Brooklyn versus the Bronx. Joe interrupted to inquire about Larkin's land, as he was looking for a good mining claim.

During the carnival there were Eskimo dances, blanket-tossing, and fireworks. Exhilarated from all the activity, we dashed from one event to the other, from the hockey games at the university to the ski-jumping on a ramp set up near the Chena River bridge to a baseball game on snowshoes!

The Fairbanks Folk Dance gave a folk dance exhibition, and there were bingo games and special movies at the Lacey Street Theatre.

In the Nordale Hotel, I was able to visit with Eva

McGown at the Beta Sigma Phi Tea. She was as beautiful as ever in her suit and pearls. As we sat and drank our tea, I asked her about Arthur, her husband, and how she managed without him all these years.

"Some called me a mail-order bride, but I hated that name. For Arthur I left all I had known. My family could not understand how I could go to the end of the world for him. They gave me up for dead. My love was a grief to everyone in Ireland.

"Arthur was a proud, silent man, but not that way with me. I would walk along the Chena River, look at the snow and the frontier town, and ask myself, 'What am I doing in this wilderness?' I stopped in front of my own house and the front window was lighted up, and I could see my husband inside. A love that had compassion in it for him and for me, and for everyone on the earth, came up in my heart — and I said, 'This is why I am here. To show mercy.' From then on, Lass, I lived with all my soul in Fairbanks, and the green island faded like an old ribbon.

"When he died, I knew about loneliness; it was a heavy load. I heard no sound in our cabin but the clock ticking and the wind. I went to church and knelt, 'Lord, I am ready for thy work.'"

Eva visited the sick at the hospital and worked at her desk at the Nordale Hotel, helping newcomers. When the city of Fairbanks gave her a gold watch, she said, "The bread I cast on the water came back with butter and jam on it."

Cindy Pearson, a vivacious redhead and my friend in Beta Sigma Phi, was the mistress of ceremonies at the crowning of Miss Alaska. "Cindy," said Sandy Fenton, "has a heart as big as all outdoors." She brought gifts to the needy, giving food from her garden and kitchen. Before Mark was born, she brought a basket containing a blue blanket and some home-baked goodies for me. You couldn't admire anything in her house or she would give it to you.

Laura Hagberg, popular Eskimo waitress at the Model Cafe, won the Miss Popularity title at the Miss Alaska contest. Her prize was a ticket to New York and back. I gave her my parents' address. My family was captivated with Laura, for she was good-humored, bubbling over with joy.

The Chena River was frozen to a depth of seven feet, and the ice was able to withstand the weight of the crowds and dog teams. Natives had flown in from the villages with their dog teams for the chance to win the North American Sled Dog Championship jackpot. Villages had sent their best racers and pooled their fastest dogs. Eskimo and Indian mushers looked splendid in their handmade fur garments; even their dogs wore braided yarn tassels.

Some of the Eskimos had never been in Fairbanks before, had never seen so many people gathered at one time, or so many stores displaying such a variety of goods.

Mike Agababa, who had raised his dogs in Fairbanks in his Third Avenue kennels, was on the Chena River ice watching the starting line. The Marshall, Fabian Carey, in a marten trapper's hat, flaps dangling around his lean face, fired the starting gunshot. Townspeople in corduroy parkas stomped their feet; everyone's breath steamed. A university professor wore an unusual outfit made of a Hudson Bay blanket; a banker wore a coonskin coat; military men wore white "bunny boots." Eskimo children looked like large lollipops with huge fur ruffs framing their faces.

It was a northern fashion show. Lolla Hudson wore her new black seal fur coat trimmed in white fur; Hildur wore her raccoon fur coat. Sandy Fenton, whose team had won the curling trophy against the Dawson City Challengers, wore a ski suit and an old-fashioned aviator's hat with a scarf flung over her shoulder, à la Amelia Earhart. No matter what anyone wore in those days, you rarely saw a mink coat in a place where trappers caught plenty of mink, marten, and beaver — only the prostitutes wore mink in those days!

Frantic spectators stamped their frozen feet as they cheered their favorites. We lined up on the Chena River bank and pressed for vantage points on the bridge as the dog teams took off, one after the other. We admired the huskies' thick double coats, their tough feet and well-furred tails, which protected their faces when they slept.

Andy Kokrines and his brother Bergman won, as did Gareth Wright and Howard Luke, all Indians. Trophies were awarded for the best times. The town feted the winners like bullfighters, and their names were spoken throughout the year by aficionados. Mushers traded and sold dogs and exchanged stories. Bars raked in the customers. Bets were won and lost and whiskey flowed.

The Ice Carnival brought the excitement of winter sports to our small town, a needed winter break.

The influx of racing teams enlivened everyone. At night when we went to bed we could hear the huskies yelping and howling and the answering chorus from the neighborhood dogs all over town.

My mother
and father

★

27

Father

*Art is a collaboration between
God and the artist, and the less
the artist does, the better.*

Andre Gide

I had written to my father and sent him an Eskimo ivory carving of a loon. A week later my family called to tell me he was sick in the hospital, suffering from pneumonia. A few days later, his heart gave out. He died in 1951 at the age of sixty-seven. It all happened so suddenly, and I was so far away. It would have taken two days to fly to New York, and they were burying him before I could get there. When I called my family, asking if I should come, they replied, "There is nothing you can do."

Instead, I went to a funeral for Phil Halupsak's father, whom I hardly knew. I sobbed bitterly in the back of the Catholic church. I thought about my father's smile and cheerful nature, and how he loved his four daughters. He always carried books in his overcoat pockets, and instilled in his children a love of learning and a love of beauty. Whether it was the curve of a branch against the sky or a mother holding a child, my father instilled in us the wonder of life.

I had been able to take Mark to New York, and I was happy my father had seen him then. I remembered him playing with Mark, laughing with joy as he stretched out on the floor and his grandchild crawled up on his chest.

My father's capacity for enjoyment was most evident when he had a day off, and stayed home to work on his scrapbooks of beautiful places. He was an armchair traveller, seeing the world through photographs. We four sisters spent many rainy days poring over his scrapbooks. Once in Verona, my sister Elaine saw a sculpture she remembered from Papa's scrapbook.

Damon Runyon, who frequented Lindy's restaurant, famous for its cheesecake, wrote about flat-footed waiters like my father. Lindy's waiters took no guff, wisecracking to their customers, white napkins tucked over their arms. No servile image there, they gave as good as they got. We lived on Dad's tips, depending on the generosity of strangers. My father's legs were strong from walking all day; he never owned a car. We had chicken on Friday nights, but rarely red meat. Yet, when he was out with friends or relatives, he would pick up the bill, play the big sport.

Sobbing for my father in the white wooden church, I wished that we had understood each other. Now it was too late. I wished I had told him how much I appreciated and loved him; how sorry I was for my childish grudges, never expressed. I wished I could ask for his forgiveness, talk with him, hear him tell me that he was proud of me — that he would have sent me to college if he could have afforded it.

I had wanted to go to college with a terrible yearning, and when I went to work in the morning hanging on to the subway strap — there never were any seats on that hour-long trip from the Bronx to Manhattan — I envied the schoolgirls going to college, carrying a load of books. My family had needed my small income during the Depression, and most of the girls in our neighborhood worked to help their families.

On my father's day off, he lit his cigar, went into the kitchen, and cooked. He loved to give parties for our relatives. "Come stand by me, Clara, you bring me luck," Papa would say after dinner, as he downed a slug of slivovitz, the

Yugoslavian plum brandy he loved. Soon our small living room would be filled with laughter and cigar smoke and the slapping of pinochle cards.

It was my father who bought me my first paint set; who took me to the museums, to the free opera in Central Park, to the Botanical Gardens; who bought the opera and symphony records to play on our windup Victrola. It was my father who bought original oil paintings for our walls. He also hung a Renoir reproduction of a nude and "Two Lovers Fleeing a Storm," by Cot, a popular painter in the forties. He introduced me to his favorite authors in the library: Goethe, Thomas Mann, and Romain Rolland. He could not pass a bookstore without browsing, a talent I inherited.

For years he was the invisible figure leaning over my shoulder as I painted or wrote. My father loved me so; in all my life he had never raised his voice or struck me. The worst punishment I received as a child was to be banned once from the table. Now that I had my own family, I realized more than ever how hard he had worked to put bread on the table, doing menial work beneath his talents for tips. I felt he was Willy Loman, in *Death of a Salesman*, used up in the big city, "cast aside like an orange sucked out."

However, my father knew how to enjoy life, and on his days off, we travelled by train to Coney Island. One summer we lived near the ocean. Leaping into that great ocean and feeling the sun and salt on my skin is a memory that has never left me.

My father told us about his favorite brother, who had given his life for a friend. They had gone ice-skating on a pond when the friend fell through the ice. My father's brother jumped in, pulled his friend out, and covered him with his own jacket. Subsequently, my father's brother died of pneumonia.

The grandparents I never knew owned a little grocery store in Lemberg, Austria. My aunt once told me that lunch at their home on Sundays took three hours, including coffee in their garden. Father had no head for business, my mother used to say, but he had an intellectual curiosity, a love of books and music. He spoke seven languages and wrote poetry.

Sitting in the church at another man's funeral, I grieved for my father. The priest, a tall man with expressive hands, officiated the Catholic ritual of death and sorrow, his hands reminding me of the drawing by Dürer. Father George Boileau, in his forties, had trained as a Jesuit missionary to work in remote villages, but the bishop appointed him pastor of the Fairbanks Catholic Church.

Father Boileau had the manner of a just person, and his robes and demeanor came right out of the Bible. He greeted everyone along the street. It did not matter who you were, what religion or color, rich or poor. He helped Eva McGown find help for alcoholics and homes for people who needed shelter. Glasses gave his face a stern look, but his smile was warm and generous. An attentive listener, he was a man of great personal charisma.

My father was not religious at all, but both men were tall and walked proudly with vigorous strides. Both were well-read and intelligent, my father a self-educated man, a constant reader.

The priest, of course, had no wife who was losing her memory, no four kids to support on a waiter's tips, nor personal financial worries like my father.

The children of my art class were spread out along the banks of the Chena painting the Catholic Church and its steeple across the river. The church had stained glass windows and a madonna in a cupola. Father Boileau walked by and encouraged the children, admiring their work, really looking at their first attempts at watercolor.

When he came to dinner, we talked about books and poetry, especially Roethke's poetry. Boileau confessed that he also wrote poetry, and encouraged me to study with Roethke through the University of Washington's correspondence course, as the University of Alaska had no poetry course then. Unfortunately, I was given another teacher who stressed iambic pentameter, which served to discourage me.

My Catholic neighbor said, "You wouldn't think Boileau so wonderful if he told you to keep having babies." She had six, and complained, "I can't afford the high school fees and the church's financial demands."

I once asked Father Boileau what he wanted when he prayed. He put his head down in his hands, and said quietly, "Grace." He told me, "Until we understand who we are, why we are here, where we are going, we cannot genuinely create, let alone see the creative hand of God in this Universe." A good friend, he understood the role of a creative artist, and like my father, encouraged my painting and writing.

Nest Polinski held the Theosophist view that my father had not died, but had gone on to another life. It made me understand why so many people of the world, including the Eskimos and Indians, believed in reincarnation. It was a comforting view, but it did not lessen my grief. Joe and my friends consoled me, and holding Mark close was a comfort. I was thankful my father had lived to see his first grandson. I missed my father and the rest of my family more than ever and looked at the one road leading south with deep longing.

＊

28

——

Disaster

There are strange things done in the midnight sun
By the men who moil for gold.
The Arctic trails have their secret tales
That would make your blood run cold.

The Cremation of Sam McGee
Robert Service

Joe flew to Rampart, an Indian village on the Yukon River, to see Pete Larkin's mining claims on Ruby Creek, eleven miles out of Rampart.

A week later, Pete Larkin came to Fairbanks, wearing his old sweat-stained fedora and baggy pants held up by suspenders. The old man had done a little prospecting throughout the years, barely existing on gold, his Social Security, moose, and beans. All he wanted was ten percent of the take, "a thousand dollars down with another thousand due later." They sealed the deal with a handshake, and Joe was in the mining business. A man's word was as "good as gold" in those days!

Joe found two partners, the Strand Brothers. Herb, an electrician, and Chet, who worked in the powerhouse. They bought two second-hand bulldozers and other mining equipment. The machinery was sixty miles out of town at Nome Creek Mine. It needed to be brought into Fairbanks for overhauling; they intended to use the parts from one bulldozer to fix the other. Dick Zhender, a trucker, was hired to bring in the equipment.

On a cold March morning, Dick woke Joe, "I'm flying in to my cabin to get my machine, and you could bring yours in at the same time. Come and help me!"

I made breakfast while Joe dressed. He grabbed a can of Argentine beef as he kissed me goodbye. "Dick's got plenty of food," he mumbled.

The trip was to take a few days, but it was eight days later when Joe came home in a police car. I had been worried sick over each day's delay.

Joe had lost ten pounds, he looked haggard, his clothes were filthy, and he smelled of diesel oil. He was totally exhausted. He ate some hot chicken soup, took a shower, and fell into bed.

The next morning over breakfast, he told me what had happened.

The pilot landed on a ridge five miles from Dick's cabin. We set out on snowshoes, with batteries roped to our backs, sliding and cursing till we got to Dick's cabin.

"We'll have a good meal and sleep, and hit it in the morning," said Dick, as he lit the gasoline lamp. "I'm starved." He opened his staple box, and let loose, "Damn if those mice haven't eaten my side of bacon. All they left is this empty shell! All we got is hotcake flour and a few cans of peaches. Some hunters must have used my shack, and ate up all my grub!"

We had a hell of a time getting his bulldozer started. We should have started out the next day, but it was a week before we got it moving. Then we snowshoed four miles to Nome Creek Mining Company, whose equipment I had bought. The camp was empty. Cleaned out. The only thing we found to eat was, you guessed it, hotcake flour! "Son of a bitch," Dick said, "I'm so sick I could vomit."

We charged the batteries on one of my machines. During the night, the engine blew a rod, so the next day we went back to Dick's cabin to get another six-and-one-half horse-power engine, which we dragged back in a big bread pan. Dick had a bad back and knee, so I did most of the work.

After endless meals of peaches and hotcakes, we were ready to travel. Dick would drive his machine and I would drive one of mine, with the second cabled to the first.

Dick came over to me and asked, "What do you think, Joe, should we stay in the valley and use the winter trail or should we take to the road?" He hadn't asked my advice since we left Fairbanks. I suggested we use the winter trail, since it was level. On the hillside road, we'd have to fight the snow drifts on the steep climb — it wouldn't be fast or safe.

"But I don't know the winter trail," he said.

I pointed it out. Although made years ago, the trail was visible through the trees.

"No, we'll take the road," Dick decided. He climbed on and took off out of sight around a curve in the steep road.

Well, that's that, I thought, as I mounted my machine. I hoped he could make it, but it didn't look too good.

We heard Ray Woolford's plane flying low. He tossed out a weighted note. "Wives worried. Do you need anything?" We stamped out an O.K. in the snow, and he flapped his wings and flew on.

I started to move my bulldozer, but I knew immediately that I was in trouble. The engine spit and sputtered. The automatic throttle was wide open and there was absolutely no power. The exhaust was spewing a fine mist of oil. Oh, boy, a cracked head! "What's wrong?" Dick shouted, throttling down.

"After all this trouble, I may have to leave one of the machines here. This one hasn't got the guts to pull the other one."

"Let me pull you," he suggested. "You can pull one and

I'll hook onto you with the cable and we'll make good headway."

Dick took up the slack, leaving twenty-five feet between the bulldozers. I signaled O.K. Dick started off slowly. I pulled my clutch in and we both pushed our throttles on full. We climbed several hundred feet above the valley; the drop-off was precipitous. Suddenly my bulldozer slid to the left as if an invisible force were pushing me to the edge of a glaciered road. I felt no assisting pull from Dick. I stopped, throwing the clutch. Zhender leapt from his seat. His bull-dozer had slid sideways on the glacier, and the rear third of the track was out in space. There we stood, mouths agape. Had the dozer gone over the edge, I would have been dragged with it.

Dick stood there trembling. I pulled the can of Argentine beef from my parka pocket and handed it to him. Staring at it with a blank, shocked looked, he reached into his pocket for his knife. Leaning against the track, we munched the beef, each lost in his own thoughts.

"Well," Dick blurted, "We'll have to get moving. We'll have to trench into the ice." The sun had dropped behind the hill and it was cold.

Lying down on the ice, I reached over the edge to feel a lip of ice extending out two feet. "Hey, Dick," I shouted, "we'd better step on it. If this ice breaks we'll lose the whole outfit."

Trenching into the ice was a slow and tiresome process, and it was late afternoon before we started moving. We sat on the right arm of the bulldozer, ready to bail out in case the slide started again. We crossed the glaciated area. It was near ten at night, and bitterly cold as we came to another glaciated stretch about 200 feet long.

"The hell with it. We'll finish in the morning. Let's get some sleep." Dick took the comforter and laid it on the ice, lying in the middle, covering himself. I lay next to him, half on the ice and half on the comforter. It was damned uncomfort-able. Dick snored. I got up and climbed the snow-covered hill, looking for windfalls, or dead trees. Soon I had a small pile of firewood. I drained some oil from the tank and poured it on the wood. It blazed, throwing a blanket of heat. When I awoke, the fire had died down. It was four o'clock in the morning. Even hotcakes would have been good now.

I got up and started trenching again. When Dick woke, he joined me, and after a few more hours of digging, there was about thirty feet of glacial ice left. "We'll make a run for it, and we'll get over it O.K.," Dick said. So we ate our last can of peaches, and fueled up the machines — they'd been running steadily for twenty hours.

We raced at what seemed a tremendous speed, bumping and clanging out of the trench and over the glacier. We made it. It was Sunday, Zhender's birthday, and he'd promised to take his wife and daughter out for dinner.

The tracks clanked, the motor roared, the oily spray from the exhaust splashed me as the wind blew. We started climbing again over steep, glaciated ice, the engines lugging down.

Before us was a giant knoll of ice right across the road. Dick thundered up the grade to the crown of ice and we both dismounted.

"Are you planning to go right over this ice?"

"That's right," Dick answered.

With that, Dick climbed back into his seat and clanked up the ice hill. As he reached the sanctuary of the other side, his bulldozer started a slow slide. He vacated his seat with amazing speed, releasing his clutch. The cable tightened, the slide stopped. The left front end of his bulldozer was again in space, hanging over the edge.

Dick came back to me, and, for the second time, asked my advice. "How the hell am I going to get out of there?"

I reversed my gears and slowly backed up, pulling Dick's machine to a safer position.

I offered to pull him farther back against the hillside, but Dick waved no and took his seat again under the corrugated roofing bearing his snowshoes and rifle. The trees that usually lined the road had been cut back the previous summer, and there was a clear view down the steep slope to the flat of the valley below. It was high noon when Dick let up on the clutch. Then, as if a giant, invisible hand pushed him, he started to slide — faster as he reached the edge of the road.

"Jump!" I screamed as I watched his bulldozer slide in a wide arc held only by the cable. He looked back at me as he slid. The look in his eyes was one of fear and dread. I felt helpless. I covered my eyes. My machine moved convulsively toward the edge. I heard two loud thuds. Dick's machine had gained momentum and hit a clump of willows. It flipped and then bounced back upright. There was an eerie silence. Even my running bulldozer seemed noiseless.

When I opened my eyes, Dick's bulldozer, the corrugated roof, and Dick were gone. I looked in the snow, expecting to see him lying there, but he wasn't.

"Why did you do it, Dick?" I shouted as I clambered down the icy hillside. He lay on the right track, face down. His right arm was grotesquely long. His legs were twisted like the roots of a large tree. His hat was over his face. I reached up to push his hat back, and got his brains in my hand.

Dick, Dick! Why, why? I ran about in shock. I have to get him out of here! He must not spend the night here! Too many animals around.

The rifle barrel was twisted out of shape, the stock splintered. Of the two snowshoe sets, I was able to make one pair. I covered Dick with his comforter. "I'll get you out of here as soon as possible."

I clawed my way up to my running bulldozer. The blade had dropped, and was over the edge of the road. A bit more, and I could have joined Dick. Another foot! I donned the snowshoes. It was about 12:30 P.M. — Dick's birthday!

What would I tell his wife — that he was so eager to get home that he killed himself? I tied my bindings, and with a last look, started off for Long Creek just a couple of miles away. There was a road commission camp there, and, I hoped, a phone!

The glacier ahead must have been a hundred feet wide, extending fifty feet up the hillside. The ice covered the land so that the bushes, willows, and small spruce peered up through the ice. My God, we couldn't have gone another quarter of a mile even if we were safely over that last spot. I crawled on my hands and knees over the glacier, hanging on to the taller willows and spruce. Water growled beneath the glacier. I walked to the edge and looked down, imagining Dick again — his mangled legs, crushed body, and smashed skull. I would never forget the feel of his brains scattered over my hands when I took his cap off. He must have died instantly!

At Long Creek camp I found the bunkhouse and called out. No answer. Removing my snowshoes, I went in. It was the home of a trapper with all his paraphernalia. During the summer it was a road gang's bunkhouse. A pot of frozen water was on the stove. No phone. The mess house next door was locked. I splintered the window with a log, climbed in, and saw the crank-type telephone. On the wall was taped a list of ring signals for Central, Chatanika Camp, and so on.

Ringing the signal a dozen times, I cranked every number on the board, then three short, three long, three short — Morse Code for SOS — no answer!

The trapper must have gone to town for food. There wasn't even hotcake flour, but I found a small bag of raisins and a dozen malt tablets.

The Chatanika River was just a short distance away. Had we taken the winter trail, Dick would have been alive. I couldn't rest with him lying out there. I donned my snowshoes and took off, following the trail.

I climbed the mountain and descended into the valley, following the telephone wire, reaching down from time to time to pick a handful of snow to wet my thirst. I was very tired, hungry, and low in spirit from shock and lack of sleep.

About four in the afternoon, I approached old Ted Marrow's trapping cabin at Thirty-Nine Mile. Nobody answered my knock. The door was open, the cabin clean, furnished with kitchen table and chairs facing the stove. A beaver was nailed out on a round board. Ted was gone — either he was out on his line, or he had walked into town for supplies. His cupboards were also bare, except for a piece of hardtack.

The most important item was the phone on the wall! I rang a long blast, and was shocked when I heard a woman answer "Operator." I told her to get me the Fairbanks marshall's office right away, then told him about Dick's death.

He said it was too late for Search and Rescue to go out until morning. I told him I would hike into Chatanika, and get a ride from there. I was in a great fever to get home.

My shoepacks were getting waterlogged, and my snow-shoe bindings were a glob of ice. A cold, full moon followed me in a cloudless dark sky. Snowshoeing with long strides, I wiggled my toes to keep the circulation going. I walked with a hypnotic rhythm. Wolves howled. I thought I heard Dick saying, "Joe, come back, Joe, come back." The hair on my neck stood up, and I started to talk to myself. Snap out of it, snap out of it, Joe! I was cold and hungry.

At about eleven at night I saw two figures in the distance walking toward me. I recognized Andy Kokrine, a well-known Athabascan dog musher. Seeing that I was pretty near collapse, Andy offered me a choice. "I've got a bottle of booze and a loaf of bread, take your choice, and come with us."

I said I had to keep going, but would take a slug of whiskey. After the snort, I started off and realized that I had done the wrong thing. I broke out in a cold sweat. I was ready to cut my snowshoes off and start crawling when I noticed a large tent off to the right, with a smokestack and snowshoes leaning against it.

Tommy Goodwin, an Eskimo from Kotzebue who worked as a lineman, invited me in. He had a pot of moose mulligan cooking. He cut off my snowshoes, pulled off my shoe packs. My feet were blue and numb; I did not feel them. He started to massage them, and after awhile, they started to tingle. I could barely eat. The feeling of relief robbed me of my appetite, and I suddenly collapsed.

I slept fitfully during the night, wondering if Dick's body was O.K., hoping the animals had not discovered him yet. I woke to the sound of an engine. It was Bob Brant of the Alaska State Troopers, come to take me home. Search and Rescue had sent a helicopter after Dick.

I was so thankful to see Joe, but horrified at what had happened to Dick Zhender. We were so sorry for his wife, Betty, and his family. It seemed that everything had gone wrong. A close shave for Joe and a disaster that cost Dick his life.

Joe panning for gold.

★

29

___

Mining
at Rampart

Gold! We leapt from our benches. Gold!
We sprang from our stools
Gold! We wheeled in the furrow,
fired with the faith of fools.

The Trail of Ninety-Eight
Robert Service

"Why can't I go with you to the mine?" I asked.

"There's no room for you and the baby at the mine. There's only a small, one-room cabin," answered Joe. So that was that.

When the ice was off the roads, the bulldozers were hauled to Fairbanks. Joe put new heads on one of the engines, overhauling it completely. He built a "go-devil" sled on which to load all the supplies and equipment. Black Navigation barged it to Rampart in April.

Joe and Herb needed to freight everything from Rampart to the Ruby Creek Mine eleven miles up the Big Minook River on Ruby Creek. Next March, when the ground was solid, Joe and Herb flew to Rampart, started the bulldozer, and made it to the cabin hauling supplies, including a Lang woodstove. Larkin's cabin had only two bunks and a Yukon stove in it. They put a tent over the sled and called it the messhouse.

When they went back for another load, the bulldozer slid toward the edge of the high bank, a forty-foot drop-off to the river. Joe said his heart was in his mouth. He finally made it to heavy brush where there was more traction. Herb jumped off when it started to slide. When Herb lit a match and lent Joe a cigarette, his hand was shaking. They were lucky.

Joe had another narrow escape. Herb, who was an alcoholic, was sleeping off his farewell-to-Fairbanks spree in a Rampart cabin. Joe had taken two five-gallon buckets made from gas cans with wire handles to get drinking water from the Yukon. The shore line was stacked high with ice floes. Carrying the buckets, Joe slipped between two floes up to his chest in the ice water. He could not feel bottom. Luckily, the two buckets anchored him on the ice. He could have drowned, for no one could live in that icy water for long.

When they reached the mining claims, there were bears all over the hillside. Herb went to fish for grayling for their dinner, and Joe went to start the tractor engine. Herb, the cook, was an intelligent man who loved good music, but he could not stay away from the bottle. In his spare time, he was supposed to help out at the cut. He wanted to work at a mine because it was a good place to dry out. He cooked three meals a day and baked bread.

Herb always said, "My hands are in the flour," or "I can't get my hands dirty because I have to punch down the bread," or "I'm going fishing." They ate grayling and steelhead trout three times a day. One day when the fish would not bite, Herb shot near a steelhead trout with his Winchester, a 507 elephant gun. "The gunshot stunned the fish," he reported, grinning.

When Joe came in for lunch, Herb lay reading and smoking in his bunk. Joe did not say anything, but he was getting tired of doing all the heavy work. He was the Cat operator and mechanic, stripping the mining ground on the banks of Ruby Creek.

"Larkin said the gold was down ten feet," reported Joe, "but I'm down fifteen feet and no gold!" Things were getting strained between the partners.

There were as many as five bears feeding on the hillsides, and they were coming closer and closer to the cabin. The men tried to scare them off with gunshots, but they ignored them. Joe shot one of them. "He came to within two hundred feet of the cabin." Herb refused to cook or eat the meat. "They have worms," he insisted.

They had bought fresh beef in Rampart, and stored it in an ice tunnel at Weisner's store. Herb was "too busy to get it," so Joe walked in the fourteen miles and hauled the meat on his back. When they cooked it, it was spoiled. Joe was getting angrier and more discouraged each day.

One day Herb took a roll of toilet paper, a scarce item, and went out after dinner. Joe was doing a slow burn, because Herb was using up the last of the toilet paper. Peter Larkin never had an outhouse. His toilet consisted of a branch of a tree nailed to two spruces, and for twenty years he used it. Herb was gone a long time. Just as Joe was going to look for him, he walked in with a sheepish look on his face.

"The branch broke, and I fell into the shit."

"I'm sorry," Joe answered, with a barely concealed smirk.

Herb's brother, Chet, came out to help. Joe worked the day shift, and Chet worked the night shift. The first night Chet worked the bulldozer, he came back with an apologetic look. "I stripped out the transmission." After explaining he knew nothing about machinery, Chet went back to his job as an electrician in Fairbanks, leaving Joe to do the repairs.

Joe ordered the parts in Fairbanks, and waited six weeks for them to come. The pilot left the parts at the Rampart airstrip. Again, Herb would not go get them, so Joe walked the eleven miles and carried back 125 pounds of gears and shafts. Putting it together, he found that some of the parts he had ordered were not in the shipment. The supplier had to send to Nome for them, as the machine was thirty years old, and parts were not easily available.

Joe worked hard to repair the bulldozer; time was running out and he was exhausted. He began to strip ground on a hillside. Somehow, he must have passed out, because when he came to, the bulldozer was climbing a steep hillside, almost ready to roll over. He stopped it in time and backed down the hill, but when he stood up, he fell face forward.

When he recovered, Joe walked into Rampart and took the first plane to Fairbanks, sending another electrician in his place to finish stripping. Dr. Schaible told Joe he was suffering from stress, and ordered him to rest. Joe was through mining.

In spite of mosquitoes, broken machinery, bears, inexperience, and a cook as a partner, it had been a learning experience for Joe. He realized we were not going to get rich quick; we had lost all our meager savings. Joe and his partners never took much from the land. They owed money for the bulldozers and machinery, and to the Ruby Creek Company and Larkin. Joe went back to work as an electrician — cured forever of his gold fever. I was glad to have him home, and never said another word about mining. Neither did he. Last we heard, Harry Havrilack was mining the claim and finding gold nuggets.

Like hundreds of other miners, Joe's life was richer because he had lived out his dream, even though his pocket was poorer. I was happy because he had gotten the gold fever out of his system. He was soon off in other dreams, bringing music to our pioneer town.

★

30

—————

Music Trails

Elected silence sing to me
And beat upon my whorled ear,
Pipe me to pastures, still and be
The music that I care to hear.

Silence
Gerard Manley Hopkins

Music was our greatest luxury, I told a trapper friend. He answered, "The greatest luxury for me is sleeping and eating. Life is so hard on the trapline, that's all that matters."

Light was Admiral Byrd's greatest luxury. While in Antarctica, he wrote in *Alone*: "I crave light as a thirsting man craves water; and just the fact of having this lantern alive in the night makes an immense difference. I feel like a rich man."

We, too, craved light during the winter darkness, but when I painted to the music of Bach and Mozart, my heart lightened. All was forgotten but the joy of music, lost in the realm where one art created another anew. The source that moved Mozart's hand — what he heard within and put to paper — now filled my ears and poured through me as a channel onto canvas. When I listened to Bach's music, I felt it was beyond the pale of everyday life, an art deeper and richer to all the senses. I wanted to live always on that plane, to feel more intensely. However, those moments were rare, woven among the routines of life.

When I opened the door to see the snow-laden trees and the light in the sky, I lingered, listening to the fragile ice on the trees. I heard a "whoooosh," a faint, mysterious cracking, a crystalline sound.

Music had a special purity of sound in the stillness of winter, and we listened to Beethoven on the radio, to our records, or to Joe playing his violin.

One evening, Hildur, who had just been elected president of Beta Sigma Phi, said, "We're looking for a new community project to support — there's some money left in our treasury."

Joe talked to our canary as he perched on his finger, pecking at his mustache. "Why don't we have some concert musicians come here? I heard that a pianist by the name of Maxim Shapiro is playing in Juneau." Joe stood up to put the canary back in the cage. "Now that would he terrific. If we could get him and other musicians to come to Juneau, Sitka, Anchorage, and Fairbanks, then we could all share the costs."

"Gosh, that's a terrific idea." Hildur's wide grin lit up her face.

From this modest beginning grew the Alaska Music Trails, sponsored by the Beta Sigma Phi, the Soroptimists, and the American University Women — all women's organizations.

Maxim Shapiro, a friend of Governor Ernest Gruening, was a fine pianist who gave concerts all over the world. He agreed to take the responsibility of signing up musicians to come to Alaska to give five concerts a year.

All was in readiness for Maxim's concert. The local movie house was packed. He had played half his program, to great applause, when the chandeliers began swinging back and forth, the building rumbled, and people jumped from their swaying seats.

Joe stood up, shouting, "Keep calm, everyone. Do not panic!" Maxim, great showman that he was, sat down and played our national anthem. When he had finished, the rocking had stopped, and he completed the rest of the program, perhaps a *vivacissimo*.

Before he left town, Maxim confessed, "Last time I played in an earthquake, it was in Japan, and the theater was demolished."

Carol Brice was the next musician of international stature to come to our far northern town. She was magnificent; the town talked of nothing else. We were all so excited about the success of the concert that Joe wrote to Marian Anderson's manager, asking her whether Anderson could sing in Alaska. Her manager politely declined, saying that she did not fly. We probably could not have afforded Anderson's fee anyway.

The most temperamental concert artist we had was not memorable for the music, but for the consternation she caused. Jose Iturbi's sister, Ampara, played half of her concert on our new Steinway, then demanded a Baldwin. "I have a contract with them," she flatly stated. It was an impossible demand, but Joe and others conferred with Raoul Griffin, the local merchant who sold cameras and other paraphernalia. Yes, he had one Baldwin, but it was a spinet, and it was one flight up!

Since Iturbi refused to finish playing on our well-tuned, concert grand Steinway, Joe, Mac Fenton, Raoul, and two other men carried the spinet down one flight of stairs, across the street and into the theater. It was thirty degrees below zero.

Everyone was thoroughly disgusted with her when she finally sat down to play, facing the audience. She finished her concert like a barroom pianist on the tinny spinet.

The women of the town sold tickets and dragged their husbands to hear opera. Two Metropolitan Opera singers walked onstage. The baritone was so drunk he held onto the curtains, and the soprano carried on without him, "Brilliantly filling in the gaps created by his inability to continue," politely wrote the *News-Miner*. "He struggled in vain to overcome an indisposition which forced him to retire."

The most exciting evening for us was the day Marilyn Horne and Gwen Kaldofsky came to Fairbanks. Horne, a rising star, was twenty-five years old, and was accompanied by Kaldofsky. A renowned teacher at U.C.L.A., Kaldofsky had been Lotte Lehmann's accompanist. Wrapped in a red shawl, Marilyn Horne sang an unforgettable program of Spanish songs.

A day before the concert, I received a call from Madame Kaldofsky, saying that at the Governor's Mansion in Juneau, they had seen a painting of mine of a young girl. (I had given an oil painting in the name of Alaska Crippled Children, of which I was state president.) Could they come over for a half-hour to see my work while in Fairbanks?

They sat in our modest living room hung with my paintings. They represented the creative world, and as we talked about art and music, my loneliness slipped away. It was rare for me to sell a painting, and I was overjoyed when they each purchased a watercolor. "It is the first painting I've ever bought," said Marilyn Horne. She relaxed in Joe's big chair with her feet up. It had been a long, exhausting month.

I invited them to share our modest dinner, and set about stretching our stuffed green peppers, baking blueberry muffins, and preparing garden zucchini and baked potatoes. When Joe came home from work, he opened a bottle of wine, and in our small kitchen, near the stove, we toasted our distinguished visitors from Los Angeles. It was a gala evening for us, full of laughter. I proposed a toast to Marilyn, for she was on her way to sing opera in Europe, and was about to marry Henry Lewis. They responded in kind, that meeting us was the highlight of their trip. Little did we guess that evening that Marilyn would go on to become the toast of the concert and opera world, the greatest bel canto singer of her generation, perhaps of all time. By the end of the evening, I was calling her "Jackie," as she was known to friends.

When we parted, Gwen said, "I will never forget you, Claire." It was the beginning of a friendship that has lasted to this day. I have never forgotten her or the great Marilyn Horne. Their encouragement meant a lot to me as an artist, and each of them has played an important part in my life.

Miklos Gafni, a twenty-five-year-old Hungarian tenor, hailed in New York as the "New Caruso," sang for us. He had been thrown into a concentration camp by the Nazis, kept alive because he sang for them. When he was liberated from the camp, he weighed only ninety pounds. A voice teacher at the camp taught him to sing, and told him if he got out alive, to go to Milan to study. He was accepted by Milan's leading singing teacher after literally singing under his window. It led to an international opera career.

Gafni was handsome, and his beautiful, luminous voice had great power. Every woman in the audience, including me, was carried away by his magnetic voice, and we clustered about him like flies around honey.

Joe conversed with Gafni in fluent Hungarian after the concert, and we enjoyed dinner with him at the Elk's Hall. He was charmed by Eva McGown, and wound up singing Irish ballads with her. Eva, a soprano, sang "My Wild Irish Rose" to Gafni's Hungarian tenor. To our delight, he kissed her hand and charmed us all.

Gafni was deeply religious, and in spite of the brutality he had suffered, had a firm belief in the "ultimate goodness of man." "It is not nearly enough to trust and believe," he said. "One must work, one must lend one's weight whenever one can toward the realization of man's hopes."

Another musician who suffered because of the Nazis was Herman Godes, a Latvian pianist. After dinner at our home, he and Joe played a Mozart sonata. Godes was so well-liked that he was invited to tour Alaska twice. The second time he came, it was forty-five degrees below zero, and he had to perform twenty-six miles out at Eielson Air Force Base. Should the car develop trouble, Godes and the rest of us in the car could have frozen, dressed as we were, and so few houses along the road.

His playing stirred up a deep response within me, and tears ran down my cheeks. There was a silence when it was over that only great art provokes. He transformed our ordinary lives and gave us a vision of greatness.

One of the funniest incidents occurred during the Claremont String Quartet's performance. After they played the first half, one of the violinists got up and asked to be excused so that he could take off his long, woolen underwear. "They told me it would be cold," he apologized, "but they neglected to mention that it would be seventy-six degrees in the auditorium." The audience just roared. The violinists took a ten-minute break and came back to great applause.

When the Claremont Quartet came to our home for a Hungarian dinner of stuffed cabbage, I received a phone call from a student who had just arrived to attend the University of Alaska. A New York friend had told him to call us. He was surprised to be invited by complete strangers to sleep on our couch and to dine with the Claremont String Quartet.

Had I remained in New York, I would have waited in line behind a hundred people to get Isaac Stern's autograph instead of being able to invite him to have dinner at our home. I drove him and his accompanist around town on icy roads with terror in my heart. What if I skidded and he hurt his hands or bashed his Strad?

Joe turned the pages of the music for them during the rehearsal. Stern and his accompanist cursed in juicy Russian whenever they goofed. At one point, Stern suggested that Joe turn the pages faster but Joe was having difficulty separating the old, stained pages. He let loose some fancy oaths of his own. They had not known he could speak Russian!

The evening of the concert it snowed. First the great Stern walked out to thunderous applause, then his accompanist, then out walked our Joe to turn the pages. I felt so proud. Stern played the Kreutzer Sonata by Beethoven, then Mozart, Dvorak, and Shostakovich. After a standing ovation, he also played many encores. It was a thrilling evening.

Years later I waited in line for an hour after a concert of his in New York. Stern did not remember my face, but when I whispered that I was from Alaska, he called out to his accompanist Alex, "Remember we had bear and moose steak at their home?"

We met many great musicians through Music Trails: Janos Starker, Leonard Rose, Van Cliburn, Zvi Zeitlin, Vladimir Ashkanazy, Paul Olefsky, Zara Nelsova, Aldo Parisot, the Fine Arts Quartet, Yaltah Menuhin and Paul Doktor, and Jan Peerce, to mention a few. Paul Olefsky and his pianist Raymond Hanson had dinner with us and, in our living room, played my favorite Bach aria transcribed by Alan Shulman.

Music was our greatest solace, and the strongest bond between Joe and me. Our children were brought up hearing classical music daily. Music became more than a luxury to us, it was a necessity. Music was the single most important thing in Joe's life, and he practiced the violin every day.

CHAPTER

31

Going North

And I think over again
My small adventures
When with a shore wind I drifted out
In my kayak
And thought I was in danger.
My fears,
Those small ones
That I thought so big
For all the vital things
I had yet to reach
And yet, there is only one great thing,
The only thing:
To live to see in huts and on journeys
The great day that dawns,
And the light that fills the world.

Eskimo Song

On February 5, 1953, our daughter Yolande was born —
six years after Mark — after four hours of easy labor, a
beautiful birth without anesthetic. She had brown hair and
blue eyes, and weighed seven pounds, five ounces. We
named her after Joe's sister and mother. I chose her middle
name, Joy, because her birth had given me joy. (As a teenager, she decided to call herself Sam, my father's name.)

My mother died October 17, 1956, after wasting away in a hospital. She was buried near our father. My heart felt heavy as stone. I would never see her dear smile again. Oh, my beautiful mother.

I would always remember the gentle mother of my youth, her laughter and songs and the fragrance of braided bread. And how her eyes lit up when she danced.

I was living on three levels: that of wife and helpmate to Joe, mother of two children, and when I was painting, that of an artist. It was as an artist that I struggled alone. My soul hungered for revelations. It seemed an impossible quest.

One word began to flash deeply upon my consciousness. A common word. Purpose. What was purpose? Something to be achieved, to be working toward? A future goal? A series of steps? But purpose was not like blueberries waiting to be picked, it was brought into existence by human choice.

I was not going to spend my life without using the gifts within. I wanted to paint. No one cared if I did or not; it was up to me to free myself.

When I painted my Eskimo friends in my kitchen, it was not like seeing them in their own villages. If only I could connect with their source, where they lived on their own land. Part of their lives seemed missing in Fairbanks.

I began by asking questions of the pilots who flew North. Where would I go? How many people lived in the village? Where would I sleep?

It was Charlie Lucier, the anthropologist at the university, who helped me. When I met him on the street, he had just returned from the Arctic. "I know a place, but it's not on the map," he said. "It's called Sheshalik, a nomadic Eskimo camp. You won't like it, Claire. There is no store, no white people, no electricity, no running water. People live in tents and hunt. No toilet." He looked me in the eye, "If you forget something, you must do without. You'll sleep on the ground."

Without hesitation I replied, "That sounds like just the place I'd like to go." I could find a tent, borrow Joe's sleeping bag, get enough grub, and bring my paints.

I would have to fly to Kotzebue and then charter a plane to drop me off at Sheshalik. At last I had a destination, a purpose! It would be a long time before I was free to leave and arrangements made, but I knew I would do it.

The hunger to express myself as an artist was the driving force of my life. It was not that I did not love my husband and children, but that no matter what else I ever did in my life, if I could not express myself, I would never be satisfied. Once, on a camping trip, the creek bed was dried up and I had no water; I painted with spit.

The demands of the house and family left only frag-mented moments for my work. No matter if no one else in our community left their families to live with the Eskimos, I needed to do it for myself. The need was overpowering; it was as if I was compelled to go to an unknown place and find out what I needed to know for myself, not taking anyone's word, not reading about it in a book. I wanted to see how Eskimos really lived.

Joe was supportive, and never raised any objections. He taught me how to put up our tent and how to work the little, two-burner gas stove. I practiced one night in the backyard, struggling to put up the tent. Little Yola joined me — she thought it was great fun to sleep in a tent with Mom.

All my life and my twelve years in Alaska were coming to a climax. All my resolutions — the time taken in spare moments to paint all the people I had met whose lives had inspired me — now pointed the way. I had to act; it was time to fulfill my life as an artist.

In July 1958, I finally left home and flew to Kotzebue. Charlie, who had married an Eskimo girl from Noatak, gave me one name to look up at Sheshalik, that of Della Keats. (Her Eskimo name was Puyuk.)

I had a cup of coffee at Rotman's store. The man sitting on the next stool asked me what I was doing in Kotzebue.

"I'm going to Sheshalik," I responded.

"Well," he said, "If you look out of the window, you can see people from Sheshalik in their boat. Why don't you ask them if they'll take you?" I left my hot coffee and ran to ask them, and so began my adventure.

When I arrived at Sheshalik and looked up Della Keats, she befriended me. An Eskimo healer born in Noatak, she was beloved throughout the Arctic.

In later years, Della often visited us in Fairbanks. We were friends until the day she died. Della and her sister, Leela, must have had a remarkable mother. Leela was a missionary, a spiritual guide, who devoted her life to helping others. She was a calm, wise woman whose broad lap sheltered many children. They were healers with earth wisdom. The women were an inspiration to me in the self-reliance and spirituality of their lives and in their loving attitude toward me.

They had the knowledge and wisdom to make something out of nature — rope from sealskin, thread from caribou sinew, and needles from birds' wings. They could bind wounds, sew up cuts with hair, cure snow blindness, and set bones.

When I left for the Arctic, it was the first time I had traveled alone without my husband. I was seen by the Eskimos as a person, not as a mother, wife, or artist. I was accepted for myself, not judged for my social standing or my bank account.

Once an old lady with the old black tattoo marks on her chin sat in Leela's tent with us. We were eating salmon and she said in Eskimo, "What is that white woman doing in your tent?"

Leela answered, "She is no ordinary woman. She is the one who cut whale meat with us at Sheshalik."

The Eskimos could not figure out what kind of woman went North by herself without a husband. I was the first artist they had ever met, a strange white woman who cut whale meat and lived among them.

When Della first met me, she couldn't understand why I would want to get my hands dirty cutting meat. "You'll get them full of blood."

"That's all right," I had answered. "Give me a knife, a little blood won't hurt me." If I had not felt that way, I could never have painted that rare scene of the midnight sun shining on Della against the sea as she cut the cord between a beluga whale and her embryo.

That these women accepted me as one of their sisters remains a great source of pride to me. Later, when I lived at Point Hope the women gave me their grandmother's Eskimo name, "Kayoutuk," meaning a dipper of fresh water. I knew I had been given an extraordinary gift that would last me all my life. It was a rare privilege to be sharing their lives.

When I first went to Point Hope some years later, and Killigvuk befriended me in his house, I did not know that he was the last remaining shaman of the northern coast of Alaska. For twenty years, until he died, we were friends, and he came to live with us periodically in Fairbanks. He was a gentle man, and "grandpa" to my kids; a healer and medicine man. I was privileged to witness Killigvuk drumming at ceremonial dances. To the Point Hope people, he possessed power and magic songs that the hunters needed to bring them luck.

The Eskimos inspired me: the way they sat and stood and walked on the land; the simplicity of their lives and their bond with the land. They shared all the food with each other, and with strangers like me. I was fortunate to be there at that time and place to witness a proud people.

When I went to the Arctic, it did not matter if I had a proper bed, or slept on the ice, in the tents, or if I ate seal liver or whale heart. For the first time in my life, food was not important. I did not care if I had a bath, a shower, or washed in a tin basin with sea water. I was happy, words flowed from my pen like an avalanche.

I did the best drawings of my life sitting on a rock, the north wind blowing and the dogs howling. I had time to write or sketch without interruption. It was a revelation to find that I did more creative work in one month than I had accomplished in a year at home.

When I went north, I felt I was lucky to be a woman. Had I been a man, I would have had to compete with the men as a hunter; physical prowess would have been important. As a woman, I did not have to prove my ability to skin, sew, or cut fish or meat. I could just be myself.

When I returned home, my friends asked how I could eat seal liver. How could I live like that? No one understood. In the villages, I was living in a loving community of souls. The women became my friends and Eskimo children followed me everywhere. I became their art teacher and friend.

Back in Fairbanks, I painted feverishly for three months and lost ten pounds. Painting became a sacred act. I painted the people at work with blood on their hands, paintings that were as large as doors. I used oil paint on a palette knife, spreading it thickly on Masonite panels.

"Fejes' style was influenced by Gauguin, Diego Rivera, and Marsden Hartley," the art critic Sidney Tillim wrote in *Art News* after my first New York show in 1962. If Fairbanks expected me to paint like Sydney Laurence before Sheshalik, what did the townspeople think now of my large oils done with a palette knife?

In New York the language of art criticism had changed. Jackson Pollack was flinging paint on canvas from buckets. Tinguely was making self-destruct machines in the courtyard of the Museum of Modern Art. In Alaska I did not feel the cities' turbulence, the dehumanization of life, the mechanization so evident in New York. My pulse in Alaska was tuned to nature and the people and the land, and I followed my own integrity.

In a letter to my sister Elaine, I wrote:

> *I had to cut away all ways of creating that were not my own. The painting had to rise, as it were, out of its own burnt ashes, seeing and creating out of my own life's experiences.*
>
> *I want to paint the inner light, an illumination of the canvas from within so that it glowed and warmed and strengthened the onlookers, forcing them to catch their breath and say, "Aio."*

My father loved paintings and books, instilling in me a love of learning and adventure. He was a bon vivant, and lived life with joy. My father wrote poetry; perhaps with more time he could have written books.

I was living out my own and my parents' dreams. My life's journey was to integrate all the different parts of my life, to discover my spiritual heritage, and to live up to my potential. I made a beginning; I began to live a life of purpose, not just letting circumstances control my days but choosing to have a voice in the direction of my journey. I was fortunate to discover Sheshalik, where it all came together.

Out of my journal I wrote *People of the Noatak*, using the drawings I made in the Arctic. Alfred A. Knopf published the book in 1966.

If Emily Carr, my counterpart in Canada, painted the forests and totems of the Canadian coast, mine were the people of the Arctic. The people and the land of the Arctic would influence the thrust of my work for the rest of my life. Even though I did not sell a single painting for fifteen years, I kept painting.

The Eskimo and Indian women reminded me of my mother wearing her kerchief. She also was a natural earth woman without any formal education. What a loss I felt not speaking her language. Her life in Poland was a mystery to me, and because of her loss of memory and then her death, it was gone forever.

As I painted, it was not the Eskimo mothers who stood there with ulus, but my mother, who used the same knife to cut and chop fish in her wooden bowl. It was my mother singing as she worked. It was my mother I painted over and over. My mother was the Eskimo woman in her toil, standing mutely and working, scarf tied under her chin; she was the Indian woman holding her nursing baby. She inspired all of my work.

I identified with the Eskimo and Indian mothers who, like my mother, could not help their children with their schoolwork; who did not read or write, and who did not understand the alien white world thrust upon their children.

After Sheshalik, I emerged with a new persona, a creative rebirth, to find my own voice. All the banked fires within me had burst into flame, and I painted surely, without retracting a single stroke.